Teaching Academic Writing for EAP

ALSO AVAILABLE FROM BLOOMSBURY

Teaching English-Medium Instruction Courses in Higher Education,
Ruth Breeze and Carmen Sancho Guinda
On Writtenness, Joan Turner
Linguistics Approaches in English for Academic Purposes, edited by
Milada Walková

Teaching Academic Writing for EAP

Language Foundations for Practitioners

MILADA WALKOVÁ

BLOOMSBURY ACADEMIC
LONDON • NEW YORK • OXFORD • NEW DELHI • SYDNEY

BLOOMSBURY ACADEMIC
Bloomsbury Publishing Plc
50 Bedford Square, London, WC1B 3DP, UK
1385 Broadway, New York, NY 10018, USA
29 Earlsfort Terrace, Dublin 2, Ireland

BLOOMSBURY, BLOOMSBURY ACADEMIC and the Diana logo are trademarks of
Bloomsbury Publishing Plc

First published in Great Britain 2024

Copyright © Milada Walková, 2024

Milada Walková has asserted her right under the Copyright, Designs and Patents Act, 1988,
to be identified as Author of this work.

For legal purposes the Acknowledgements on p. xi constitute an extension
of this copyright page.

Cover design: Grace Ridge
Cover image © Maria Kuznetsova / Getty Images

All rights reserved. No part of this publication may be reproduced or transmitted
in any form or by any means, electronic or mechanical, including photocopying,
recording, or any information storage or retrieval system, without prior permission
in writing from the publishers.

Bloomsbury Publishing Plc does not have any control over, or responsibility for, any third-party websites referred to or in this book. All internet addresses given in this book were correct at the time of going to press. The author and publisher regret any inconvenience caused if addresses have changed or sites have ceased to exist, but can accept no responsibility for any such changes.

A catalogue record for this book is available from the British Library.

A catalog record for this book is available from the Library of Congress.

ISBN: HB: 978-1-3502-8772-3
PB: 978-1-3502-8771-6
ePDF: 978-1-3502-8773-0
eBook: 978-1-3502-8774-7

Typeset by Deanta Global Publishing Services, Chennai, India
Printed and bound in Great Britain

To find out more about our authors and books visit www.bloomsbury.com and
sign up for our newsletters.

To all EAP practitioners hungry for knowledge.

CONTENTS

List of figures viii
List of tables ix
List of teaching activities x
Acknowledgements xi
List of abbreviations xii

1 Introduction 1
2 Knowledge base of academic writing 11
3 Genres 25
4 Language and content 51
5 Structuring the text 81
6 Writer, reader, community 107
7 Formative feedback on writing 161

Notes 177
References 180
Index 208

FIGURES

4.1 Recursive embeddedness of noun phrases. Noun phrase taken from BNC EDL 223 70
6.1 Stance 115

TABLES

3.1 Move Structure and Language of the Book Review 36
3.2 Move Structure and Language of the Abstract 38
3.3 Move Structure and Language of the Introduction Section of the Research Report 39
3.4 Move Structure and Language of the Methods Section of the Research Report 42
3.5 Move Structure and Language of the Results and Discussion Section of the Research Report 44
3.6 Move Structure and Language of the Conclusion Section of the Research Report 45
3.7 Move Structure and Language of the Essay 46
3.8 Move Structure and Language of Reflective Writing 47
4.1 Model of Academic Argument 56
4.2 Tense and Voice 64

TEACHING ACTIVITIES

3.1 Genre analysis 28
3.2 Genre production 30
4.1 Paraphrasing 60
4.2 Verb phrase 64
4.3 Active or passive? 65
4.4 Participle clauses 67
4.5 Noun phrases 70
4.6 Nominalization 71
4.7 Word families 72
4.8 Formal academic style 79
5.1 Topic sentence 88
5.2 Known-to-new progression 92
5.3 Cohesion 94
5.4 Transition markers 98
5.5 Referring to text and its parts 101
5.6 Conciseness 104
6.1 Stance markers 112
6.2 Attitude markers in context 117
6.3 Using attitude markers 120
6.4 To hedge or not to hedge? 125
6.5 Hedging and boosting 126
6.6 Hedges 126
6.7 Self-mention pronouns 131
6.8 Personal and impersonal self-mention structures 134
6.9 Engagement markers 141
6.10 Referencing 144
6.11 Citation 145
6.12 Integral and non-integral citations 155
6.13 Language of integral citations 156

ACKNOWLEDGEMENTS

I would like to thank the many people who supported me in writing this book. My first and foremost thanks go to Alex Ding, without whom this book would not exist, for always being an invaluable source of inspiration, learning and encouragement. I owe a great deal to Jody Bradford for feedback on the whole manuscript and for cheering me on. I thank Bee Bond for advice and feedback on my book proposal and to Michelle Evans, Laetitia Monbec, Tatyana Karpenko-Seccombe, Hanem El-Farahaty and Ivor Timmis for advice on various aspects. I am very thankful to my coach Stephie Hoppitt for helping me see I was ready to start writing the book when I felt I was not. I am pleased to acknowledge the wonderful support of Bloomsbury editors Laura Gallon, Maria Giovanna Brauzzi and Sarah MacDonald. I am grateful to copyright holders for granting permission for content to be reused in the book or for publishing content under a license allowing free reuse. Finally, I am indebted to numerous students and colleagues who inspired the ideas in the book in one way or another.

The author and publisher gratefully acknowledge the permission granted to reproduce the copyright material in this book. Every effort has been made to trace copyright holders and to obtain their permission for the use of copyright material. However, if any have been inadvertently overlooked, the publishers will be pleased, if notified of any omissions, to make the necessary arrangement at the first opportunity.

Other third-party copyrighted material displayed in the pages of this book are done so on the basis of 'fair dealing for the purposes of criticism and review' or 'fair use for the purposes of teaching, criticism, scholarship or research' only in accordance with international copyright laws and is not intended to infringe upon the ownership rights of the original owners.

ABBREVIATIONS

AVL	Academic Vocabulary List
BAWE	British Academic Writing English Corpus
BNC	British National Corpus
CARS	Create a Research Space
CDST	Complex Dynamic Systems Theory
EAP	English for Academic Purposes
EGAP	English for General Academic Purposes
ESAP	English for Specific Academic Purposes
ESP	English for Specific Purposes
FSP	Functional Sentence Perspective
HE	Higher Education
IELTS	International English Language Testing System
IMRAD	Introduction – Methods – Results and Discussion
L1	First Language
L2	Second Language
MICUSP	Michigan Corpus of Upper-level Student Papers
SFL	Systemic Functional Linguistics
SLA	Second Language Acquisition
TECCL	Ten-Thousand English Compositions of Chinese Learners Corpus
TESOL	Teaching English to Speakers of Other Languages

CHAPTER 1

Introduction

1.1 EAP and its theoretical underpinnings

English for Academic Purposes (EAP), as defined by Flowerdew and Peacock (2001: 8), is 'the teaching of English with the specific aim of helping learners to study, conduct research or teach in that language'. The inclusion of *teaching* in the definition suggests a very practical orientation of EAP, one that perhaps overlooks the discipline's theoretical foundations. Indeed, in his 2006 book, Ken Hyland (2006: 5) noted that '[m]any EAP courses still lack a theoretical or research rationale and textbooks too often continue to depend on the writer's experience and intuition rather than on systematic research'. More than fifteen years later, the gap between theory and practice is still strongly felt. On the one hand, EAP pedagogical practice seems to be little informed by theory: Cowley-Haselden and Monbec (2019) found that only about half of EAP courses are reported to be based on theory, that the word *theory* is interpreted variously in the EAP community and that some EAP practitioners do not even feel theory is relevant. Recent evaluations of EAP textbooks (Deroey 2018; Walková 2020) confirm older findings that commercial EAP textbooks reflect research to a very limited extent (Harwood 2005b). On the other hand, the discipline tends to produce research with little pedagogical application, as criticized by Swales (2019). Even when research articles do discuss pedagogical implications, they do so rather briefly: In Riazi, Ghanbar and Fazel's (2020) study of articles published in one EAP journal, less than 40 per cent of all articles devoted more than one paragraph to the discussion of pedagogical application of their findings.

Reasons for this lack of engagement with theory in EAP are manifold. One of considerable importance is the discipline's relative infancy (see Ding & Bruce 2017 for an overview of the history of EAP), which perhaps contributes to practitioners seeing EAP 'as intuitive and practical (and, as such, atheoretical)' (Cowley-Haselden & Monbec 2019: 43) and to academia often viewing EAP as a support service rather than an academic discipline (Ding & Bruce 2017). Related to this position of EAP is another reason – that EAP practitioners are too often prevented from engaging with theory through scholarship by their institutional constraints, such as precarious teaching-only contracts and a lack of scholarship support (Ding & Bruce 2017; Davis 2019). Yet another reason for a gap between theory and practice might be a lack of standardized education in EAP – thus an EAP practitioner might have a background in English language teaching, in linguistics or in any discipline, from engineering and physics through business to sociology and fine arts. To be able to engage with EAP theory and apply it to practice, one must, therefore, venture beyond the confines of his/her own original discipline. For a specialist in a scholarly discipline, this might involve coming to terms with linguistic terminology and research methods, for a language specialist, this might be getting to grips with specificity in English for Specific Academic Purposes (ESAP).

Basing practice on theory is what makes EAP an academic discipline rather than a university support service (Ding & Bruce 2017). This understanding has in recent years increased the number of responses to the need to marry theory and practice in EAP. *A Theory into Practice* discussion list has been created in the Baleap community (Cowley-Haselden & Kukuczka 2019). *Journal of English for Academic Purposes* has started publishing *Researching EAP Practice* articles with a focus on pedagogical practice (Hu 2018). A recent volume edited by MacDiarmid and MacDonald (2021) has showcased how theory can be applied in EAP teaching practice.

Focusing on academic writing, this book hopes to contribute to the effort of bridging the gap between theory and practice in EAP. It does so by proposing that EAP pedagogy should be based on best evidence currently available. What is considered evidence here is knowledge created as a result of scholarly activity, validated by the process of peer review, and made public via dissemination. In contrast, I do not consider as evidence academic writing manuals, textbooks or websites, as these are not necessarily based upon research but possibly on intuition and even myths. (This is not to say that all academic writing manuals or textbooks are such; quite the contrary, there are excellent writing guides written by scholars active in research, e.g. Swales & Feak 2000, 2004.)

For theory and evidence to be applied in pedagogical practice, it has to become part of the EAP practitioner's knowledge base, defined by Ding and Bruce (2017: 65) as 'the theories and research that are drawn upon in the design of syllabus, development of courses, production of materials and implementation of pedagogy in the field of EAP'. Generally speaking, EAP practitioners can access theory in three ways. One is *first-hand access* by reading original academic publications. While this may be demanding and time consuming, especially for a novice EAP practitioner, it is the most direct and the most valuable way to access theory. It is my belief that an EAP practitioner should develop knowledge of his/her core areas of interest through first-hand access. This knowledge will, of course, develop over time, as there is a vast array of knowledge available. A less direct access to theory is the *second-hand* one, represented by examples of how original work has been used by others, for instance in conference presentations and published papers. The second-hand access is a quicker way to learn about theory than the first-hand one, thus enabling us to learn about theory beyond our immediate areas of interest, and helps us understand original work by giving examples of its interpretation and application (my thanks go to Laetitia Monbec for pointing this out to me). The second-hand access can thus serve as a gateway to the first-hand access. Finally, the *third-hand access* involves learning about theory from teaching materials developed by another practitioner, shared within one's institution or network, or accessed through published EAP textbooks or freely available websites for EAP students. While this might be a common way of learning about EAP for practitioners very new to EAP, I would argue against relying on the third-hand approach, as it may lead to perpetuating myths about EAP (such as the use of personal pronouns, see Chapter 6.6) and to deskilling of EAP practitioners (I owe this point to Alex Ding). This book hopes to enable second-hand access to theoretical linguistic foundations of academic writing and to arouse curiosity about various areas of academic writing that will eventually be satisfied, it is hoped, by accessing the relevant original publications first-hand.

1.2 What is academic writing?

Within EAP, academic writing typically occupies a central place, both in teaching and research, due to its centrality in higher education (HE) assessment and in research communication. This section considers a seemingly simple question: What is academic writing? It does so by pointing out that academic writing, and EAP more generally, can be conceptualized variously (cf. Kirk 2018), so it might be more suitable to talk about *EAPs* rather than a single conception of EAP. This book's conceptualization of EAP follows Bruce's (2021) in its focus on the context of academia rather than wider society, and accordingly on the use of language for academic rather than social purposes, and on the development of academic literacy and discourse competence rather than on the development of language proficiency and formal competence.

The understanding of academic writing appears to vary among teachers and institutions, depending on the context. Tribble (2009) points out that what published EAP textbooks call *academic writing* can range from five-paragraph personal essays to evidence-based postgraduate dissertations. In a similar vein, Aull (2015) proposes a cline of written academic genres ranging from school genres based on personal evidence only, through early university genres whose argument is based on both personal evidence and textual sources, to advanced academic genres based on a synthesis of views from literature, drawing on personal evidence in a limited way. Focusing on the difference between relying on personal evidence and the use of external sources, Hinkel (2002a), following Bereiter and Scardamalia (1987) (see Chapter 2.2), distinguishes between knowledge-telling type of writing that is based on information already available to the writer, such as personal beliefs and experience, and more cognitively demanding knowledge-transforming type of writing that requires the writer to collect and analyse information and consider 'content integration, expectations of the audience, conventions and form of the genre, the use of language and linguistic features, the logic of the information flow, and rhetorical organization' (Hinkel 2002a: 55). It is the latter type of writing that is the focus of this book. In contrast, personal essays not based on sources, often arguing for or against a particular case relevant to the wider society, are not considered academic writing here. A failure to distinguish personal writing of this type from academic writing has created many myths in EAP pedagogy, for instance that paragraphs need to have a topic sentence and that objective writing does not use personal pronouns. This book hopes to counter such myths.

One example of personal writing is International English Language Testing System (IELTS) Academic writing. IELTS Academic is an international test of English language proficiency used as a language requirement test for university admission for international students in the UK and elsewhere (cf. British Council 2023). In my experience, students coming to EAP courses who have spent considerable time preparing for the IELTS test and improving their score often believe that the type of writing they practised and mastered for IELTS *is* academic writing, which led to this conclusion by the test's name, or rather, misnomer. However, there are significant differences between IELTS Academic writing and university writing. Moor and Morton (2005) analysed and compared instructions for IELTS Academic writing Task 2 and a range of undergraduate and postgraduate university assignments from various disciplines and found the following differences between the two types of writing. First, while IELTS writing Task 2 always includes an essay, university writing is characterized by a variety of genres, including not only essays but also research reports and literature reviews, among others. Second, university assignments draw on a greater variety of rhetorical functions, including description, summarization and instruction, all lacking in the IELTS task. Third, while the objects of enquiry in IELTS are always real-world entities (e.g. technology and education), university writing deals with both real-world (e.g. historical events and physical phenomena) and abstract (e.g. theoretical frameworks) entities. Finally, university writing almost always requires students to use external sources, while IELTS writing always relies solely on the writer's prior knowledge, thus reflecting Hinkel's (2002a) distinction cited above.

The difference in the use of sources leads Moor and Morton (2005) to conclude that what is of primary importance in university writing is content, while in IELTS it is language proficiency. As Molinari (2022: 78) puts it, IELTS essays (and similar ones written for testing purposes) 'are written to display language and mimic essay forms, not to advance truthful, or real, accounts of the world'. It has to be pointed out that Moor and Morton (2005) analysed only task instructions but not actual samples of assignments: the latter type of analysis would likely reveal specific differences in language use, such as frequent sweeping generalizations and vague language in IELTS essays in contrast to carefully hedged and term-loaded language in university assignments. Moreover, the difference in the length of the two genres (250 words for IELTS and around 2,000 words for a university essay) has a significant impact on the level of depth required (Moor & Morton 2005), leading to, for instance, a relatively high frequency of transition markers (see Chapter 5.5) in IELTS essays.

Drawing on the above discussion, this book understands academic writing taught in EAP classes as characterized by the following features:

1. **Intertextuality**, which involves explicit reference to scholarly work, acknowledged with academic citations, interwoven into one's text and used as evidence for one's argumentation.
2. **Content** (often abstract) characterized by complexity of ideas and requiring criticality on the part of the writer, one that typically goes beyond everyday issues relevant to the general public, one that is specific to a scholarly topic and possibly to a particular discipline. What I understand as content in this book is the meaning communicated through language.
3. A context that typically includes an academic **audience** and the **purpose** of developing and demonstrating knowledge and/or research skills, or contributing to knowledge.
4. **Genre variety** that includes genres of the upper end of Aull's (2015) continuum, such as university essays, lab reports, literature reviews, abstracts and theses.
5. **Language** that is specific, objective and formal.

Admittedly, while most academic genres fit the above criteria easily, some genres written in academia digress from the criteria to some extent. For instance, reflective writing will make reference to a specific event or to experience more heavily than to scholarly work. Some of the genres that university students will write in preparation for their profession will be addressed to a non-academic audience, e.g. clients. These differences will in turn impact on the language used in the respective genres. This book is concerned with the language and rhetorical strategies in central academic genres.

1.3 Aims and scope

This book is aimed not only at teachers relatively or completely new to EAP seeking to learn about fundamental linguistic concepts in academic writing, but also, in line with the belief that learning about EAP is a lifelong process (Campion 2016), at experienced EAP practitioners wishing to broaden and deepen their knowledge base of EAP writing theory. This book is thus not an introductory book for EAP teachers: I feel that while there are many introductory books available, the literature for more advanced professional development is relatively limited. This book thus hopes to serve the needs of both novice and experienced EAP practitioners and it is expected that they will read the book in a depth appropriate to their career stage.

The book's aim is twofold. The first aim is to provide a systematic overview of core concepts related to the language of academic writing, challenging some common practices in teaching by providing evidence from published research and from authentic examples of academic writing. The book's second aim is to demonstrate how the theories under study can be applied in teaching practice. To this end, I provide examples of teaching activities. These, however, are not to be understood as one-size-fits-all recipes for teaching academic writing, but rather as activities to be adapted and contextualized for particular students, or better yet, as inspiration for one's own application of theory in practice.

The lens through which I view theory is linguistic, given my background and interests. I illustrate the language points discussed with examples from published academic writing and from corpora. My selection of corpora was admittedly influenced by their availability and ease of use, but it was primarily motivated by the pedagogical usefulness of the extracts rather than research rigour.[1] The corpora selected thus represent a lower (Ten-Thousand English Compositions of Chinese Learners Corpus (TECCL)) and higher level (British Academic Writing English Corpus (BAWE) and Michigan Corpus of Upper-level Student Papers (MICUSP)) student writing as well as expert writing (British National Corpus (BNC)).[2]

The book is necessarily selective in its treatment of various theories and there are admittedly many areas of approaches to academic writing that are not included, e.g. Legitimation Code Theory, or only touched upon lightly here, such as Systemic Functional Linguistics (SFL). The reason for this is that the book presents my personal perspectives of application of theory into teaching practice. This, of course, does not preclude EAP application of theories not included here. On the contrary, the reader is invited to fill such gaps in the presented book and to share such applications with the EAP practitioner community. Equally, the book hopes to inspire further research into yet under-explored areas of academic writing. Throughout the book, I point out what areas require further research – but in doing so I am not speaking to researchers detached from EAP teaching practice; rather, I call on EAP practitioners involved in both teaching and scholarship to conduct research and scholarship that will further inform both the theory and the practice of EAP.

To draw implications for evidence-based practice, the book relies on evidence from published research into academic texts, second language writing and second language acquisition (SLA). Using this evidence is not without problems, however, and in what follows I outline these as caveats for the reader to bear in mind when reading the book. One caveat is that some of the research drawn upon comes from Teaching English to Speakers of Other Languages (TESOL) rather than from EAP or from conceptualizations of EAP that see personal writing of the knowledge-telling type as academic, contrary to how academic writing is understood here (see Section 1.2). It could be argued that using such studies of personal writing can potentially skew our understanding of learner issues in academic writing. One reason for including these studies here is that it is often impossible to tell what genres are analysed, unless sample writing and/or task instructions are provided, since the authors of these studies talk about *academic* writing rather than personal writing or simply about *essays*. This conflation makes comparison between different studies difficult, which provides further justification for distinguishing between academic and personal writing, and for EAP practitioners to conduct research into the student genres they actually teach in EAP classes. Another reason for including these studies is that I feel it would be wrong to ignore them in EAP completely, as they offer valuable insights into the process of learning English. Nevertheless, where I feel the available literature is biased towards TESOL rather than EAP, I explicitly point this out (Chapter 7). Moreover, in order to avoid skewing the depiction of learner issues in academic writing, I often present evidence for one point from several studies, even though it means that the book is rather heavily referenced.

The second caveat is that some quantitative studies reported here, although peer reviewed and published in reputable journals, fail to provide information on the statistical significance of their findings. In my view, a lack of statistical testing is a widespread problem in research in EAP and language teaching more generally: too many studies do not present statistical analyses of their data. Regardless of whether this is given by a lack of expertise in statistical methods or by limited robustness of the data themselves, quantitative findings lacking inferential statistics need to be viewed with caution, and as tendencies that might not be confirmed on larger data samples. Additionally, when results of statistical tests are provided, any apparent differences between two samples that are shown not to be statistically significant need to be considered as a result of mere chance rather than due to a factor that is observed, and thus disregarded. In the remainder of the book I point out occasional problems of interpretation of statistical testing (or of its lack), and I would call on EAP researchers to include statistical testing in their papers.

Finally, evidence from published research selected for this book includes analyses and comparisons of first language (L1) English and second language (L2) English writing, student/novice and expert writing, and low-scoring and high-scoring student writing. Such comparisons, however, need to be treated with caution. To start with, comparisons between L1 and L2 writers tacitly assume that L1 English writers' texts serve as a model of academic writing and that L1 English writers are better writers than L2 English writers by default (cf. McKinley & Rose 2018: 9). These assumptions are not only wrong but also disempowering and demotivating, as they carry the implication that L2 writers, no matter how skilled, will always be second-rate compared to L1 writers. Moreover, comparisons of L1 and L2 writing disregard the writers' audience and cultural background: Evidence shows that scholars write differently for local and international audiences (e.g. Yakhontova 2002; Belcher & Yang 2020), for instance. Such comparisons, therefore, need to be put into perspective by considering what the differences between L1 and L2 writing might indicate. Differences in quantitative counts of selected features, especially, do not necessarily imply a learning issue – such accounts should be accompanied with qualitative interpretations of why a particular observed difference might be an issue. I will illustrate my points with two examples from Hinkel (2002a). One of Hinkel's (2002a: 125) findings is that Vietnamese writers use more adverbs of frequency, e.g. *usually*, in their writing than L1 English writers. Although Hinkel claims frequency adverbs are problematic because they are vague, she does not comment on whether the overuse found in learner writing results in stylistic inappropriateness, a lack of relevant details or hindered flow of writing – all of which would indicate a learning issue – or whether this difference in frequency is in fact mere variation without pedagogical implications. Another of Hinkel's (2002a: 126) findings is that most L2 English student writers use hedging in a rate similar to that of L1 English student writers. This, however, does not necessarily mean that these student writers use hedging appropriately in their academic writing – this would need to be confirmed with a qualitative analysis of hedging in context.

Comparisons between student and expert writing, in turn, are equally problematic but for different reasons, namely differences in genre, the purpose of text and the writer–reader relationship. First, unlike expert writing, student writing is submitted for the purpose of assessment, with the reader being the assessor with more knowledge and power. This affects how willing students are to assume authority in their writing (e.g. Hyland 2002b). For instance, the PhD students in Jomaa and Bidin's (2017) study were reluctant to critique sources in their dissertation for fear that the authors of these sources might become their dissertation examiners. Second, the differences in language use between student and expert writing may also be due to differences in the genres compared, e.g. student essays and journal articles. In other words, if student writing differs from expert writing, this might not indicate a lack of awareness of discourse conventions on the part of student writers but actually students' skilful use of language for their given purposes. To help us better understand the relationship between discourse and genre, further research is needed into similarities and differences between student and expert genres. Differences between the two types of genres also beg the question to what extent it is appropriate to present expert writing addressed to peers as a suitable model and benchmark for student writers (see Chapter 3.3).

The fairest comparison, then, seems to be between low-scoring and high-scoring student writing. Such comparisons should be matched for purpose, audience and genre, and perhaps also for task and discipline, enabling us to uncover differences between successful and less successful writing and between writing strategies of skilled and less skilled writers. Taking the above reservations into account, this book draws on all the three types of comparisons, together with qualitative analyses of writing. The EAP learners as envisaged in the book include pre-undergraduate, undergraduate and postgraduate students, postgraduate researchers and academic faculty writing for publication.

The rest of the book is organized as follows. Chapter 2 focuses on the knowledge base for EAP practitioners which is drawn upon in the remainder of the book. It reviews and critiques selected long-established as well as more recent theoretical frameworks and approaches. The chapter is organized around four themes: theories of epistemology, theories of language, theories of and approaches to language teaching and teaching writing in particular and theories and approaches to EAP.

Chapter 3 discusses the concept of genre from the point of view of several genre theories and explores the application of genre analysis in writing pedagogy. The chapter also discusses power relations between the writer and the reader in student genres, and a mismatch between model genres and target genres in student education, which I call *the EAP genre paradox*. The rest of the chapter focuses on the textual organization and language of selected written academic genres.

Chapter 4 explores the language and content in academic writing and the relationship between the two. The main themes include criticality and argument, paraphrasing, grammar, lexis and style. Grammar and lexis are deliberately treated together as they are understood to be on one continuum. I advocate the primacy of content over formalism and the contextualization of content and language within discipline and genre.

Chapter 5 considers local textual organization, both in terms of content – ordering and presentation of information (paragraph development, coherence, conciseness and clarity) – and language (cohesion and the use of discourse markers). The chapter thus distinguishes between coherence and cohesion as two separate concepts. I also propose that the topic sentence is a pedagogical concept rather than an authentic feature of academic texts, and I call for more scholarship on paragraph development, conciseness and clarity.

Chapter 6 views academic writing as an interaction between the writer, the reader and the academic community. I propose a model of stance composed of four aspects and show how metadiscourse is used to signal each of these aspects. The chapter discusses controversial points related to stance and questions the usefulness of some common pedagogical approaches.

Chapter 7 reviews existing research on formative feedback on academic writing, coming from second language researchers as well as scholars in HE more generally. Drawing on this research, the chapter provides recommendations for teaching practice in the form of pedagogical principles to be followed when giving formative feedback. The chapter also provides suggestions for the development of feedback literacy within curriculum and calls for more EAP-oriented scholarship on feedback.

CHAPTER 2

Knowledge base of academic writing

2.1 Introduction

This chapter is a brief overview of the theoretical frameworks and approaches, both long-established and more recent, which I believe should form part of EAP practitioners' knowledge base for teaching academic writing. In no way does the chapter aspire to be exhaustive; instead, the selection presents theories on which I draw in the rest of the book, organized into four groups. I start with theories of epistemology (Section 2.2). These include, on the one hand, cognitive processes related to the acquisition of knowledge at the individual level – Bloom's revised taxonomy of cognitive skills (Anderson et al. 2001) and models of knowledge transmission in written discourse by Flower (1979) and Bereiter and Scardamalia (1987), and on the other hand, production of knowledge at the collective level – disciplinary differences from Becher and Trowler (2001) applied to writing in, e.g. Hyland (2004). The second group includes theories of language use (Section 2.3), namely SFL originally developed by Halliday (e.g. Halliday & Matthiessen 2013), Functional Sentence Perspective (FSP) (e.g. Firbas 1992) by the Prague School of Linguistics, politeness theory by Brown and Levinson (1987) and Hyland's (2019a) metadiscourse model. The third group includes theories of and approaches to teaching language in general and teaching writing in particular: Larsen-Freeman's (2003) grammaring, writing as a process or product/genre (cf. e.g. Badger & White 2000) and Complex Dynamic Systems Theory (CDST) applied to writing (Fogal & Verspoor 2020). Finally, the fourth group includes approaches within EAP – Academic Literacies (Lea & Street 1998) as opposed to study skills and academic socialization, Critical EAP (Benesch 1993) and Critical Pragmatic EAP (Harwood & Hadley 2004) and intercultural rhetoric (e.g. Connor, Nagelhout & Rozycki 2008). Obviously missing from this list are theories of genre, which will be reviewed in Chapter 3.

2.2 Theories of epistemology

This section reviews theories of epistemology, i.e. theories of the nature of knowledge, both at the individual and collective level. At the individual level, it is important to consider how a learner processes and communicates knowledge. A useful model to help us understand the processing of knowledge is **Bloom's revised taxonomy for learning** (Anderson et al. 2001). The revised version of the taxonomy is mapped not as a pyramid with six levels, as it is popularly known, but as a four-by-six grid with two dimensions. One is the knowledge dimension that consists of four categories – *factual* (comprising isolated facts), *conceptual* (comprising classifications, principles and models), *procedural* (discipline-specific skills) and *metacognitive* (general study skills and reflection). Let me illustrate this dimension with an example from academic writing, in particular with hedging. *Factual* knowledge refers to knowing what hedging is, *conceptual* knowledge might include the relationship of hedging to boosting, *procedural* knowledge means using hedging appropriately in writing and *metacognitive* knowledge encompasses learner's awareness of his/her ability to use hedging appropriately. It can thus be seen that being able to define hedging and to use it are two very different types of knowledge, and while the latter assumes the knowledge of the former, the former does not necessarily lead to the latter, which has implications for the need to practise writing.

The second dimension of Bloom's revised taxonomy includes six categories of cognitive processes, ordered with increasing complexity: *remember* (which comprises recognizing and recalling), *understand* (classifying, exemplifying, paraphrasing, summarizing, comparing, explaining and inferring), *apply* (using a procedure in a particular situation, executing and implementing), *analyse* (differentiating, organizing and attributing), *evaluate* (checking and critiquing) and *create* (generating, planning and producing). For instance, in academic writing, *remember* might include the ability to spell words, *understand* paraphrasing a source, *apply* choosing an appropriate tense, *analyse* identifying move structure in a text, *evaluate* judging a text against a set of criteria and *create* writing a text. Similarly to the knowledge dimension, the more complex cognitive processes build on the less complex ones, yet the less complex ones do not automatically lead to the more complex ones. For instance, learners might evaluate sample texts as successful or less successful with ease yet still find it difficult to write their own text. Bloom's revised taxonomy thus reminds educators of the complexity of the learning process.

Let us now turn to communicating knowledge in writing, represented by two models. Flower (1979) distinguishes between what she calls **writer-based and reader-based prose**. Writer-based prose, characteristic of many novice writers, is constructed without consideration of the reader and as such is written for the writer like an internal monologue. Content-wise, it focuses on the writer's knowledge and the process of acquiring this knowledge. Structurally, then, writer-based prose is narrative and organized chronologically and/or by associations with the topic. The contexts are undefined and changing; the text contains (often irrelevant) details rather than generalizations and abstractions; inferencing thus rests with the reader. Some linguistic signs of writer-based prose include sentence fragments (see Chapter 4.6), which run counter to the reader's expectations, and ambiguous third person pronouns, e.g. *he* in (1), which according to Flower refer to the *psychological subject* of a sentence.

(1) On the one hand , about the social progress , every people is in charge of the pressure more large , so people think the job is important , at the same time , we have to hard , can not life after all , It is said that the government employees test is hardly passd , in my opinion face the chellange , we can work on others job , not all people is sure *he* can pass the exam. (TECCL 05366)

Reader-based prose, in contrast, is written for the reader. Its purpose is to communicate information to the audience in a way that meets the audience's needs and expectations. The content is analytical and focuses on abstract and generalized propositions about the topic, which are organized logically and hierarchically. Reader-based prose is built on contexts shared between the writer and the audience. Flower suggests that moving from writer-based prose to reader-based prose requires planning and organizing the content of a text for the reader, supplying further information and making connections explicit.

Similarly to Flower's (1979) model, Bereiter and Scardamalia (1987) propose that writers can approach writing in two ways – **knowledge-telling or knowledge-transforming**. Novice writers typically produce texts through the knowledge-telling process, which involves writing everything one knows about the topic of the composition. Knowledge-telling writers' concern is the immediate context, typically a sentence to follow. Expert writers, in contrast, routinely rely on the knowledge-transforming process. This involves setting up overall goals for their text and producing the text achieving these goals in terms of both content and discourse, selecting and generating new ideas and reformulating the goals if necessary. Clearly, EAP instruction aims to help writers move from writer-based/knowledge-telling type of writing to reader-based/knowledge-transforming writing. This includes considering the audience's knowledge and expectations, selecting relevant content and making its relevance explicit, and planning and organizing the overall text accordingly.

The models reviewed so far consider processing and communicating knowledge by individuals. I will now turn to a model of knowledge production at the collective level, one which distinguishes **epistemological and social differences between disciplines**. Becher and Trowler (2001) divide disciplines into four groups, along two dimensions. The hard–soft dimension refers to the degree of exactitude, rigour and replicability. Hard sciences are typically characterized by more collaborative research, shorter research articles, faster publication process, larger publication output and greater competitiveness than soft sciences. The pure–applied dimension, in turn, distinguishes between disciplines largely focusing on creating theoretical knowledge and disciplines applying knowledge to solve problems. With a degree of simplification and overlaps, these two dimensions create four groups of disciplines. Hard-pure disciplines include natural sciences such as physics and chemistry; hard-applied disciplines include technical and medical fields such as mechanical engineering and pharmacology; soft-pure disciplines include humanities and some social sciences, e.g. history and anthropology; and finally, soft-applied disciplines include social sciences such as law and education.

Epistemological and social differences among disciplines have been used to interpret the differences in the use of language in academic writing. For instance, Hyland, K. (1998) explains the higher frequency of hedging in soft disciplines compared to hard disciplines as a reflex of the rather subjective and interpretative character of soft disciplines. When teaching disciplinary discourse, one must be careful not to overgeneralize disciplinary differences. For a start, the hard–soft distinction is a continuum rather than a dichotomy, as Hyland, K. (1998) cautions. Moreover, a low frequency of a particular language feature in certain disciplines does not mean that the feature does not occur in academic writing of those disciplines at all. Therefore, EAP teachers should not 'prohibit' students from using the given features but instead they should strive to develop students' awareness and sensitivity to how common such features are in their discipline. Disciplinary differences can be particularly well explored in groups of students from mixed disciplines. Equally, it has to be borne in mind that disciplines are far from homogenous, and that sub-disciplines can vary in their use of language. For instance, Harwood's (2006) study found differences in the use of personal pronouns between sub-disciplines of political science. A final word of caution is that the occurrence of many linguistic features is not aligned with a classification of disciplines. For instance, Swales et al. (1998) found no correlation between the frequency of imperatives and a type of discipline; however, they noticed that imperatives are used mostly in disciplines which refer the reader to equations, cited examples or other similar material. In sum, it can thus be seen that epistemology affects the use of language yet the observed characteristics are tendencies rather than rules. Epistemological, social and linguistic characteristics of academic disciplines, as briefly sketched above, should be part of practitioners' knowledge base, as proposed by Ferguson (1997).

2.3 Theories of language use

In this section I review four different theories of language use, starting with **Systemic Functional Linguistics** originally developed by Michael Halliday (e.g. Halliday & Matthiessen 2013). This approach views language as an inventory of options that language users choose from for the particular meaning they wish to communicate. In SFL, language use is multi-stratal and multifunctional as follows. Language has three strata – graphology/phonology, lexico-grammar and discourse semantics, while context creates two additional strata – register and genre. Language has three main functions: *ideational* (to convey information about experience, e.g. *theories of language use* and *language as an inventory of options* used in this paragraph), *interpersonal* (to establish and maintain social relations, e.g. *I review* and *widespread popularity*) and *textual* (to organize and contextualize text, e.g. *in this section* and *starting with*). To these three functions correspond, respectively, *field* (what discourse is about), *tenor* (the relationship between the participants of communication) and *mode* (channel of communication – spoken or written). These are three aspects of register that influence language choices that participants make in a communicative exchange. Overall, SFL is a complex framework that has gained widespread popularity in EAP.

Another functional approach to language is the theory of **Functional Sentence Perspective** developed by the Prague School of Linguistics (e.g. Firbas 1992). FSP explores information structure at the level of sentence (and extended to the level of paragraph, see Chapter 5) by introducing the notion of communicative dynamism or 'constant development towards . . . the fulfilment of a communicative purpose' (Firbas 1992: 7). Linguistic elements in a sentence vary in the degree of communicative dynamism that they carry; in other words, different parts of sentences vary in the degree they advance communication. Some sentence elements provide information that is retrievable from the context – these present the *theme* of a sentence or given information. Some other sentence elements, called *rheme*, advance communication by presenting new information that is not retrievable from the context. Between theme and rheme is *transition* with a degree of communicative dynamism that is higher than the theme's but lower than the rheme's. Stylistically neutral, well-composed sentences proceed linearly in the order *theme – transition – rheme*.

To illustrate, in the main clause in Example (2), the theme is *the most influential framework*, as it provides given information (cf. the definite article *the*) retrievable from the context, which is provided in the example by *from among functional approaches to the study of academic discourse*. The verb *has been* provides a transition to the rheme, namely *SFL*, as this noun phrase provides the highest degree of communicative dynamism in the sentence. This principle of linear ordering of theme and rheme, however, may interfere with the grammatical principle of fixed word order in English (subject–verb–object). Thus, (3) as a sentence following (2) is ordered from rheme (*Michael Halliday* as the new information in the sentence) to theme (*it* referring to *SFL* in the previous sentence), hence its pragmatic appropriateness is questionable (as marked by ?). One structure that allows the two principles to align is the passive voice, as presented in (4).

(2) From among functional approaches to the study of academic discourse, the most influential framework has been SFL. (constructed example)

(3) ?Michael Halliday developed it. (constructed)

(4) It was developed by Michael Halliday. (constructed)

The notions of theme and rheme from FSP have been further elaborated by SFL. Nevertheless, it has to be pointed out here that the notion of *theme* is understood very differently in FSP and SFL. In FSP, it is understood in relation to the preceding context: theme is the element that presents information retrievable from the context, regardless of its syntactic realization or position in a sentence, e.g. *the most influential framework* in (2) and *it* in (3). In contrast, theme in SFL is defined formally, as the elements at the beginning of a clause, i.e. typically the sentence subject and any linguistic material preceding it, e.g. *from among functional approaches to the study of academic discourse, the most influential framework* in (2) and *Michael Halliday* in (3). This book draws on the FSP understanding of theme and rheme to explore coherence as information structure (see Chapter 5).

Another theory of language use reviewed in this section is **metadiscourse** – an approach to the study of language that, in line with SFL, recognizes that communication involves not only the transmission of ideas but also interaction between participants of a communicative exchange and a commentary on the discourse itself. Crismore, Markkanen and Steffensen (1993: 40) define metadiscourse as 'the linguistic material in texts, whether spoken or written, that does not add anything to the propositional content but that is intended to help the listener or reader organize, interpret and evaluate the information given'. In other words, metadiscourse involves language elements that do not serve the ideational function as outlined in SFL.

Several models of metadiscourse have been proposed in the literature. In the narrow view of metadiscourse (e.g. Ädel 2023), only language referring to *the world of discourse* (i.e. comments on the use of language in the given text and on the interaction with the reader) but not language referring to the real world (including personal experience and views on the real-world phenomena) is considered metadiscourse. The broad view of metadiscourse, in contrast, considers as metadiscourse any language that is manifestation of the writer's presence in the text, including language showing logical connections between ideas presented in the text, the writer's attitude towards what is being said (stance markers) and language used to refer to other texts. Most of the models adopting such a broad view of metadiscourse (e.g. Vande Kopple 1985; Crismore, Markkanen & Steffensen 1993; Dafouz-Milne 2008) follow the SFL approach to language functions (other than ideational) and accordingly recognize two types of metadiscourse – textual and interpersonal. Contra these models, Hyland (2019a) argues that all metadiscourse is interpersonal, as it anticipates the readers' knowledge and expectations. Therefore, his model recognizes two categories of metadiscourse, each with five subcategories:

1. Interactive metadiscourse, which helps the reader navigate through the text:
   a. Transition markers, e.g. *therefore, similarly,*
   b. Frame markers, e.g. *to summarize, first,*
   c. Endophoric markers, e.g. *in Table 1, (see) below,*
   d. Evidentials, e.g. reporting verbs and *according to,*
   e. Code glosses, e.g. *for instance, which means.*

2. Interactional metadiscourse, which involves the reader in the text:
   a. Hedges, e.g. *likely, approximately,*
   b. Boosters, e.g. *obviously, in fact,*
   c. Attitude markers, e.g. *admittedly, important,*
   d. Engagement markers, e.g. *see (below), let us,*
   e. Self-mention, e.g. *we* and *my.*

When teaching metadiscourse, we have to bear in mind Hyland's (2017) admonition that metadiscourse is a fuzzy concept. One reason is that metadiscourse can be realized in various forms of varying length. What this means is that no category of metadiscourse can be equated to, for instance, a particular word class. For instance, hedges include some modal verbs, e.g. *can*; lexical verbs, e.g. *suggest*; adjectives, e.g. *possible*; adverbs, e.g. *probably*; nouns, e.g. *indication*; and phrases, e.g. *to my knowledge.* Another reason is that the same form can have metadiscoursal or other meaning, depending on the context. For instance, *however* functions as metadiscourse (namely a transition marker) in (5) but not in (6), where it is a modifier of the adjective *remote.*

(5) Behrens's book, *however,* pays no attention to politics or to public matters. (BNC A05 861)

(6) Clues, *however remote,* may be crucial. (BNC A6B 797)

What follows is that metadiscourse is a functional, not a formal, category, and EAP pedagogy should make this clear to learners. Hyland's model of metadiscourse has been very influential in the study of academic writing, EAP, and it will also be used in this book due to its comprehensiveness and simplicity. Interactive and interactional metadiscourse will be discussed in detail in Chapters 5 and 6.

The last theory mentioned in this section is the **theory of politeness** by Brown and Levinson (1987), which deals with interpersonal aspects of communication. The central notion of the theory is the concept of *face*, or the self-image that members of society wish to maintain during communication. There are two aspects of face: negative face, i.e. the desire for one's actions to be unimpeded by others, and positive face, i.e. the desire to be perceived positively, approved of and appreciated. Some communicative acts threaten the face of the speaker/writer or the addressee, e.g. suggestions, disagreement and criticism – these are the so-called *face-threatening acts*. In order to save face in such situations, speakers can draw on a variety of politeness strategies, such as white lies, jokes, indirectness and references to in-group membership. The theory of politeness has been used to explain various phenomena in academic writing, such as hedging as a strategy that acknowledges the need for the reader to accept the proposed claims (Myers 1989) and the use of inclusive personal pronouns, e.g. *we* referring to the writer and audience, as a strategy conveying in-group membership (Harwood 2005a).

2.4 Approaches to teaching language and writing

This section will briefly outline selected approaches to teaching language and writing. To begin with teaching writing, several pedagogical approaches have been identified in literature (see e.g. Ivanič 2004 for an overview). One of these is **the process approach,** which focuses on processes involved in writing, such as generation of ideas, planning, drafting, revising and editing (Badger & White 2000), consulting resources and inserting references (Wingate & Harper 2021). In contrast, **the product approach** to writing focuses on language features of particular texts that learners strive to imitate (Badger & White 2000). The product approach has been extended to **the genre approach,** which additionally focuses on different social contexts in which texts are written (Badger & 2000). Genre approaches to academic writing are discussed in greater detail in Chapter 3. All the approaches have their limitations: while the process approach pays limited attention to the contexts, purposes, structure and language of texts (Badger & White 2000; Ivanič 2004; Hyland 2003a), the product and genre approaches pay limited attention to processes involved in writing. As successful writing requires the development of language, genre awareness and writing strategies, Badger and White (2000) propose that writing pedagogy should combine these approaches – and call this synthesis **the process genre approach**.

Moving now to teaching vocabulary, an approach that has gained some currency in EAP is based on using **academic vocabulary lists** (AVLs) – lists of word families frequently occurring in academic texts. There are several AVLs based on various principles (see Therova 2020 for a short overview) but they all appear to be too general to be useful for students in particular disciplines (Hyland & Tse 2007). Even though discipline-specific AVLs have been compiled, all AVLs suffer from two major problems related to the fact that they present vocabulary in a decontextualized way. One of these problems is that AVLs are purely form based and disregard the polysemy of words: One entry in an AVL thus might have very different meanings in different contexts (Hyland & Tse 2007). For instance, *acquisition* will refer to *language acquisition* in linguistics and *mergers and acquisitions* in business. Therefore, vocabulary teaching should raise awareness of polysemy (Logan & Kieffer 2018).

Another problem is that AVLs do not illustrate grammatical or collocational behaviour of the listed words. For instance, an AVL listing the word *research* does not provide information on its uncountability (e.g. *?researches*), collocations (e.g. *to conduct research*) or phrases in which it appears (e.g. *the research so far*). What follows is that vocabulary needs to be taught within larger structures, as has been recently recognized in the creation of the Oxford Phrasal Academic Lexicon (OPAL n.d.), which lists not only words but also phrases common in academic discourse. OPAL is related to previous research on lexical bundles in academic writing (see Chapter 4.5). This approach to vocabulary follows Sinclair (1991), who proposed that text is constructed through two opposing principles. *The open choice principle* stipulates that language choices for text construction are only restricted by grammaticality. In contrast, **the idiom principle** stipulates that 'the choice of one word affects the choice of others in its vicinity' (Sinclair 1991: 173), and that text is constructed from semi-preconstructed phrases which can be varied to some extent lexically and syntactically, e.g. *it is important to, as a result* and *in the case of*. As text is constructed by the application of both principles, grammar and lexis are one continuum rather than two separate systems – an understanding that is reflected in the SFL's (see Section 2.3) term *lexico-grammar*.

Turning now to grammar, it could be argued that EAP should focus on the development of academic literacy rather than on teaching grammar – after all, EAP students will typically have been learning the grammar of English for several years. Nevertheless, unless the learners use a good range of grammatical structures accurately, EAP classes should aim to raise awareness of relevant grammar, in particular if the students are assessed on their language. However, this is not to suggest that EAP courses should follow a structural (lexico-grammatical) syllabus. Rather, grammatical structures to be taught should be carefully selected in relation to the target genres (see

Chapter 3) and to the learner issues, in particular the structures that the learners misuse or underuse (see Chapter 4). If the learners have indeed been learning grammar for an extended period of time, time for the presentation of a structure can be reduced and more time can be devoted to transferring the students' existing knowledge to the context of academic texts and to scaffolded practice before application into students' own writing.

An approach to teaching grammar advocated by Diane Larsen-Freeman (2001) views the development of the use of grammar as a skill, called **grammaring**, through the acquisition of language patterns rather than through the acquisition of a set of rules. Similarly to SFL, Larsen-Freeman (2015: 272) sees the system of grammar as a set of options that enables language users 'to realize meanings and position themselves ideologically and socially'. For instance, academic writers can choose to introduce previous literature with reporting verbs in the present simple as presently relevant or in the past simple to distance themselves from particular sources (see Chapter 6.8). Reflecting this view of grammar, Larsen-Freeman (2001, 2015) argues that, rather than giving students arbitrary grammatical rules, teachers should give learners reasons why a particular grammatical structure is used in a particular context. In her framework, teaching grammar should thus include not only focus on form (the morpho-syntactic aspect) and meaning (the semantic aspect) but also focus on use (the pragmatic aspect – when and why a particular structure is used in lieu of an alternative structure with the same meaning).

Nevertheless, Larsen-Freeman (2001) points out that learner grammar develops in a long-lasting process characterized by occasional relapses. This insight is based on applying the **Complex Dynamic Systems Theory** into language teaching (Larsen-Freeman 1997). CDST studies systems characterized by changing behaviour which 'emerges from the interactions of its components' (Larsen-Freeman 1997: 143) rather than from the components alone and which can be disproportionally affected by numerous factors, including initial conditions and feedback, making the systems' behaviour unpredictable. CDST research (e.g. Fogal & Verspoor 2020) shows that the development of L2 writing might include periods during which the learning of one area is negatively affected by the learning of another area before both areas are acquired, leading to developmental peaks and regressions in learners' writing. CDST reveals that 'learning linguistic items is not a linear process – learners do not master one item and then move on to another' (Larsen-Freeman 1997: 151). Instead, '[l]earning takes place through continually revisiting the same space over and over again' (Larsen-Freeman 2012: 210). The pedagogical implications are obvious: rather than expecting students to have mastered a new area of academic writing after input and practice, EAP classes should regularly revise previously taught language and skills, support learning with formative feedback (see Chapter 7) and accept that students' writing will develop in a non-linear way.

2.5 Approaches to EAP

This section reviews approaches that have had an impact on how EAP is conceptualized and taught, although some of these approaches might not have originated within EAP. Such is the case of Academic Literacies, an approach proposed by Lea and Street (1998). In their seminal paper, Lea and Street recognize three models of developing academic literacy – academic skills, academic socialization and Academic Literacies – with each subsequent model building on and expanding the previous one. I will now review these models briefly.

The academic skills, or **study skills**, approach views academic literacy as a set of discrete skills which, once developed, can be transferred across various contexts; its pedagogy is remedial and focused on surface language issues such as grammar, spelling and punctuation and on generic study skills such as time management and revising for exams (Lea & Street 1998; Lillis 2003; Wingate 2006). Within the framework of the study skills approach, academic communication can be viewed as a transferrable skill and taught without reference to a particular subject, such as essay writing and giving presentations. Wingate (2006) argues that such skills should be seen as communication skills and developed within the context of disciplines. This, however, might prove difficult for English for General Academic Purposes (EGAP) courses with students from mixed disciplines.

Academic socialization, in turn, is characterized by Lea and Street (1998, 2006) as an approach to the development of literacy that recognizes disciplinary differences and enables students to adopt disciplinary practices through genre and discourse analysis. According to Lea and Street, academic socialization fails to see disciplines and genres as dynamically changing and influenced by power relations. This presentation of socialization into disciplines, however, does not acknowledge that learning about a discipline can be not only explicit, through focused instruction, but also implicit, through observation and participation (Lillis 2003; Wingate & Tribble 2012). Wingate and Tribble (2012) also point out that Academic Literacies' critique of academic socialization does not take into account critical approaches or the importance of context in the teaching of academic writing in EAP.

The final model in Lea and Street's (1998) framework is **Academic Literacies**, which 'conceptualises student writing as a socially situated discourse practice which is ideologically inscribed' (Lillis 2003: 192) and which is considered by its proponents to be superior to the other two models. This approach suggests that students struggle with academic writing not due to a lack of skills but due to multiplicity of academic literacies across disciplines and teachers and due to different interpretations of effective writing by teachers and students. Therefore, power relations should be shifted in order to make language practices visible and to redefine acceptable ways of meaning-making collaboratively with students. This would involve letting students express their personal interests and identities and allowing non-traditional forms of meaning-making (Lillis 2003). In summarizing differences between Academic Literacies and mainstream EAP, Lillis and Tuck (2016) list the following: while EAP focuses primarily on text in standard English and normative ways to help a novice writer become an expert writer, Academic Literacies focuses on the writer and his/her identities, transformative multilingual and multimodal ways of meaning-making, and challenging and negotiating academic writing practices. Nevertheless, the pedagogical application of Academic Literacies is somewhat limited. For instance, Gardner (2012) points out that Academic Literacies' focus on practices lacks in providing students with language resources. In addition, Wingate (2012b) questions how students could challenge literacy practices without understanding them first, and her findings suggest that students are more ready to adopt dominant literacy practices rather than to challenge them.

In spite of Academic Literacies literature portraying EAP as normative, some approaches in EAP have recognized that possible side effects of socialization into academia might involve accepting dominant practices in education and society without questioning, and expecting EAP students to adjust to the existing norms – what has been called the 'vulgar pragmatism' of EAP (Pennycook 1997: 256). In response to *Pragmatic EAP*, an alternative position – **Critical EAP** – has evolved as an attempt to problematize power relations and social conditions, to challenge the status quo and ultimately to bring about educational and social change (Benesch 1993). As Pennycook (1997: 263) puts it, 'it is crucial to see English classes not as mere adjuncts to the knowledge curricula but rather as important sites of change and resistance'.

One danger of this approach, as pointed out in literature (Allison 1994; Burbules & Berk 1999), is enforcing values and ideology on students. For instance, if students' ideological positions stemming from their culture are considered oppressive by their EAP teacher, is it ethical for him/her to challenge these positions (cf. Appleby 2009)? Another issue is that Critical EAP might not always work in students' favour: What if students themselves are to benefit from the status quo because gaining access to the dominant norms enables their social mobility (Canagarajah 1993) or participation in mainstream academia (Harwood & Hadley 2004)? It is this last issue that has led Harwood and Hadley (2004) to propose **Critical Pragmatic EAP**, which they define as an approach which 'acknowledges that students should be exposed to dominant discourse norms, in line with Pragmatic EAP; while on the other hand, like Critical EAP, it stresses that students have choices and should be free to adopt or subvert the dominant practices as they wish' (Harwood & Hadley 2004: 357). In this book I adopt the Critical Pragmatic approach to teaching academic writing, and I see the role of EAP teacher as that of assisting EAP learners to make informed decisions about aligning with or challenging dominant practices in particular situations while enabling them to access and produce academic texts.

The last approach reviewed in this chapter is **Intercultural Rhetoric**, or 'the study of written discourse between and among individuals with different cultural backgrounds', as defined by Connor (2011: 1). Intercultural Rhetoric originated as Contrastive Rhetoric with Robert Kaplan's (1966) paper in which he suggested that the structures of texts written by international students of various L1s differ from the linear organization expected in English. Although Kaplan's paper suffered from numerous problems of methodology and interpretation (cf. Connor 1996), it inspired further research into organizational and linguistic strategies applied in writing by various academic cultures. Intercultural research has shown, for instance, that non-anglophone rhetorical cultures might value imitation over originality (Ho 1998, cited in Ramanathan & Atkinson 1999) and moral message over criticality (Sullivan, Zhang & Zheng 2012), they may delay the statement of the purpose of writing (Čmejrková 1996) or not justify their research by a niche in the literature (Belcher & Yang 2020).

Of particular interest is John Hinds's (1987) distinction between writer-responsible and reader-responsible languages – or rather, rhetorical cultures, depending on whether the responsibility for effective communication rests mostly on the writer or reader. English, being writer-responsible, values clarity and meeting readers' expectations. In contrast, academic writing in reader-responsible rhetorical cultures tends to be associative rather than straightforward and to lack the rigid rhetorical structure found in English academic texts (Čmejrková 1996). In sum, what is considered effective writing is not universal across rhetorical cultures. The main pedagogical implication of intercultural rhetoric is that L2 writers cannot rely on transfer of rhetorical strategies from their L1. Instead, they need to become aware of differences between the rhetorical cultures of their L1 and L2 and write for each culture accordingly (cf. Belcher & Yang 2020). The role of EAP practitioners, then, is to help EAP students understand rhetorical conventions in English academic writing, while recognizing the value of other rhetorical conventions in other academic cultures.

2.6 Summary

This chapter has reviewed selected theories of epistemology and language use and approaches to teaching language and writing and to EAP. It is my belief that these theories should be part of EAP practitioners' knowledge base informing the syllabus design, materials design and teaching delivery. The rest of the book will, to varying degree, draw on these theories and approaches and discuss their relevance for and application to the pedagogy of academic writing. As previously pointed out, the presentation of theories and approaches is by no means exhaustive but selective, and its selection is influenced by my background and experience. The reader is encouraged to be unsatisfied with this subjective selection and to seek to learn about further theories and approaches to inform his/her practice.

CHAPTER 3

Genres

3.1 Introduction

The previous chapter reviewed selected theoretical frameworks and approaches relevant to the teaching of academic writing. I pointed out that genre theories were purposefully left out, as these deserve a separate, in-depth treatment. It is thus in this chapter that I focus on written genres in academia. I start by briefly introducing several approaches to the concept of genre in Section 3.2 (the SFL, English for Specific Purposes (ESP), rhetorical, socio-cognitive and cognitive metaphor approaches). Section 3.3 discusses principles of teaching genres in EAP classes and highlights power relations between the writer and the reader in student genres and a mismatch between model genres and target genres in the acquisition of academic language, which I call *the EAP genre paradox*. Section 3.4 then describes a variety of selected (sub)genres: book review, research report (composed of abstract, introduction, methods, results and discussion, and conclusion), essay and reflective writing. For each of these genres, the section gives not only a simplified move structure but also a list of relevant linguistic structures. These models of genres, however, are to be adapted for particular writers, readers, purposes and contexts. Finally, Section 3.5 concludes the chapter.

3.2 Genre

The concept of genre, defined in Richards and Schmidt (2010: 245) as 'a type of discourse that occurs in a particular setting, that has distinctive and recognizable patterns and norms of organization and structure, and that has particular and distinctive communicative functions', has been approached variously in different traditions. Bawarshi and Reiff (2010) give a detailed overview of a number of approaches to genre. Of these, three approaches, as identified by Hyon (1996), hold a central position in teaching academic writing: SFL (see Chapter 2.3), ESP and rhetorical genre approaches. To start with, **rhetorical genre studies** see texts as instruments not only for communicating but also for social acting, and it is the social context, rather than structural and linguistic description, that is the central interest of rhetorical genre studies. Consequently, rhetorical approaches see socialization rather than classroom teaching as a way of learning about genres, and as such, their pedagogical application is rather limited.

In contrast, **genre studies within SFL** stress the importance not only of social aspects of genres but also of their structural and linguistic aspects. Pedagogically, the SFL approach originally focused on school genres and later included genres relevant to adult L2 English migrants with the aim of countering social injustice. Examples of genres within SFL include, for instance, explanation, narrative and description.

Similarly to SFL, **ESP genre studies**, influenced by the work of John Swales (1990), explore how social context determines the structure and language of genres. However, in contrast to the SFL approach, the ESP approach is oriented at an L2 English university student and therefore considers such genres as research article, conference abstract and dissertation. These genres are analysed primarily through the identification and ordering of its *moves*. Move, as defined by Swales (2004: 228), is 'a discoursal or rhetorical unit that performs a coherent communicative function in a written or spoken discourse', and that can be linguistically realized in various ways and its length can vary from one clause to several sentences.

Another **socio-cognitive approach** to genre has been developed by Ian Bruce (2008a), who distinguishes between two conceptions of genre – social genre and cognitive genre. Social genres, such as personal letters and research articles, are 'socially recognized constructs according to which whole texts are classified in terms of their overall social purpose' (Bruce 2008a: 8). Cognitive genres, such as narration and explanation, 'refer to the overall cognitive orientation of a piece of writing in terms of its realization of a particular rhetorical purpose' (Bruce 2008a: 8). While the ESP and rhetorical approaches study the former type of genres and the SFL approach focuses on the latter type, Bruce combines the two conceptions in his work, pointing out that a single social genre might have multiple rhetorical purposes and thus be realized by a combination of several cognitive genres. His three-level model thus incorporates the level of social genre (e.g. results and discussion section), the level of cognitive genres (e.g. explanation) and the level of linguistic realization (e.g. cause and effect expressions). A major limitation of Bruce's model, in my view, is that only four cognitive genres are considered in academic writing, namely report, explanation, discussion and recount. These might not account for all rhetorical purposes of written academic discourse, such as orientation, argumentation and persuasion, as pointed out by Cotos, Huffman and Link (2017).

Yet another, radically different approach to genre is proposed by Sawaki (2024), who analyses academic writing not from the point of view of structure or lexico-grammatical features but from the point of view of **conceptual metaphors and cognitive images**. She demonstrates how research articles draw on cognitive images such as *lack [of something]* (e.g. to justify current research) and conceptual metaphors presenting research as an everyday domain (e.g. JOURNEY in *The goal of this study is . . .*). Sawaki's model thus offers a way of analysing genres not from the structural point of view but from the viewpoint of figurative language. As such, it is compatible with other genre approaches.

Whichever approach to genre one follows, it is important to bear in mind the notion of **prototypicality**, as pointed out by a number of scholars (Swales 1990; Paltridge 1997; Bruce 2008a; Sawaki 2024). To put it simply, prototypicality of genres means that a certain genre is characterized by a number of social, rhetorical, cognitive, structural and linguistic features but not all instances of the genre have these features to the same degree; instead, individual texts are more or less typical representatives of their genre. In other words, genres are characterized by flexible conventions rather than rigid rules (Tardy 2019). The implications for EAP classes involve pedagogy that is explorative and creative rather than prescriptive: the goal of genre analysis in class should be to provide a toolkit from which student writers will be able to choose and combine individual tools serving their own purposes rather than to provide a template-like form for the production of a target genre. Such a pedagogical approach, in the spirit of critical pragmatism (see Chapter 2), enables students both to participate in the genres of their academic community and to use genre knowledge in an original way (cf. Bruce 2008a: 10).

With this caveat in mind, in this book I follow the Swalesian (ESP) approach to genre and genre analysis due to its clear focus on academic genres, strong impact on EAP and easy application in teaching practice. Mindful of Cheng's (2021) admonition that lexico-grammatical features of particular genres are inseparable from the given genres' rhetorical organization, in Section 3.4 I provide simplified structural and linguistic models for selected academic genres. However, in recognition of genre prototypicality and variation, these models need to be adapted for students in specific contexts, as not all moves and language structures will be relevant to their context, and they might need to be substituted with other moves and linguistic devices. Moreover, EAP classes should not only present the genre models as a product but also facilitate the processes involved in producing the genres, thus applying the process genre approach to teaching writing (see Chapter 2.4).

3.3 Teaching genre analysis and the EAP genre paradox

This section starts with the applications of genre theories in pedagogical practice. It has to be pointed out that not all approaches to genre see classroom teaching as a valuable way of mastering writing genres: as mentioned in the previous section, for many scholars working within the framework of rhetorical genre approaches, only socialization into the given discourse community leads to an effective mastery of genres. I would argue, however, that socialization into academia can be facilitated through an analysis of the social context, communicative purpose and language of academic genres, and that genre analysis is thus a valuable way of learning about one's discourse community.

Most genre approaches thus see the value of explicit teaching of genres through various teaching tasks. For instance, the SFL genre pedagogy is built around the cycle of (i) contextualizing the genre, (ii) modelling through an analysis of exemplars of a given genre, (iii) joint negotiation – or collaborative construction of a text of the given genre, (iv) independent construction of a text by individual students and finally (v) linking the given genre to other texts for comparison and contrast (Bawarshi & Reiff 2010). Similarly, Bruce (2008a: 154) illustrates teaching written genres through an exploration of the extra-linguistic and linguistic context, collaborative and individual analysis of exemplar texts, and collaborative and individual writing of the given genre. Swalesian approaches are often based on awareness-raising through analysing sample texts' move structure and related language, and possibly comparing the results of the analysis across different disciplines (e.g. Swales & Feak 2004). For some practitioners, linguistic analysis involves the use of genre-specific corpora and examining concordance lines for language reuse in students' own writing (e.g. Burgess & Cargill 2013). Examples of genre teaching activities can be found in Teaching activity 3.1 and 3.2.

Teaching activity 3.1. Genre analysis

This activity is composed of three steps, presented as Teaching activities 3.1a–3.1c. This particular example focuses on the methods section of the research report.

Teaching activity 3.1a. Independent move analysis
In pairs, reread the methods section of Text 1 and identify what information is included in general. Make a list for each subsection.

Teaching activity 3.1b. Language analysis
Now reread the methods section of Text 1 again, focusing on the language used, and answer the following questions:

1. What tense is used?
2. When is the active voice used and why? When is the passive voice used and why?
3. What type of question is the research question – a *yes/no* or a *wh-*question?
4. Find non-finite participle clauses. How are they used?
5. What language structure is used to give justification for a particular choice of method?
6. Which words are used in the section to indicate:
   a) contrast,
   b) temporal sequence,
   c) cause and effect?

Teaching activity 3.1c. Guided move analysis
Look at the list of moves for the methods section and quickly reread the methods section of Text 2:

1. Which of the moves listed can you identify in the text and where?
2. Which moves are missing? Why do you think they were not included?

Commentary
Two examples of the given genre are used in this activity (example texts are not provided here due to limitations of space), and it is assumed students have read and processed these for meaning (see Section 3.3) – hence the instructions to *reread*. Move analysis is done here in two ways – independently without a reference to the move structure uncovered by published research (Teaching activity 3.1a), and scaffolded with students referring to the move structure see Section 3.4.5 (Teaching activity 3.1c). The former intends to develop students' learner autonomy by developing their genre analytic ability as a transferrable skill. It is more suitable for simpler, shorter texts – in this case a clipped methods section. The latter is suitable not only for shorter but also for longer and more complex texts, such as an elaborated methods section. The scaffolding fine-tunes the move awareness developed in Teaching activity 3.1a and prepares for the productive stage.

Teaching activity 3.1b focuses on linguistic devices of the target genre (cf. Section 3.4.5) selected as relevant to the example text analysed. Both Teaching activities 3.1a and 3.1b are conducted before providing students with a list of moves and useful language, in order to foster inductive learning.

Teaching activity 3.2. Genre production

Following the analytic activities 3.1a–c, these productive activities include three steps, 3.2a–c.

Teaching activity 3.2a. Collaborative writing

Think about the yoghurt data we analysed in the previous class. Let's write up a methods section describing our research methods.

- Research question: Which brand of dairy yoghurt has the highest content of protein?
- Open data by Sutton et al. (2019).
- Three brands: Zott, Isey, Ski.
- Protein content in the three brands: mean, median, mode – MS Excel.

Teaching activity 3.2b. Planning independent writing

Look at the list of moves and choose which of the moves:

a) You're going to include in your methods section.
b) You're not going to include in your methods section because they don't apply.
c) You might include in your methods section.

Teaching activity 3.2c. Drafting independent writing

Draft your own methods section, following the moves selected in the previous activity and using some of the language introduced earlier.

Commentary

This activity follows the genre process approach to writing (see Chapter 2.4) and proceeds from collaborative to individual writing (see Section 3.3). The collaborative writing is based on the shared points of reference – in this case content to be used for writing. As envisaged here, it is led by the teacher, who types up class suggestions for the text sentence by sentence, or phrase by phrase, for all the class to see. The teacher also encourages the class to provide other suggestions, reformulate and revise what has been written and provides assistance and instant feedback to help the class improve the text in progress. The activity should thus model the planning and drafting of a text, pursued individually in Teaching activities 3.2b–c. The independent activities refer to the move structure and language provided earlier and highlight that these are to be used as a toolkit rather than a template.

In the remainder of this section I will discuss what I call the *EAP genre paradox* – a set of mismatches between the student genres student writers need to produce (e.g. essay, dissertation) and the expert genres which students read for content and which they might use as models for their writing (e.g. textbooks, journal articles). While it has long been recognized that student and expert genres differ in multiple ways, I will argue that the common solution – that of providing student exemplars of target genres – only accentuates the problem.

One type of mismatch between student and expert genres is social, namely mismatch in purpose and audience. While expert genres are typically produced for peers (journal articles) or for readers with less knowledge than the writers (textbooks), assessed student genres are typically produced for a teacher assessor with more knowledge and more power: it is typically the teacher who determines the text's topic, length, deadline and mark given to the writer (Tardy 2019). In the words of Shaw (1992: 304), 'textbooks inform downwards from a position of authority, and articles report horizontally to peers, while writers of theses are required to display their knowledge and grasp of the subject "culture" to superiors'.

Related to the audience is the purpose of writing. Expert genres are produced to disseminate knowledge (journal articles) or inform the reader (textbooks). In contrast, student writing may have a variety of communicative purposes, e.g. to propose a research plan (cf. Goulart, Biber & Reppen 2022), but ultimately its social purpose is to display knowledge and skills (cf. Nesi & Gardner 2012). As Hyland (2012: 141) puts it, students have 'to demonstrate an appropriate degree of rhetorical sophistication while recognizing readers' greater knowledge of the field and power to evaluate their text'. To illustrate, the authentic purpose of a published academic book review is 'to introduce and evaluate new publications in the field' (Motta-Roth 1995: 4), yet when students produce a book review for assessment, its actual purpose is to demonstrate independent reasoning (cf. Nesi & Gardner 2012).

These social mismatches between student and expert genres are reflected in discoursal mismatches, that is in terms of textual organization (e.g. the use of topic sentences expected from students but infrequent in expert writing, see Chapter 5.2) and use of language, especially metadiscourse to assert writer authority (e.g. Hyland 2002b). As Harwood and Hadley (2004: 360) point out, 'a dominant norm for expert writers may not be a dominant norm for student writers'.

The implications of the mismatches between expert and student genres are not trivial, and they can be detrimental to the quality of student writing. First, student writers can be reluctant to assume authority in their writing, as they feel authority is appropriate only for established writers (e.g. Hyland 2002b), and to critique scholars who might become examiners of their work (Jomaa & Bidin 2017). Second, as Wong (2005) shows, a writer whose primary purpose in writing is knowledge display for evaluation might engage in less risk-taking compared to a writer whose primary purpose is to receive feedback in order to improve his or her draft. This may become particularly problematic in reflective writing, if students write what they think their assessors expect rather than what they actually believe (see Section 3.4.9). Third, when student writers know they share background knowledge with their teacher reader, they might not develop content in depth as this would result in redundant information or they might not cite the respective sources (Chandrasoma, Thompson & Pennycook 2004; Parkinson 2017). Finally, novice student writers tend to use spoken register when writing for an audience they know personally (Puma 1986, cited in Aull 2015: 'The FYW corpus and the analysis' section). In sum, student writers play it safe or write for a particular teacher rather than for an abstract academic audience.

EAP genre paradox is the reason why research exploring the frequency of particular language devices in student writing should not compare it to the frequency of the devices in expert writing (see Chapter 1.3), and why expert writing might not be a realistic model of writing for student writers. As regards teaching implications, the paradox cannot be avoided altogether – it can only be mitigated in several ways. First, we need to acknowledge the paradox and 'multiple and conflicting purposes, audiences, occasions' (Coe 2002: 203) of student writing rather than a single purpose and a single audience. Second, as Wong (2005: 44) suggests, 'the intended audience should be clarified and explained to students' as part of task instructions. This could be an imaginary peer audience, and students should engage in peer feedback to receive an authentic response from this intended peer audience. Third, in line with Critical Pragmatic EAP (Harwood & Hadley 2004), students should be empowered to follow or flout conventions, understanding both the rationale for a particular convention (or a lack thereof) and the potential consequences of flouting it.

One obvious solution to the EAP genre paradox might be the use of student exemplars. While I am supportive of their use in writing pedagogy, I argue that they do not mitigate the problem of the EAP genre paradox, which essentially involves mismatches between the genres students *read* and the genres students *write*. Students normally read expert genres such as journal articles and textbooks. They seldom have access to student genres such as dissertations and essays (cf. Thompson 2005: 311, Nesi & Gardner 2012: 134), be it due to data protection or tutors' fear that seeing other students' successful work might lead to plagiarism. Such access, then, typically needs to be enabled by a teacher with power to do so. Even then, students might consult a handful of exemplars to notice particular discoursal features, yet their exposure to the target genres is limited and they do not read the texts for content in the sense of extracting information from the texts and using it in their own writing. Student exemplars are thus exploited as mere instances of form rather than repositories of knowledge.

Student writers, thus, will have seen multiple examples of expert genres but few, if any, target genres. This means student writers will have developed formal schemata, i.e. 'knowledge relative to the formal, rhetorical organizational structures' (Carrell 1987: 461), of expert genres.[1] These schemata, however, are not entirely relevant to the target genres students need to write, given the social and discoursal mismatches discussed above. Using student exemplars to develop relevant schemata might help to some extent (although for robust schemata, frequent exposure rather than seeing a few exemplars is needed).

Nevertheless, student exemplars are normally only used for genre and language analysis but not for content. This arguably limits the acquisition of the rhetorical patterns and language used in student genres as during the analysis students might be pre-occupied with processing the content of the texts. A more effective approach to teaching language would be the approach advocated by Timmis (2018), drawing on language naturally occurring in authentic texts which are selected for their content and which are processed for meaning before being utilized for language work. This, indeed, is how EAP pedagogy approaches expert genres – texts are selected for content and the discussion of content precedes genre and language analysis.

However, as the value of content in student exemplars might be limited for EAP classes, the EAP genre paradox remains a problem. The only solution to it, then, is acknowledging the paradox and openly discussing it with students, raising their awareness of different types of academic writing and empowering them to make informed choices in their writing, in line with Critical Pragmatic EAP (see Chapter 2.5).

3.4 Genre analysis of selected genres

As mentioned in Chapter 1, academic writing involves a variety of genres. A comprehensive overview of university student genres is given by Nesi and Gardner (2012), who divide these genres into five groups according to their purpose. The first group involves genres whose purpose is **to demonstrate knowledge and understanding**, such as *exercise* and *explanation*. As they draw on less complex cognitive skills (cf. Anderson et al. 2001; see Chapter 2.2), they are used especially with lower undergraduate students. They are typical of hard sciences, rather descriptive and frequently supported with visuals.

The second group of genres requires students **to demonstrate criticality**, and as such complex cognitive skills. This group includes *essay* and *critique*. Essay has, in Nesi and Gardner's (2012) framework, six subtypes, including *exposition* and *commentary*. A critique is both descriptive and evaluative and can focus on, for instance, a book, a journal article, a research method, research results or a product.

The purpose of the third group of genres, including *literature surveys, methodology recounts* and *research reports*, is **to demonstrate research skills**. Literature surveys include a variety of subtypes, including *annotated bibliography* and *literature review*. Methodology recounts, typical for hard sciences, describe research methods used to carry out an assigned experiment, e.g. *lab report*. Research reports, e.g. *dissertations*, present independent research firmly grounded in theory.

The purpose of the fourth group of genres is **to prepare university students for professional practice**. These genres, for instance *case study* and *design specification*, require students to apply disciplinary theory into practice. The final group is **writing for self and others** and includes *empathy writing* that communicates specialist knowledge to a non-specialist audience, e.g. *leaflets for the public*, and *narrative recounts* that chronologically report on events or provide personal accounts of events, e.g. *accident reports* and *reflective recounts*, respectively.

Nesi and Gardner's (2012) overview shows the breadth of writing that might be expected from university students. It is therefore imperative that EAP courses prepare students for this breadth and the complexity of the genres involved and avoid overemphasis on writing text summaries or argumentative essays.

In the remaining of this section I briefly introduce a range of selected genres: book review; abstract; research report as composed of introduction, literature review, methods section, results and discussion section, conclusion; essay and reflective writing. These include stand-alone genres, e.g. essay; sub-genres that are part of a larger genre, e.g. introduction of a research report; and genres that can be stand-alone or part of another genre, e.g. literature review. Each selected genre is presented through its move analysis and relevant language, yet, as discussed in Section 3.2, this is meant for adaptation to fit the specific requirements of a particular group of students rather than a one-size-fits-all template. The language structures referred to throughout the section will be discussed in detail in Chapters 4–6.

3.4.1 Book review

One genre that seems to be rather popular in EAP courses is the summary. While writing a summary of an academic text might seem like a good exercise in identifying and paraphrasing key ideas in a text, I would question the value of having students write a summary due to its limited authenticity – How many times do university students have to produce a summary of a single text for a reader (other than for oneself, perhaps, in which case they are likely to use artificial intelligence to write it for them)? As Dovey (2010: 49) puts it, 'summary writing, as a classroom genre, rarely has an authentic purpose'. Moreover, summary writing may give students the impression that academia values regurgitating ideas, when instead, it is synthesizing and critiquing ideas that university students should aim for. Therefore, I propose that, rather than focusing on summaries, EAP classes should focus on writing *evaluative genres* (see Hyland & Diani 2009), such as book reviews and literature reviews.

For this reason, I do not discuss the summary here but turn instead to the book review. The purpose of an authentic book review is 'to introduce and evaluate new publications in the field' (Motta-Roth 1995: 4). The rationale for writing book reviews in EAP classes is that students engage with an extended academic text, concisely summarize its content and develop a critical stance on the book's content and suitability for its target audience. For researchers hoping to write for publication, book reviews also present a relatively easy entry into publishing. The move structure and useful language for the book review are presented in Table 3.1.

3.4.2 Abstract

The abstract can be a stand-alone genre (e.g. abstract as a conference proposal) or a sub-genre of the research report (e.g. abstract of a journal article). In the latter case, however, the abstract will frequently function also as stand-alone genre in databases. The purpose of the abstract is to briefly summarize a research study and to arouse the reader's interest in the full study.

Research has uncovered two main types of the abstract, with a third, rather infrequent, mixed type combining the other two types (Lorés 2004; cf. also Samraj 2005). *Informative* abstracts give a succinct overview of an entire research study. As such, their move structure reflects the structure of research reports (see Table 3.2 for an overview of moves and language). In contrast, *indicative* abstracts merely inform the reader of the topic and scope of research without giving details of the methods or findings, and their move structure is the same as Swales's (1990) model for introductions (see Section 3.4.3). This type is not further discussed here, and the reader is referred to the move analysis of introductions below. While Dos Santos (1996) points out that a mere indication of conclusions fails to meet the readers' expectations and to serve the purpose of the genre, it can be argued that indicative abstracts may suit argumentative studies better than informative abstracts, which will best fit data-driven research studies. Further research is needed to elucidate authors' purposes in a particular type of the abstract and the respective effects on the readership. Nevertheless, a more recent trend in academic communication is to produce abstracts in modes additional to writing, such as graphical abstract and video abstract (Florek & Hendges 2023; Liu 2020).

TABLE 3.1 Move Structure and Language of the Book Review

Moves	Language
Introduce the book: • What is its topic? • What is its purpose? • Who is the book for? • Who is the author? • Define key terms or give background information on the topic • How does the book contribute to the field?	Introducing the book with the verb *to be* in present simple, e.g. *[Book title] is . . . This book/volume is . . .* *For* + complex noun phrases to refer to the intended audience, e.g. *for researchers working in the field of nanoscience* Positive attitude markers, e.g. *outstanding, a welcome contribution* Non-finite clauses with *to*-infinitive of purpose: *(the book's) purpose is to advocate a novel approach to the study of*
Describe the book: • How is it organized into (parts and) chapters? • What is each part/chapter about? • Is there any additional material, such as graphs and appendices?	Endophoric markers[a] referring to the book reviewed and its parts, e.g. *In the following chapter, Chapter 5 explores* Present simple with active or passive voice, e.g. *the author explores, The book is divided into*
Evaluate the book: • How important or innovative is it? • Is the topic current and are the references up-to-date? • Is the book convincing? Is anything missing from the discussion? • Is it useful to readers? Why (not), how and to what kinds of readers? • How easy to read is it? Is it clear? • How could the book be improved?	Attitude markers: positive and negative adjectives, e.g. *detailed, restricted* Hedging to soften criticism, e.g. *we might expect* Self-mention, e.g. *in my opinion* Engagement markers – reader references, e.g. *provide the reader with* Unreal conditionals: modal verb + have + past participle, e.g. *the book would have benefitted from*

The evaluation should concern both:

A) selected individual chapters, for instance regarding particular arguments. The evaluation of particular chapters appears immediately after their description in the body paragraphs concerned with the relevant chapter(s), and

B) the whole book, for instance regarding value for the audiences. The evaluation of the whole book appears in the concluding paragraphs.

TABLE 3.1 (Continued)

Moves	Language
Give recommendation: • Do you recommend the book to a specific readership (possibly despite its limitations)?	Frame markers, e.g. *In summary* Transition markers of contrast, e.g. *in spite of* Recommendations with the modal verb *should*, e.g. *The book should be of interest to*, or with future simple tense, e.g. *The book will appeal to*

Based on: Belcher (1995), Hyland (2004b), Moreno and Suárez (2008) and Motta-Roth (1995).

[a] Endophoric markers are not really used endophorically here, as they refer to another text. I use the term endophoric markers for simplicity, however, as these devices are discussed in Chapter 5.

I now turn to discussing sub-genres of the research report, i.e. introduction, methods, results and discussion (the so-called IMRAD structure) and the conclusion section. With some adaptation (e.g. no indication of a research gap in the introduction section), these can also be used to teach the genre of laboratory reports, given the similarities between research reports and laboratory reports (cf. Parkinson 2017).

3.4.3 Introduction

The purpose of the research report introduction is to provide background to and rationale for a research study. Although the introduction of a research report can vary in length, depending on the type and length of the respective research report (e.g. journal article or dissertation), research has shown that introductions tend to be fairly similar across research report types and disciplines (Anthony 1999; Bunton 2002; Samraj 2002), with only slight variations from Swales's (1990) Create a Research Space (CARS) model. The move structure and respective language are presented in Table 3.3. Again, it must be stressed that this is to be used as a toolkit rather than as a template, and writers need to adjust the move structure in Table 3.3 to suit their particular context. For instance, doctoral dissertations will include more information than journal articles, and various disciplines may identify different types of gaps (in research or in real life) and present different kinds of research (e.g. reporting on students' perceptions in education and developing a product in engineering).

TABLE 3.2 Move Structure and Language of the Abstract

Moves	Language
Contextualize the research: • What is known about the topic? Why is it important? • What research has been done so far?	Topic + present simple, e.g. *genre awareness is an important area of EAP* Reference to a body of literature with present perfect, e.g. *recent research has found* Evidentials with present or past simple, e.g. *Pho (2008) shows that*
Present your research: • What is its purpose? • What are the research questions or hypotheses?	Endophoric markers referring to the work with present simple, e.g. *This/The present study/paper focuses on*
Describe the methodology • What methods and data sources were used? • How were the data collected and analysed?	Past simple tense and passive voice, e.g. *25 participants were interviewed*
Summarize the findings • What are the main findings of the research?	Vocabulary referring to research, e.g. *the results, the findings, the study* Hedges, e.g. *The results support earlier findings that, students appear to prefer* Boosters, e.g. *The results strongly indicate, The study found* Positive attitude markers, e.g. *show the positive effect of intervention* Vocabulary referring to statistical testing, e.g. *significant difference*
Draw conclusions: • What do the findings mean? • What recommendations can you give?	Self-mention, e.g. *We suggest that*

Source: Dos Santos (1996), Obeng, Wornyo and Hammond (2023) and Pho (2008).

3.4.4 *Literature review*

The literature review can be a stand-alone genre (e.g. review articles) but typically it is part of a research report as a sub-genre. In the former case, the literature review provides a state-of-the-art overview of research into

TABLE 3.3 Move Structure and Language of the Introduction Section of the Research Report

Moves	Language
Provide background: • Why is the topic important/interesting in real life or for research? • What do we know about the topic from previous research? • Define and exemplify relevant terms.	Positive attitude markers, e.g. *important, well-established, plays a central role in* Temporal adjectives or adverbs, e.g. *recent research* Present perfect tense to refer to a body of literature, e.g. *a number of studies have investigated/found/shown that, it has been suggested that* Evidentials with present simple to show current relevance, e.g. *Swales (2019) suggests*
Establish a gap: • What do we not know about the topic from previous research? How can the previous research be extended? • What problem in real life remains to be solved? Note. Only include here a gap that your study addresses.	Transition markers of contrast, e.g. *however, nevertheless, yet* Quantifiers specifying limited quantity, e.g. *little research has been conducted, few studies investigate, little is known about* Negation, e.g. *no systematic investigation, it is not clear whether* Negative attitude markers, e.g. *time consuming, research is limited, existing studies suffer from*
Present your work: • What is the aim of your work? What are your research questions? • What theoretical framework do you use? (in introductions to longer research reports) • What methods did you use? (in introductions to longer research reports) • What are your main findings? What do you propose or what have you developed? • How does your work fill the gap identified above? How does it extend previous research? • How is your work organized?	Non-finite *to*-infinitive clauses to refer to the aim, e.g. *the aim/goal/purpose/objective of the present/this study/paper/article is to determine* Self-mention, e.g. *In this paper we explore/propose that* Passive voice to refer to the overall organization of the text, e.g. *The remainder/rest of the paper is organized as follows.* Endophoric markers and present simple to refer to the more detailed organization of the text, e.g. *This paper argues that, Section 2 presents*

Source: Anthony (1999), Bunton (2002), Cortes (2013), Lu, Yoon and Kisselev (2021), Maher and Milligan (2019), Samraj (2002), Swales (1990).

a particular area. In the latter case, its 'purpose is to justify the value of the research, and to show why it is distinct from what is documented in the literature' (Kwan 2006: 32), and its move structure is fairly similar to the introduction sub-genre (Kwan 2006; Tseng 2018) – and in fact the literature review is sometimes embedded within the introduction instead of being a separate section. Due to these overlaps between the introduction and the literature review, I do not offer a separate overview of moves for the literature review.

Nevertheless, as shown by Dovey (2010), focusing on the structure and language of the literature review only via the product/genre teaching approach (see Chapter 2.4) is not effective enough, as it might result in students over-relying on summaries of individual sources at the expense of synthesizing them. Dovey concludes that to teach writing literature reviews, it is more suitable to apply the process approach (see Chapter 2.4), which guides students through the process of selecting information from sources and synthesizing it appropriately. I would therefore suggest that rather than by move structure, the organization of the literature review should be guided by hierarchical ordering of information. This hierarchy is controlled by 'a focus – an overarching purpose . . . guid[ing] . . . the process of meaningful selection and organisation' (Dovey 2010: 51).

An effective literature review presents selected relevant information related to its overarching purpose from general to specific, with increasing branching of information. It focuses on concepts rather than individual sources, showing similarities, overlaps and differences between various frameworks and studies, and taking stance (see Chapter 6) towards the works presented. An ineffective literature review, in contrast, reviews sources in excessive detail rather linearly, moving from a summary of one source to another. In other words, an effective literature review reflects knowledge-transforming rather than knowledge-telling (see Chapter 2.2). To organize their literature review appropriately, writers should incorporate hierarchical structure in their planning, as exemplified below (based on Walková 2020):

(1) Transition markers (TMs)
    a. TMs as linguistic devices
        i. TMs as a type of metadiscourse
        ii. Definitions of TMs
        iii. The use of TMs in academic writing
    b. Learner issues with TMs
        i. Frequency
            • Overuse
            • Underuse

ii. Accuracy and appropriacy
- Semantic misuse
- Stylistic misuse

3.4.5 Methods

The methods, or methodology, section 'details . . . the progression of procedural steps and provides sufficient specification for replication studies' (Cotos, Huffman & Link 2017: 92). It is a sub-genre that is part of the research report, but the methodology recount can also be a stand-alone student genre (the lab report). Although in most disciplines the methods section follows the introduction (and the literature review if not part of the introduction) and precedes the results and conclusion section(s), in some disciplines which rely on common methodology, such as chemistry, the methods section follows the conclusion. The move structure and useful language for the methods section are presented in Table 3.4. It has to be pointed out, however, that longer and more complex methods sections reporting on several experiments draw on individual moves in a cyclical fashion, and a combination of two or more moves might be repeated (Peacock 2011).

The literature (Bloor 1998; Swales 2004) also distinguishes between *clipped* and *elaborated* methods as two extremes of a continuum of detailing the research procedure. Towards one end of the continuum are clipped methods, typically in hard sciences, that rely on a large amount of shared knowledge between the writers and the audience and that present little justification or exemplification. The resulting methods sections are thus short and lexically dense. Towards the other end of the continuum are elaborated methods, typical for soft disciplines but also used in hard disciplines where the methods used are innovative or controversial. Elaborated methods sections are characterized by explicitness and a large amount of detail, with definitions of terms, justification of the choice of methods and exemplification. The resulting sections are longer and possibly divided into subsections. EAP classes should therefore be sensitive to disciplinary differences in the presentation of the methods section.

3.4.6 Results and discussion

The results and discussion are treated here together as one section, although in some research reports they may be treated separately as two sections. This will depend to some extent on the nature of the research and on disciplinary conventions. The purpose of the results and discussion section(s) is to report and interpret the results of one's research. The move structure and language

TABLE 3.4 Move Structure and Language of the Methods Section of the Research Report

Moves	Language
Give background information: • What is the purpose of the research study? What are the research questions or hypotheses? • What methodological approach was used? (Reference as appropriate.) Why?	Non-finite clauses with *to*-infinitive of purpose: e.g. *The aim was to explore the potential of, In order to investigate* Research questions: *Wh-* questions, e.g. *To what extent, How does x affect, What are some of the mechanisms* or Yes/No questions, e.g. *Does x impact y, Is there a connection between, Is it feasible to*
Report on the research conditions and/or sources of data: • What was the research environment like (e.g. geographical location, temperature)? • What materials were used (e.g. supplies, instruments, statistical packages)? • What (human or animate) subjects participated in the study? • What steps were taken to ensure ethicality of the research? • Why was the research conducted in these conditions and using these sources of data?	Description: Past simple, e.g. *this study examined* The passive voice, e.g. *no statistically significant differences were found* Self-mention, e.g. *we measured* Non-finite clauses with present participle to express means, e.g. *was measured using the contour method* Preposition *by* introducing a complex noun phrase or a non-finite present participle clause to express means, e.g. *we identified exits by searching* Frame markers: sequencers, e.g. *then* Verbs of composition, e.g. *contain, comprise, include*
Report on the data and data collection procedure: • How was the data/sample collected? Why? • What was the experimental procedure like (step-by-step recount)? Why was this procedure used? • What is the data/sample like (e.g. qualitative description, descriptive statistics)?	Justification: Non-finite *to*-infinitive clauses to express purpose, e.g. *(in order) to ensure* Preposition *for* introducing a complex noun or a non-finite present participle clause to express purpose, e.g. *for the analysis of, for preparing* Transition markers of consequence: cause, e.g. *because*
Report on the data analysis procedure • How was the data analysed? Why? • Do the methodological choices present any limitations?	

Source: Bruce (2008b), Cotos, Huffman and Link (2017), Lim (2006), Peacock (2011).

for results and discussion are presented in Table 3.5. If two separate sections are required, the *report on the results* move for the results section can be separated from the *comment on the results* move for the discussion section.

The first move, *link back and forward*, is optional, and its usefulness might depend on the length of the results and discussion sections(s). As with the methods section, the results and discussion moves are often cyclical (Peacock 2002). Table 3.5 also includes the language used in captions of figures; these are not part of the main text of the results and discussion section(s) but instead accompany figures so that they can be interpretable stand-alone.

3.4.7 Conclusion

The conclusion section discussed here is a sub-genre that is part of research reports. (Other genres, e.g. book review and essay, have concluding parts as well yet in this book these are dealt with as part of the respective genre.) The purpose of the conclusion section is to summarize and conclude a research report. It can be presented as a separate section or it can be merged with the preceding discussion section. The move structure and language for the conclusion section are presented in Table 3.6. Naturally, the order of the moves is not fixed: it might be more appropriate to discuss practical application and implications for practice after discussing significance. Similarly, recommendations for future research may be linked to the study's limitations.

3.4.8 Essay

The essay appears to be the most frequent student genre at universities in some contexts (e.g. Moore & Morton 2005 for Australia; Nesi & Gardner 2012 for the UK). However, what is referred to as *essay* can in fact represent a variety of genres and purposes (Coffin & Hewings 2003; Bruce 2010). Coffin and Hewings (2003) therefore distinguish three essay types: (i) exposition, which puts forward a claim; (ii) discussion, which considers alternatives to put forward a claim and (iii) challenge, which challenges an established claim. To these types, Nesi and Gardner (2012) add three more types: (iv) factorial essay and (v) consequential essay, which explain and evaluate factors or consequences, respectively, related to an issue, and (vi) commentary, which analyses, and possibly compares and contrasts, texts. The variability of essays needs to be borne in mind when analysing the move structure and language of essays. Table 3.7 provides an attempt to generalize over the main types of essay, and as such needs to be adapted for particular essay type and purpose, using authentic student exemplars as samples for analysis and models for writing.

TABLE 3.5 Move Structure and Language of the Results and Discussion Section of the Research Report

Moves	Language
Link back and forward • What were the research aims and/or methods used? • How is the rest of this section organized?	Past simple tense, e.g. *the present study sought to* Future simple tense, e.g. *I will discuss each of x in turn*
Report on the results • What are the results? Highlight trends and give evidence, referring to examples, statistics and visuals as appropriate. Are the results statistically significant? • Are the results surprising? Do they confirm the hypothesis?	Lexical bundles with present simple tense, e.g. *the(se) results/findings suggest that* Frame markers: sequencers, e.g. *first,* and topicalizers, e.g. *with regard to* Code glosses, e.g. *for example* Endophoric markers, e.g. *see Figure 1* Attitude markers, e.g. *surprisingly*
Comment on the results • How can the results be explained? • Do the results agree with previous literature? If not, how can the difference be explained? • How do the results contribute to the field?	As above plus: Lexical bundles and evidentials, e.g. *this finding is consistent with, lends support to, the findings support the previous results by Shaw (2008)* Transition markers, e.g. *as a result, due to the fact that* Hedges, e.g. *one possible explanation is* Boosters, e.g. *the results clearly demonstrate*
Figure captions and legends (separate from the main text) • What does the figure show? What do its parts mean?	Captions: Complex noun phrases rather than finite clauses, e.g. *the move structure and language of the results and discussion section* Legends: Vocabulary referring to the colours and shapes in figures, e.g. *the red bar, the dashed curves* Vocabulary showing connections and comparisons, e.g. *normalized frequency, versus, respectively* The passive voice, often with prepositions, e.g. *levels are indicated by, are shown along, the black curves were obtained using, are given in*

Source: Brett (1994), Du, Jiang and Liu (2021), Hopkins and Dudley-Evans (1988), Le and Harrington (2015), Liu and Buckingham (2018), Yang and Allison (2003).

TABLE 3.6 Move Structure and Language of the Conclusion Section of the Research Report

Moves	Language
Briefly summarize the study: • What was the study's aim/hypotheses/ research questions? What gap did the study try to address? • What methods were used? • What are the findings?	Frame markers: discourse labels, e.g. *In summary* In chapter-long conclusions in dissertations: endophoric markers, e.g. *Chapter 3* Present perfect or past simple, e.g. *this work has explored . . . Chapter 5 discussed . . .*
Evaluate the study: • What is its significance? • What are its limitations?	Attitude markers, e.g. *make a significant contribution to, the main limitation*
Show the study's implications: • What is the practical application of the findings? What recommendations for practice/policy can you give? • What recommendations for future research can you give?	Hedges and/or boosters, e.g. *can be of benefit to, should be taken into account* Vocabulary referring to future research, e.g. *Future research needs to be undertaken, further studies might*

Source: Bunton (2005), Liu and Buckingham (2018), Soler-Monreal (2016), Yang and Allison (2003).

As with the literature review, an important organizational feature of essays not captured in their move structure is the hierarchical ordering of information. The overarching principle controlling the organization of the essay is the proposition related to the essay title, stated in the introduction and conclusion section. The body of the essay, then, provides supporting claims subordinate to the proposition, which are in turn supported with evidence in the form of data, cited sources and examples. Hounsell (1997) shows that writers of high-scoring essays organize data in a particular order to show their own interpretation of the material used, in contrast to writers of low-scoring essays, who present information in their essays discretely, without a particular organizing principle and without an overarching proposition. This difference in approaching essay writing, reflecting the difference between knowledge-transforming and knowledge-telling strategies discussed in Chapter 2.2, thus seems crucial for successful essay writing. Nevertheless, this hierarchical organization cannot be achieved by move structure: as Bruce (2010: 160) acknowledges, essay 'body sections are not amenable to analysis in terms

TABLE 3.7 Move Structure and Language of the Essay

Moves	Language
Provide background: • What is known about the topic? Give facts, definitions and examples. Why is the topic important? • What is your proposition in relation to the essay question/title? OR What issue will you consider in the essay? OR What position will you challenge? • How is the rest of the essay organized?	Complex noun phrases referring to the topic with present simple tense, e.g. *international students represent a significant proportion of enrolments in UK higher education* or with past simple tense for historical perspective, e.g. *free elementary education was introduced* Self-mention *I* or inanimate subjects with present simple or future simple, e.g. *(in this essay) I (will) argue that, this essay argues that* Frame markers: sequencers, e.g. *this essay will first examine . . . It will then*
Provide data: • What evidence in support of your proposition can you give? How do you respond to opposing ideas? • OR What alternative positions do you consider? • OR What evidence against the position challenged can you give? • OR What factors or consequences need to be taken into account?	Transition markers, e.g. *furthermore, however* Structures expressing causative links to support argumentation, e.g. *this shows that, it can be seen that* Conditional sentences to support argumentation, e.g. *if generic structure of text types can be taught, then it follows that* Evidentials, e.g. *Bruce (2010) uses an original framework* Frame markers to move from one point to another, e.g. *I will now discuss* Hedges, e.g. *perhaps, it could be argued that*
Summarize and conclude: • What alternative positions has the essay considered? • What is your position on the essay question? • What implications can you draw? What recommendations can you give? What predictions can you make?	Complex noun phrases referring to the topic with present simple tense, e.g. *it is important to continue increasing diversity in higher education*

Source: Bruce (2010), Coffin and Hewings (2003), Henry and Roseberry (1997), Nesi and Gardner (2012).

TABLE 3.8 Move Structure and Language of Reflective Writing

Moves	Language
Briefly describe a selected incident: • What happened? • How did you feel? • Why is the incident important?	Self-mention, e.g. *I, my* Past simple tense, e.g. *I administered a test* Temporal adverbials, e.g. *during the semester* Cognition and affective verbs, e.g. *I believe, I felt* Adjectives describing emotions, e.g. *comfortable, anxious*
Analyse the incident: • Why did it happen? • How does it relate to your subject knowledge, your previous professional experience and your skills? • Was your action in line with ethical principles? • How can the incident be viewed from different perspectives (e.g. by others involved in the incident with different roles)?	Transition markers of comparison, e.g. *similarly, unlike* and consequence, e.g. *therefore, as a result of* Hedges, e.g. *perhaps*
Evaluate the incident: • What was positive and what was negative about the incident from your point of view? • What was positive and what was negative about the incident from the perspectives of others? • What could you have done differently?	Attitude markers, e.g. *benefits* Unreal conditionals: modal verb + *have* + past participle, e.g. *I could have used, it would have been beneficial, I should have considered*
Plan future action: • What have you learnt from the experience? • What options for action do you have in future? • What will you do differently in future?	Future simple, e.g. *I will ask*

Source: Bowman (2021), Nesi and Gardner (2012), Ryan (2011), Ryan and Ryan (2013).

of such content-organising moves'. For this reason, in teaching essay writing it is imperative to combine the product/genre approach with the process approach (see Chapter 2.4), focusing on providing evidence, making claims and formulating one's position (see Hewings 2010 for an illustration).

3.4.9 Reflective writing

The final genre to be discussed is reflective writing, which aims to enhance professional practice in certain disciplines, especially within health care and education. Unlike most academic writing (see Chapter 1.2), reflective writing is much more personal in terms of content and language, and intertextuality is not its essential feature (Bowman 2021). Its move structure and language devices are presented in Table 3.8.

Reflective writing belongs to the *narrative recount* category of writing for self and others in Nesi and Gardner's (2012) framework, and it is an example of the EAP genre paradox (see Section 3.3): On the one hand, reflective writing serves to develop metacognitive skills and as such is authentically written for oneself. On the other hand, when reflective writing is produced for assessment, it is written for others and its purpose becomes to demonstrate learning and/or compliance with disciplinary practices. This power imbalance, as Bowerman (2021: 113) suggests, might lead students 'to write to satisfy the perceived reader, but not to include their genuine thoughts'. I therefore propose that, in the spirit of Critical Pragmatic EAP (see Chapter 2.5), EAP classes should open up discussions of power structures related to reflective writing.

3.5 Summary

This chapter briefly discussed a number of genre theories and approaches to teaching academic genres. Recognizing the social context of student genres, I highlighted knowledge and power imbalance related to assessed student writing. I introduced the concept of the EAP genre paradox, which is a set of social and discoursal mismatches between expert genres that students read for content and target genres that students need to write, and discussed its implications for learning and producing writing. To partially mitigate the negative impact of this social context, I advocated Critical Pragmatic approach to teaching genres. For an effective genre pedagogy, I advocated the process genre approach to teaching writing. Recognizing the importance of structural and linguistic features of genres, I presented the move structure and language of selected academic genres, while recognizing that for some genres, such as essay and literature review, move structure might not be sufficient, and that hierarchical cognitive organization of information is more appropriate.

The chapter's selection of genres is necessarily limited and a review of additional genres would be beneficial. As I have stressed throughout the chapter, however, the analyses of genres presented here are not intended as formulas to be followed but rather as a starting point for adaptation. As such, they can also serve as models for practitioners' own genre analysis of additional genres. The language introduced in this chapter in relation to particular genres will be discussed in detail in the following three chapters.

CHAPTER 4

Language and content

4.1 Introduction

Moving on from specific genres discussed in the previous chapter, this chapter focuses on content and language in academic writing more generally. I consider these two as inseparable parts of communication, just as meaning and form are inseparable parts of words and structures. Starting with content, Section 4.2 explores the rather elusive concept of criticality and Section 4.3 centres on argument as an outcome of argumentation and persuasion. I advocate teaching criticality and the development of argument as embedded within disciplines and genres. At the interface of content and language sits paraphrasing (Section 4.4), which mediates content expressed in a source in a language alternative to the one used in the source. I argue in favour of the pedagogical approach to paraphrasing that gives primacy to content: in other words, writers should paraphrase ideas, not sentences. Section 4.5 then moves on to language, with grammar and lexis treated together as interrelated components rather than as independent systems of language (see Chapter 2.4). The section discusses selected lexico-grammatical features, following up on those identified as relevant across a variety of genres in Chapter 3. The chapter closes with a discussion of formal academic style in Section 4.6, recognizing that some stylistic conventions can and should be contested.

4.2 Criticality

Criticality is one of the cornerstones of academic discourse (see Chapter 1.2), yet its understanding varies. According to Davies's (2015) review, the literature recognizes three main components of criticality:

(1) criticality as critical thinking, that is, as a cognitive skill;

(2) affective dispositions that are a prerequisite for critical thinking, such as inquisitiveness, scepticism, ability to entertain alternative viewpoints, upholding ethical standards and intellectual humility as well as intellectual courage and

(3) critical action, which includes being critical members of an academic community and challenging oppressive ideologies (cf. Critical EAP in Chapter 2.5).

In terms of cognition, critical thinking processes include analysis, evaluation, problem solving, drawing inferences, interpretation and explanation, identifying assumptions, predicting, seeing alternative viewpoints and argumentation (Davies 2015; Facione 1990; Lai 2011). Taking into account the affect and action components of criticality, EAP pedagogy should encourage students to see themselves as valid members of academic community who have a legitimate right to take stance on previous literature and to put forward their own claims, as long as these are well supported with evidence.

Difficulties that L2 English students have with criticality include a lack of understanding what criticality is, a lack of language that expresses criticality, a lack of subject knowledge, treating published literature as facts that cannot be contested, cultural discomfort with criticizing other researchers' work and fear that the authors to be criticized might become the writer's dissertation examiners (Jomaa & Bidin 2017). These difficulties reflect all the three components of criticality outlined above: cognitive in terms of understanding criticality and adequate subject knowledge, affective in terms of intellectual courage and confidence to critique others, and action in terms of challenging power relations. What is missing in Davies's (2015) framework, however, is the use of language to express criticality, suggesting that the importance of language, so central to EAP, can be overlooked in HE more generally.

Textual approaches provide a clearer understanding of how criticality is manifested in academic writing. A simple and pedagogically useful model of criticality is Leader's (2019) Scope model with five components:

(1) Selection of relevant sources,

(2) Care in accurate acknowledgement of sources,

(3) Organization of information in such a way that it logically leads to one's argument,

(4) Positioning of sources, highlighting similarities and differences between them and

(5) Evaluation of the sources in the sense of aligning oneself with particular sources and disagreeing with others, and stating one's own position.

The SCOPE model thus incorporates some of the cognitive components of criticality, specifically analysis, evaluation and argumentation, as well as one of critical dispositions, namely adhering to ethical standards of acknowledging sources.

Humphrey and Economou (2015) propose the Onion model of criticality, which includes four layers, with the lower layers supporting the higher ones. The basic layer is description, which provides uncontested, established information from cited sources. The second layer, analysis, reorganizes information from sources into categories and/or highlights logical relations such as similarity and contrast. The next layer, persuasion – or argumentation in Gomez-Laich, Miller and Pessoa's (2019) adaptation of the Onion model – argues for and supports the position of the writer. The final layer, critique, challenges positions of others or points out limitations of sources and offers the writer's alternative. The Onion model includes cognitive processes of analysis, argumentation and evaluation, and like the SCOPE model, incorporates the use of sources.

These two models can be used to help students understand criticality. Nonetheless, I would suggest that, rather than teaching criticality as a decontextualized transferrable skill, it should be taught in relation to students' discipline and/or a particular genre, to the extent possible. The literature disagrees on whether criticality as a skill is transferrable across different domains, whether it is tied to a specific domain or whether it has elements of both (Lai 2011). Davies (2015), for instance, suggests that an individual's cognitive skills and dispositions in general are transferrable across disciplines, whereas critical action that is part of one's socialization into a particular discipline is discipline specific. It is unclear, however, how to separate the two: although Davies (2015: 87) considers 'argumentation . . . very much a general skill, congruent with many disciplines (as all disciplines use arguments)', research suggests that argument is constructed very differently across disciplines (Walková & Bradford 2022). General argumentation skills might therefore not be successfully applied in the context of a particular discipline. Indeed, pedagogical approaches seem to be more effective when teaching criticality specifically for a particular discipline rather than in general, and intra-disciplinary transfer of criticality is more likely than interdisciplinary one (Lai 2011). It follows that EAP pedagogy should enable and encourage students to explore the content of their discipline, either within an ESAP course, or within an EGAP course with an interdisciplinary focus, as described by Bodin-Galvez and Ding (2019). An example of the latter approach is an interdisciplinary class in which students write a literature review within their particular discipline, supporting their development of subject knowledge by reading subject-specific sources.

In addition to teaching criticality within the context of students' disciplines, criticality should be embedded in genre pedagogy (cf. Bruce 2020), as it is manifested variously across genres, for instance in the book review as evaluation of an entire book, in the literature review as analysis of relations and evaluation of selected information from a number of sources and in the research report primarily as persuasion and evaluation of one's findings. Disciplinary and genre contextualization of criticality should be coupled with teaching the linguistic realization of criticality. Language for expressing criticality includes abstract vocabulary realized as nominalizations (see Section 4.5), attitude markers (Chapter 6.4), transition markers of contrast and of consequence (Chapter 5.5) and hedging (Chapter 6.5) (Bruce 2020; Gomez-Laich, Miller & Pessoa 2019; Humphrey & Economou 2015). The following section zeroes in on a prominent aspect of criticality – the development of an argument.

4.3 Developing argument

As most university writing requires students to develop an argument (Wolfe 2011), the presentation of an argument should be central to teaching academic writing (Wingate 2012a). Lee and Deakin (2016: 21) define argument as 'developing and defending a position; appealing to a reader's logic and emotion; anticipating and countering a reader's reactions; and aligning with or distancing oneself from cited sources'. Following this definition, this book understands argument not just as taking a side in an argumentative essay (as interpreted by some EAP practices), but as an outcome of reasoning and persuasion in a variety of academic genres, which is closely connected to the genre's purpose.

Rhetorical studies have developed several theoretical models of argument (see, e.g. Andrews 2005 and Wolfe 2011 for overviews). Toulmin's ([1958] 2003) classic model involves a number of interrelated components: a *claim* is supported with *data*; the connections between the claim and the data are *warrants*, whose authority rests on *backing*; *qualifiers* limit the degree to which the claim applies; and the conditions of *rebuttal* specify when the claim does not hold. Toulmin (2003: 97) illustrates his model with the following example: *Harry was born in Bermuda* (data). Since *a person born in Bermuda will generally be a British subject* (warrant) *on account of legal provisions* (backing), then, *presumably* (qualifier) *Harry is a British subject* (claim) *unless both his parents were not Bermudians* (rebuttal). While Toulmin's model has been very influential, it has also attracted some criticism. Thus, for instance, Andrews (2005) considers the model as useful for theoretical analysis but not for pedagogical application. Its problems lie in overlaps between the individual components, inapplicability to macrostructure and to arguments composed of several claims, as well as superficial treatment of the relevance or accuracy of the data (Stapleton & Wu 2015; Wingate 2012a).

In contrast to Toulmin's theoretical–analytical model, Wingate (2012a) proposes a pedagogical model of argument with three components: position, presentation of the position by logical sequencing of propositions and selection of relevant evidence. Thus, position is the overall argument, typically expressed in a thesis statement, supported by individual claims (propositions), in turn supported with evidence. Wingate's (2012a) model, however, does not include a counterargument, i.e. an opposing claim. According to Wolfe, Britt and Buttler (2009), this is problematic because the absence of a counterargument makes a weak argument. Their model of argument, therefore, contains a claim, reasons for the claim and a counterargument with a rebuttal. In this model, the claim is composed of theme, side of the argument,[1] predicate and qualifiers, e.g. in the argument *Talking on cell phones while driving should be outlawed*, the theme is *talking on cell phones while driving*, the side is against, with the predicate being *should be outlawed* (the authors give no example of a qualifier). Each component of an argument – theme, side, predicate, qualifier and reasons – can generate a counterargument. Rather than agreeing with it, ignoring it or dismissing it without supporting evidence, the writer needs to rebut the counterargument in order to make his/her writing persuasive.

It follows, then, that a strong argument will contain an acknowledgement and a rebuttal of a counterargument. The rebuttal, however, must meet certain criteria for the argument to be strong: According to Stapleton and Wu (2015), the counterargument must be strong and valid, reflecting a genuine reaction of a critical reader, and each counterargument must be dismissed with a relevant rebuttal.

Nevertheless, models of argument based on claims and counterarguments are not used universally across disciplines: Walková and Bradford (2022) have identified three models of argument in journal articles in four disciplines. *Premise-based argument* in philosophy and literature proceeds inductively from evidence to claims, followed by counterarguments and rebuttals. *Exposition-based argument* in chemistry is also inductive, but it does not involve claims or counterarguments: instead, it includes justification of research, description of research process and of findings and explanation of the findings. Finally, *hypothesis-based argument* in computational science does not contain claims and counterarguments either, but it is not inductive. Instead, it is deductive, starting with a hypothesis, theorem or rule, presented also as an equation, followed by explanation and proof. While it remains to be seen what further models of argument are used in other disciplines, and to what extent these models, based on expert writing, are used by student writers, Walková and Bradford question the usefulness of teaching argument out of the context of disciplinary epistemology.

A model of argument applicable across disciplines and genres, therefore, needs to be sufficiently abstract to allow for application in manifold contexts and sufficiently flexible to allow writers to select parts relevant for a given piece of writing. An attempt at such a model is presented in Table 4.1. It is largely based on Moore and Morton's (2005) list of rhetorical functions in university writing assignments and influenced by Bruce's (2008a) cognitive genres and Fahnestock and Secor's (1988) stases.[2] Following Humphrey and Economou (2015) in recognizing criticality as a continuum rather than

TABLE 4.1 Model of Academic Argument

CRITICAL
Proposition: What is your answer to the research question/essay question?
Evaluation: Why is X valid/relevant/important? Why is the opposite of your proposition not valid? What is missing about X? What weaknesses does X have?
Implications: What should be done about X? How can X be improved?
Explanation and prediction: Why is X like this? What may happen as a result of X? Why did you choose to do Z?
Comparison and contrast: How are parts of X similar to or different from each other? How is X similar to or different from Y?
Evidence: How do your data support your proposition? How do your sources support your proposition? How does your personal experience support your proposition?
Background: What is X? What features does X have? How is Z done?
DESCRIPTIVE

a dichotomy between descriptive and critical, the model maps potential elements of argument against a continuum from the most descriptive to the most critical.

In its determination of the order of the elements on the scale, the model loosely follows Bloom's revised taxonomy (Anderson et al. 2001, see Chapter 2.2) and Humphrey and Economou's (2015) Onion model of criticality (see Section 4.2). The model thus equates:

- *background* with understanding (Bloom's taxonomy)/ description (the Onion model),
- *evidence* with applying,

- *comparison and contrast, explanation and prediction* and *implications* with an increasing level of analysing/analytical layer,
- followed by *evaluation* as evaluating/critical layer,
- reserving *proposition*, equated with creating/persuasion in Bloom's taxonomy and the Onion model, respectively, to the extreme end of the spectrum, in line with Bloom's revised taxonomy and contra the Onion model.

The reason why I consider proposition the most critical is that this is the backbone of argument, which is supported by the other components of argument.

Writers, however, should not try to draw on all the components – instead, they can select the components relevant to the context of the topic, (sub)genre and discipline. For instance, in a research report, *proposition* will be present in the form of the main finding in the abstract, results and discussion, conclusion and possibly introduction; *evaluation* will occur as highlighting the importance of research in the abstract and introduction, rejecting alternative interpretations of findings in the discussion section and acknowledging limitations in the conclusion; *implications* for practice and/or future research in the conclusion; *explanation and prediction* in the discussion and methods; *comparison and contrast* in the literature review and discussion; *evidence* by sources and data in the literature review and the results and discussion section; and *background* in the introduction, literature review and methods.

4.4 Effective paraphrasing

As mentioned in the previous two sections, criticality and argument require the use of sources in line with academic integrity. Indeed, academic integrity is a fundamental feature of academic writing and many novice writers find it difficult to avoid plagiarism. Although the proliferation of online classes and rapid advancements in artificial intelligence have led to growing concerns about intentional plagiarism (Bubaš & Čižmešija 2023), only a minority of students choose to cheat – plagiarism is often committed unintentionally. The literature therefore argues that intentional plagiarism should be distinguished from misuse of sources, and that, while the former should be addressed with disciplinary action, the latter requires pedagogical intervention and long-term student development (Hamilton 2016; Jamieson 2013; Pecorari 2003).

The reasons why students misuse sources are manifold, including different understanding of the use of sources across education systems in various cultures (Abasi, Akbari & Graves 2006), different understanding of acknowledging sources between secondary school and university (Chanock 2008) or even among different university lecturers (Chandrasoma, Thompson

& Pennycook 2004; Roig 2001), different understanding of what constitutes shared knowledge that does not need support of citations (Abasi, Akbari & Graves 2006; Chandrasoma, Thompson & Pennycook 2004), a lack of criticality on the part of the writers who feel they cannot contest expert writers' claims (Abasi, Akbari & Graves 2006; Chanock 2008) and language issues (Howard 1992; Pecorari 2008). Some of these causes are related to citation practices being occluded to student writers (Pecorari 2006), to multiplicity of academic literacies (Lea & Street 1998, see Chapter 2.5) and to knowledge imbalance between the writer and the reader of student genres (see the EAP genre paradox in Chapter 3.3). Students also fail to acknowledge sources when they do not understand that any information in a text that is not attributed to a source is taken to be the writer's original idea (Tadros 1993, see Chapter 6.8) or when they do not understand that a non-integral citation can have scope over only one sentence, not over several sentences or paragraphs earlier in the text – only an integral citation at the beginning of information taken from a source can have scope over several sentences (see Chapter 6.8). All of these causes of plagiarism, therefore, need to be addressed in EAP pedagogy, rather than language issues only.

Language issues are indeed the main concern of teaching paraphrasing in EAP. In transitioning from reliance on copying to effective paraphrasing, novice writers have been shown to pass through at least two natural stages of the development of writing. The first one is identified by Howard (1992: 233) as follows: 'a composing strategy which I call "patchwriting": copying from a source text and then deleting some words, altering grammatical structures, or plugging in one-for-one synonym substitutes'. A constructed example of patchwriting is given in Example (1), which uses Howard's definition as its source:

(1) A composition strategy called patchwriting includes copying the original text, omitting some words, changing grammar, or using synonyms. (constructed)[3]

Another stage is described by Petrić (2012: 111) as a 'painstaking creation of a mosaic out of the appropriated material and one's own words, where each is clearly marked', which she refers to as legitimate but excessive textual borrowing. This stage involves overuse of properly acknowledged fragmentary direct quotations including terms and common, easily paraphrasable chunks (Example 2).

(2) The strategy called 'patchwriting' involves lexical omission, grammatical alteration and 'plugging in one-for-one synonym substitutes' (Howard 1992: 233). (constructed)

To move beyond these stages, Macqueen and Knoch (2020) suggest that writers need to learn to distinguish between terms, lexical bundles (see Section 4.5) and text that requires paraphrasing. First, terms need to remain the same in the paraphrase; however, students new to a particular academic culture and/or epistemology of a particular discipline may struggle to identify terms in a source (Magyar 2012). EAP pedagogy should therefore help students recognize how terminology might be signalled in a text, such as by providing a definition, e.g. (3); by attributing the term to another author, e.g. *following* in (4); or by the writer's voice introducing his or her own term, e.g. *which I call* in Howard's (1992) definition cited above.

(3) Do they represent their source through copying (whether cited or uncited), summary, paraphrase or patchwriting – '[c]opying from a source text and then deleting some words, altering grammatical structures, or plugging in one-for-one synonym-substitutes' (Howard 1993: 233)? (Howard, Serviss & Rodrigue 2010: 178)

(4) Following Howard (1993), we define patchwriting as reproducing source language with some words deleted or added, some grammatical structures altered, or some synonyms used. (Howard, Serviss & Rodrigue 2010: 178)

Second, lexical bundles can and should be reused by students – but paradoxically, elsewhere, not in the paraphrase of the given text, as it would be unnecessarily close to the original, e.g. changing *a good deal of* to *a great deal of*. EAP classes should therefore help students build a repertoire of lexical bundles which they can automatically draw on in their writing without being prompted by a source.

Finally, the remaining chunks of text that are neither terms nor lexical bundles need to be paraphrased. It is tricky, however, to know how to do this and what makes an acceptable paraphrase (especially given the varying views of lecturers, as mentioned above). In an attempt to address these questions, EAP practice draws on several strategies. One is to advise students to avoid copying chunks of a certain length, e.g. chunks of five words or more (Flowerdew & Li 2007; Roig 2001). This approach, however, ignores the function of these chunks (as terms, lexical bundles or material to be paraphrased), thus potentially ignoring long lexical bundles as language that can be reused, e.g. *the rest of the paper is organized as follows*, and also legitimizing patchwriting as an effective paraphrasing strategy, e.g. changing *a good deal of* to *a great deal of* reduces the length of the string of words copied but is not effective paraphrasing.

Another approach common in pedagogical literature is to distinguish between summarizing and paraphrasing (Dubois 1988), the differences being in the focus on the key points and a select point, respectively, and in terms of length compared to the original. I would argue that such a distinction is neither authentic (expert writers unlikely consider whether they should summarize or paraphrase a text) nor does it help novice writers to express ideas from sources in their own words more effectively. Therefore, I use the term paraphrasing broadly, to cover the traditional understanding of both paraphrasing and summarizing.

I would further argue that the distinction between summarizing and paraphrasing might have a detrimental impact on student writing. On the one hand, practising summarizing a source in its entirety might impede criticality, as students reproduce the main ideas of a text without considering their own purpose in writing, i.e. they are being exhaustive instead of selective. In addition, it might impede synthesizing, as students focus on individual sources rather than on ideas within them, with a potential result of presenting a summary after a summary instead of a synthesis of ideas taken from several sources. On the other hand, practising paraphrasing in the sense of students selecting any sentence from a text to put into their own words is overtly formalistic and might give an impression that paraphrasing is a mere exercise in language manipulation in order to avoid punishment for plagiarism, disconnected from the writer's purpose. It is precisely this formalistic approach that results in misuse of sources, when '*students are not writing from sources; they are writing from sentences selected from sources*', as found by Howard, Serviss and Rodrigue (2010: 188, original italics).

A different approach is presented by Walsh Marr (2019), who proposes a focus on nominalizations to paraphrase sources in a more abstract or a less abstract language, e.g. *throwing out food – food waste*. While her approach recognizes the importance of understanding the content of a source before employing language operations, it nevertheless seems to be based on sentence-long extracts from a source rather than on longer stretches of text. It is also unclear why (and by whom) these particular sentence-long extracts have been selected for paraphrasing. Moreover, if students are to paraphrase expert texts, typically written in abstract language using nominalizations (e.g. *food waste*), the language of the paraphrase might end up lacking in formality and language complexity (e.g. *throwing out food*).

What follows from the above discussion is that teaching paraphrasing should refrain from formalism and accentuate content as serving a particular purpose. The implication for the teaching of paraphrasing is that content must always come before language and students thus need to select information they wish to include in their writing first, depending on their purpose. The selection, however, must focus on ideas rather than sentences – in fact, students should be encouraged to *paraphrase ideas, not sentences*, thus adopting a content-focused rather than form-focused approach. This approach to paraphrasing is presented in Teaching activity 4.1.

Teaching activity 4.1. Paraphrasing

You are writing a paper about female underrepresentation in STEM. Read the text by Fisher et al. (2020: 1) below and find the following information for your paper. Then paraphrase the information you found in the text in your own words:

1. You want to point out the length of PhD study for women compared to men;
2. You want to list the factors that are likely to hinder women's academic progress;
3. You want to list the factors that are likely to promote women's academic progress;
4. You want to discuss recommendations given in literature for increasing female participation in STEM.

Women's underrepresentation in science, technology, engineering, and mathematics (STEM) impedes progress in solving Africa's complex development problems. As in other regions, women's participation in STEM drops progressively moving up the education and career ladder, with women currently constituting 30% of Africa's STEM researchers. This study elucidates gender-based differences in PhD performance using new survey data from 227 alumni of STEM PhD programs in 17 African countries. We find that, compared to their male counterparts, sampled women had about one less paper accepted for publication during their doctoral studies and took about half a year longer to finish their PhD training. Negative binomial regression models provide insights on the observed differences in women's and men's PhD performance. Results indicate that the correlates of publication productivity and time to PhD completion are very similar for women and men, but some gender-based differences are observed. For publication output, we find that good supervision had a stronger impact for men than women; and getting married during the PhD reduced women's publication productivity but increased that of men. Becoming a parent during the PhD training was a key reason that women took longer to complete the PhD, according to our results. Findings suggest that having a female supervisor, attending an institution with gender policies in place, and pursuing the PhD in a department where sexual harassment by faculty was perceived as uncommon were enabling factors for women's timely completion of their doctoral studies. Two priority interventions emerge from this study: (1) family-friendly policies and facilities that are supportive of women's roles as wives and mothers and (2) fostering broader linkages and networks for women in STEM, including ensuring mentoring and supervisory support that is tailored to their specific needs and circumstances.

(Fisher et al. 2020: 1)

Sample answers
1. According to Fisher et al. (2020), female doctoral candidates need about six months more to complete their study than male PhD students.

2. Women are likely to need additional time for the completion of their PhD if they get married and have a child during their study (Fisher et al. 2020).
3. Women are likely to finish their PhD on time if they undertake their training under the supervision of a woman in an institution that promotes gender equality and prevents sexual harassment (Fisher et al. 2020).
4. Fisher et al. (2020) recommend the implementation of policies that enable married women and mothers to conduct research, and supervision and mentoring schemes that address women's specific needs.

Commentary
The text included here is an abstract because it is for illustrative purposes only. Naturally, students would be expected to work with a full text article. The activity is structured in such a way that it is linked to student's (imagined) purpose of writing, promoting selection of relevant information rather than summarizing the entire text. The information needed is not necessarily found in a single sentence: the answer to number 2 spans across two sentences. In contrast, the answer to number 1 does not require all the information from the respective sentence, so students have to select the relevant information rather than paraphrase the sentence in its entirety.

The sample answers can be shown to students for comparison after they have attempted their paraphrases. Several language devices can be pointed out to them, e.g. the use of synonymy at the level of words and phrases (*finish – complete, PhD students – doctoral candidates, study – training, half a year – six months, becoming a parent – having a child*), verb collocations drawn on for the nouns used in the text (*undertake training, promote gender equality, address needs*) and nominalization (*completion, supervision, implementation*).

The activity can be further extended to discuss the use of integral and non-integral citations and to further contextualize the paraphrased sentences to include additional sources.

4.5 Grammar and lexis

Sections 4.2 and 4.3 focused on content rather than language, Section 4.4 attempted to bridge content and language and Sections 4.5 and 4.6 will focus on language rather than content. This section reviews a number of lexico-grammatical areas relevant to teaching academic writing. I treat grammar and lexis together in one section to reflect the view that grammar and lexis are a continuum rather than two separate, independent systems (see Chapter

2.4). I propose that the teaching of lexico-grammar can be *corrective*, in order to increase learners' language accuracy and/or appropriateness to academic conventions, or *developmental*, in order to increase complexity. In other words, teaching lexico-grammar should aim not only to rectify learner errors but also to increase the range of structures that learners use. Various teaching activities focusing on lexico-grammar are presented in Teaching activities 4.2–4.7.

I propose that the selection of target lexico-grammatical areas should be based on their occurrence in target genres and/or issues in student writing. Therefore, the discussion of lexico-grammar presented here does not attempt to be comprehensive: Since grammar teaching in EAP should never be exhaustive but selective, focusing on features of academic discourse and student needs, as suggested by Hinkel (2013), the areas presented here are selected on the basis of their use in academic genres (see Chapter 3) and learner issues (Farley 2018; Hewings 2006; Koyalan & Mumford 2011).

Let us start with **tense and voice**. In my experience, students – but also some EAP teachers – often confuse these two terms. Tense relates to time (present, past, future; or up to a certain point in time – perfect) and combines with aspect, which views situations as a whole or in progress (simple or progressive/continuous). The four tenses most common in academic writing (as identified in Chapter 2; cf. also Biber et al. 1999) are as follows:

- **present simple** – to describe facts with present relevance, to report on individual sources and to signal the organization of a text;
- **past simple** – to narrate past events, to recount methods used, to summarize a text in a conclusion and occasionally to report on individual sources when the author wishes to distance him/herself from them (see Chapter 6.8);
- **present perfect** – to refer to a body of recent literature and to summarize a text in a conclusion;
- **future simple** – to make predictions and to signal the organization of a text.

It can be seen that for some functions more than one tense can be used. As a general rule, present tenses give an impression of closer proximity and/or present relevance than past and future tenses.

All of these tenses can be used with either **the active or the passive voice**: while the former typically places focus on the doer of the action, the latter tends to emphasize the effects of action. That said, not all verbs can be used in both the active and passive voice: only transitive verbs (verbs that can take a direct object), e.g. *to report results*, can form the passive voice but not intransitive, e.g. *to originate *work*,[4] or linking verbs, e.g. *seem likely* but not *seem *an explanation*. For this reason, Hinkel (2002b) recommends

TABLE 4.2 Tense and Voice

Tense/voice	Active voice	Passive voice
Present simple	Students *write* an essay on this module.	An essay *is written* on this module.
Past simple	Students *wrote* an essay last week.	An essay *was written* last week.
Present perfect	Students *have written* an essay this week.	An essay *has been written* this week.
Future simple	Students *will write* an essay next week.	An essay *will be written* next week.

teaching transitivity of verbs. While the active and passive voice are often treated as formal alternatives, EAP classes should highlight the different effects of the choice of one voice over another, and in particular achieving coherence (see Examples 2–4 in Chapter 2.3). Different combinations of tense and voice are presented in Table 4.2, which highlights the fact that tense and voice are two different concepts.

A grammatical phenomenon related to tense and voice is **subject–verb agreement**, or the principle that the subject and the verb have to agree in number, e.g. *recent research has shown – recent studies have shown*. Agreement can be particularly problematic for learners with uncountable nouns, e.g. *information is (*are)*; plurals of words of Latin and Greek origin, e.g. *such criteria are (*is) considered*; nouns that can be used both in singular and plural but with a different meaning, e.g. *statistics is a prerequisite for this course – the statistics show*; and with subjects formed by complex noun phrases in which the head noun does not immediately precede the verb, e.g. *recent studies of the use of metadiscourse in academic writing have (*has) shown*.

Teaching activity 4.2. Verb phrase

Complete the text with the correct form of the verb in brackets in the active or passive voice in an appropriate tense.

Yoghurt ___ (**consume**) daily by many people of various ages. Stores ___ (**offer**) a large range of yoghurts, and consumers' choice ___ (**depend**) on flavour, nutritional value and price. This study ___ (**compare**) the nutritional value of yoghurts which ___ (**sell**) in five major supermarkets in the UK. Data ___ (**collect**) from the supermarkets' websites. The results ___ (**present**) in Table 1, which ___ (**list**) the healthiest yoghurts in the sample. It ___ (**recommend**) that nutritionists ___ (**promote**) these yoghurts to the elderly as healthy choices.

Answers

is consumed, offer, depends, compares, are sold, was/were collected, are presented, lists, is recommended, promote

Commentary

This short text provides a context for a controlled practice of verbs. The verbs are used in present simple, with the exception of the one referring to research methods. Both active and passive voice forms are employed, and the use of the subject *data* can lead to the discussion of subject–verb agreement. Overall, the activity focuses on increasing grammatical accuracy.

Teaching activity 4.3. Active or passive?

For each of the sentences below, decide whether an active or a passive sentence is preferable in a text. Either option is grammatically correct but one option is more appropriate in terms of focus and structure.

1.
A: In this section we examine the types of written teacher feedback which students prefer.
P: In this section the types of written teacher feedback which students prefer are examined.

2.
A: For this study, we designed a questionnaire with ten questions about student preferences of feedback. We administered the questionnaire to sixty student participants.
P: For this study, we designed a questionnaire with ten questions about student preferences of feedback. The questionnaire was administered to sixty student participants.

3.
A: For this study, sixty student participants were recruited. Each participant completed a questionnaire with ten questions.
P: For this study, sixty student participants were recruited. A questionnaire with ten questions was completed by each participant.

Answers

1A to enable the long noun phrase to be placed at the end of the sentence
2P for better coherence: focus on the questionnaire
3A for better coherence: focus on participants

> This activity moves away from grammatical accuracy and raises awareness of pragmatic use of alternative structures. It can be followed up by students writing their own sentences in both the active and passive voice and deciding which alternative is more appropriate within their text.

Facts and hypothetical situations can be presented with conditional structures. *If* conditional sentences in academic writing can specify conditions under which the proposition in the main clause holds true (5) or construct the writer's argument (6) (Carter-Thomas & Rowley-Jolivet 2008; Warchał 2010). Unreal conditions can be expressed using the structure modal verb + *have* + past participle (7).

(5) If blood was taken from a bird, the blood smear number was also recorded. (MICUSP BIO.G0.21.1)

(6) If adults perceive suffering in older infant cries, and neonates are truly empathic, then one would think that neonates should also respond to older infant cries with sadness. (Ruffman et al. 2019: 2)

(7) However, I think that this term *could have been* more accessible to students if the teacher was to record a definition on the board of friction (for those students who learn visually). (MICUSP EDU.G0.02.1)

Subjects and verbs with a particular tense and voice form finite clauses. Of **subordinate (dependent) finite clauses**, two types are of particular relevance to academic writing. One is postponed subject clauses with anticipatory *it* as the subject of the main clause (8). This structure allows writers to present the material conveyed in the postponed subject as new information in the sentence (see Chapter 2.3) and to express their stance (*likely* in 8) towards this information in the main clause (see Chapter 6.4). Another type is relative clauses, which are introduced with a relative pronoun – with *which* being the most frequent in academic writing, followed by *that* and *who* (Biber et al. 1999: 611). Relative clauses typically add further information on a noun phrase (9).

(8) It is likely *that the customers recognise and reinforce aspects of this way of thinking.* (BAWE 0003)

(9) The six points *which the authors write about* are of great importance throughout the book. (BAWE 0003)

Subordinate clauses without a subject and with a verb not marked for tense but marked for voice are **non-finite clauses**. Non-finite clauses can be divided by the form of the verb into *to*-infinitive clauses (10–12), present participle *-ing* clauses (13–14) and past participle clauses (15). *To*-infinitive clauses in academic writing typically express purpose (of a research study in general or of a particular action; 10), organize discourse (11) (Thompson 1985) or complement a stance word (*necessary* in 12). Participle clauses can be used to express adverbial meanings (such as means, purpose and condition; 13–14), or they can be used as a reduced alternative to relative clauses (15, alternative to *which is shown in Fig. 11.5*). All non-finite clauses can be required by the grammatical patterns of some words (*for* in 14), and all can be used to modify noun phrases (*the main reasons* in 14, *the first-resolution conceptual model* in 15).

(10) *To determine the extent of gastric metaplasia*, multiple biopsy specimens were collected from standardised sites of the duodenal bulb. (BNC HU3 7153)

(11) *To conclude*, the role of humanism in preparing the ground enabling a reformation to take place in Germany and the rest of northern Europe was very great. (BAWE 003)

(12) It is necessary *to assess the development of these constructs within the participants over time*. (BAWE 0171)

(13) The chip was fixed to a hot plate using thermal grease and electrical resistance was measured *using the '4-point probe method'*. (MICUSP MEC.G0.08.6)

(14) The main reasons *for using expert systems in aircraft maintenance* are as follows: (BNC BP2 129)

(15) The first-resolution conceptual model *shown in Fig 11.5* was then constructed from this root definition. (BNC B2M 92)

Teaching activity 4.4. Participle clauses

Rewrite the sentences below so that each one uses a participle clause. To do this:

a) Identify which part can be re-written into a participle clause,
b) Decide if a present or past participle clause is needed,
c) Rewrite the sentence, making any other necessary adjustments.

1. This paper follows Egbert's (2019) classification of research paradigms and argues that chemistry relies on positivism in its construction of knowledge.
2. After the paper reviews relevant literature on knowledge, it will analyse Creek (2021) in terms of knowledge creation within chemistry.

3. The methods which are used include textual analysis, participant interviews and statistical testing.
4. Novice academic writers who wish to improve their writing need to consider the purpose of their text and the needs of their audience.
5. Epistemology is defined as theory of knowledge (1), and it plays a crucial part in understanding disciplinary differences.
6. Corpus analysis is considered one of key methods in applied linguistics and it has informed the field for several decades.

Answers
1. This paper follows Egbert's (2019) classification of research paradigms, *arguing* that chemistry relies on positivism in its construction of knowledge.; *Following* Egbert's (2019) classification of research paradigms, this paper argues that chemistry relies on positivism in its construction of knowledge.
2. After *reviewing* relevant literature on knowledge, the paper will analyse Creek (2021) in terms of knowledge creation within chemistry.
3. The methods *used* include textual analysis, participant interviews and statistical testing.
4. Novice academic writers *wishing* to improve their writing need to consider the purpose of their text and the needs of their audience.
5. Epistemology, *defined* as theory of knowledge (1), plays a crucial part in understanding disciplinary differences.; Epistemology, *playing* a crucial part in understanding disciplinary differences, is defined as theory of knowledge (1).; *Defined* as theory of knowledge (1), epistemology plays a crucial part in understanding disciplinary differences.
6. Corpus analysis, *considered* one of key methods in applied linguistics, has informed the field for several decades.

Commentary
This activity, necessarily decontextualized to enable several instances of the target structure, provides controlled practice of non-finite clauses. Both present and past participle clauses are used. For some sentences, more than one answer is possible, opening up a discussion on how different alternatives highlight different pieces of information. Overall, the activity focuses on increasing grammatical complexity.

Much syntactic complexity in expert academic writing is phrasal rather than clausal, making academic texts informationally dense (Biber, Gray & Poonpon 2022). Available research has shown that the mastery of academic language by both L1 and L2 English student writers progresses from finite clauses through non-finite clauses to complex noun phrases (Parkinson & Musgrave 2014; Staples et al. 2022). A **noun phrase** can be composed of the following elements: determiner + pre-modifier + head noun + post-modifier, e.g. *a* + *long, complex noun* + *phrase* + *in which the head noun does not immediately precede the verb*. Of these, the head noun is central and thus obligatory, and the other elements can be added to the noun to create complex noun phrases.

Determiners identify or specify the head noun in the noun phrase. Determiners most relevant to academic writing are articles (*a/an*, *the*, zero article), demonstratives (*this/these, that/those*) and quantifiers (e.g. *many, several*). The most common type of use of articles in academic writing is the definite article *the* with cataphoric reference (Biber et al. 1999: 266), i.e. with a noun that is specified by material following the article and the noun (post-modification, see below), *the examples that follow*. Learner issues with determiners include misuse of articles; agreement in number with the head noun, e.g. *many research; and use of distal demonstratives for anaphoric reference in lieu of proximal ones (Leńko-Szymańska 2004), e.g. *this (*that) observation* referring to preceding text.

Pre-modifiers in academic writing are most frequently adjectives, e.g. *endangered species*, and nouns, e.g. *data point*, followed by present and past participles, e.g. *a triggering event* and *the represented party* (Biber et al. 1999: 589). EAP instruction should focus on participle and nominal pre-modifiers, as learners tend to underuse these (Parkinson & Musgrave 2014).

Post-modifiers, in turn, are typically prepositional phrases (composed of a preposition and a noun phrase), e.g. *the behaviour of primates*; relative clauses, e.g. *factors which influence the choice of treatment*; non-finite clauses, e.g. *a reason to doubt their validity, accidents involving children, problems associated with cancer treatment*; and appositive noun phrases, often separated by brackets, as in *a noun phrase (a group of words headed by a noun)*. Of these post-modifiers, prepositional phrases and appositive noun phrases are typically underused by learners and should become focus of instruction (Parkinson & Musgrave 2014).

We can see that grammatical structures are recursively embedded within other grammatical structures. For example, nouns can function not only as heads of noun phrases but also as modifiers of other nouns. This recursive embeddedness is illustrated in Figure 4.1 on a noun phrase taken from BNC EDL 223.

```
┌─ noun phrase ─────────────────────────────────────────────────────────────┐
│ ┌─ prepositional phrase ──────────────────────────────────────────────┐  │
│ │ ┌─ noun phrase ──────────────────────────────────────────────────┐  │  │
│ │ │ ┌─ relative clause ───────────────────────────────────────────┐│  │  │
│ │ │ │ ┌─ prepositional phrase ──────────────────────────────────┐ ││  │  │
│ │ │ │ │ ┌─ noun phrase ──────────────────────────────────────┐  │ ││  │  │
│ │ │ │ │ │ ┌─ prepositional phrase ──────────────────────────┐│  │ ││  │  │
│ │ │ │ │ │ │ ┌─ noun phrase ─┐ ┌─ non-finite clause: present ┐││  │ ││  │  │
│ │ │ │ │ │ │ │               │ │   participle passive voice  │││  │ ││  │  │
│ │ │ │ │ │ │ │               │ │ ┌─ prepositional phrase ──┐ │││  │ ││  │  │
│ │ │ │ │ │ │ │               │ │ │   ┌─ pronoun =       ─┐ │ │││  │ ││  │  │
│ │ │ │ │ │ │ │               │ │ │   │   noun phrase     │ │ │││  │ ││  │  │
│ the position of defendants who remained in ignorance of the proceedings being taken against them
└──────────────────────────────────────────────────────────────────────────┘
```

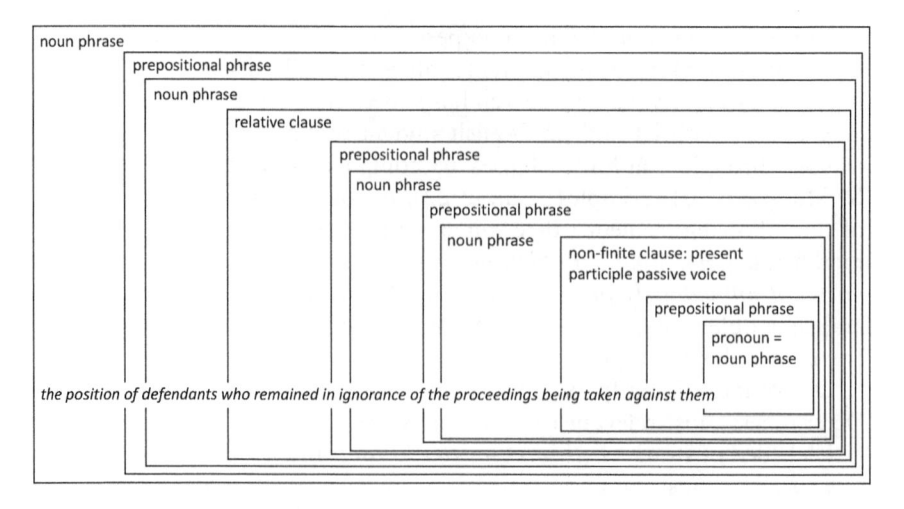

FIGURE 4.1 *Recursive embeddedness of noun phrases. Noun phrase taken from BNC EDL 223.*

Teaching activity 4.5. Noun phrases

In the following sentences, identify all the nouns and expand them into noun phrases.

1. Students attend a lecture.
2. Students' marks are forwarded to their department.
3. Students can experience symptoms.

Sample answers
1. *All first-year students* attend *a compulsory lecture on academic integrity*.
2. *Pre-sessional students' final marks* are forwarded to *their receiving department*.
3. *International students arriving to the country for the first time* can experience *some symptoms of culture shock*.

Commentary
This activity enables controlled practice of expanding noun phrases. The sentences are deliberately circumscribed to enable scope for expansion. Students should be encouraged to use a variety of pre- and post-modifiers (determiners, adjectives, participles, prepositional phrases, non-finite clauses), as illustrated in the sample answers. The activity can be followed by students writing their own sentences and expanding the respective nouns into complex noun phrases.

In academic writing, nouns are the main carriers of content. One group of nouns of particular importance is **shell nouns** or abstract nouns which can be used either with their basic dictionary meaning or with a meaning specified by the linguistic context, in which case they serve as cohesive devices and often as stance markers, e.g. *fact, effect, problem* (Schmid 2018). While expert writers typically use them to refer forward (cataphoric reference) in the pattern *the* + shell noun + *that* + finite clause (16), L2 English and novice writers overuse them to refer back to information in a previous sentence as in 17 (Aktas & Cortes 2008; Nesi & Moreton 2012). Aktas and Cortes (2008: 2013) conclude that 'students do not need to be taught these nouns as vocabulary items [but with] the cohesive functions . . . in the appropriate lexico-grammatical patterns to help them more efficiently organize the communicative purposes of their texts'.

(16) The problem is compounded by *the fact that children in the junior school are increasingly expected to read silently, and thus without help*. (BNC EF8 1617)

(17) Hence, *many boys over age 15 drop out of school to work, or are encouraged to do so by their families*. This fact is compounded slightly by one additional child in the family, increasing the negative effect of being male on schooling in larger families. (MICUSP ECO. G0.06.1)

Other important types of nouns are **nominalizations** or abstract nouns derived from adjectives and verbs denoting qualities and processes. The most common formation patterns of nominalizations in academic writing are verb+-*tion*, e.g. *formation*; adjective+-*ity*, e.g. *possibility*; verb+-*er*, e.g. *transformer*; adjective+-*ness*, e.g. *effectiveness*; adjective/noun+-*ism*, e.g. *feminism*; and verb+-*ment*, e.g. *treatment* (Biber et al. 1999: 323).

> **Teaching activity 4.6. Nominalization**
>
> Rewrite the following sentences in such a way that you turn the *italicized* verb or adjective into a nominalization and make any other grammatical changes that are necessary.
>
> 1. The university *banned* smoking on its premises and this reflects how *committed* it is to the well-being of staff and students.
> 2. We *analyse* the data and show that university students frequently find teacher feedback confusing.
> 3. This study explores how students *interpret* teacher feedback.
> 4. The use of grammatically *subordinated* sentences is a sign of *complex* language in students' academic writing.

> **Answers**
> 1. The university's *ban* on smoking on its premises reflects its *commitment* to the well-being of staff and students.
> 2. The data *analysis* shows that university students frequently find teacher feedback confusing.
> 3. This study explores the students' *interpretation* of teacher feedback.
> 4. The use of grammatical sentence *subordination* is a sign of language *complexity* in students' academic writing.
>
> **Commentary**
> This activity enables controlled practice of nominalization, derived from both verbs and adjectives. It is decontextualized to enable several instances of the target structure. Overall, the activity focuses on increasing grammatical complexity.

A common error related to word classes (parts of speech) in learner writing is the use of the wrong word form, e.g. the use of an adjective instead of a noun in 18:

(18) The *significant* of university is not only to get a degree, more often, university can improve our personality. (TECCL 00084)

Therefore, EAP instruction should help students recognize what word form is required in a particular syntactic environment on the one hand, and learn vocabulary in word families on the other hand, e.g. *analyse* verb – *analysis* noun – *analytical* adjective. To this end, it might be beneficial for students to learn word formation affixes as a vocabulary-building tool (cf. Tarasova & Baliaeva, 2024).

> ### Teaching activity 4.7. Word families
>
> For the words below, write a corresponding word family member:
>
> 1. ADJ: accountable – N:
> 2. N: apprentice – N:
> 3. V: contest – ADJ:
> 4. V: enact – N:
> 5. N: quantity – V:

> **Answers**
> 1. accountability, 2. apprenticeship, 3. contestable, 4. enactment, 5. quantify
>
> **Commentary**
> This activity should follow on working with a text: the words should be selected from the text, and thus contextualized. The corresponding family member should be a word the teacher believes the students do not actively use. Overall, the activity focuses on increasing lexical range.

Teaching vocabulary should focus not only on individual words and word families but also on the use of words in linguistic context. This will include the following combinations:

- **Collocations,** which are 'combination[s] of two lexical (as opposed to grammatical) words often found together or in close proximity' (Timmis 2015: 24), e.g. *conduct research*. The words in a collocation can be inflected, e.g. *conducting research*; separated by other linguistic material, e.g. *conduct collaborative research*; and their order is often flexible, e.g. *research was conducted*.[5] For pedagogical purposes, the term collocation can be extended to include combinations of a lexical and a grammatical word, as done in Oxford Collocations Dictionary (2002), e.g. *focus on*.

- **Lexical bundles** (lexical chunks), or sequences of three or more words which occur frequently in a particular register (Biber et al. 1999), e.g. *the effect of the*, *a great deal of*. It can be seen that lexical bundles contain both lexical and grammatical words, and that they can be semantically incomplete.[6] Shorter bundles can be part of longer bundles, e.g. *has been shown to* and *has been shown to be* (Cortes 2013). As frequency is a defining characteristic of lexical bundles, if a sequence becomes altered, it becomes another bundle with a different frequency, e.g. *a good deal of* is less frequent than *a great deal of*. In other words, lexical bundles are fixed sequences, not flexible combinations like collocations.

- **Semantico-syntactic patterns** associated with a particular word, such as *seek + to +* verb in the infinitive, e.g. *the paper seeks to establish*, and determiner + adjective + *impact + on*, e.g. *a significant effect on education* (e.g. Green, C. 2019; Hunston & Francis 2000).

The knowledge of words' collocations, bundles and syntactic patterns increases learners' accuracy and fluency. For instance, Shin, Cortes and Yoo

(2018) propose that learners' use of the definite article *the* can be improved by teaching it as part of lexical bundles common in academic writing, e.g. *the purpose of the*. Similarly, much language associated with moves of particular genres (see Chapter 3) can be taught as lexical bundles, e.g. *the results suggest that*, and evaluative language (see Chapter 6) can be taught as patterns, e.g. *it is* + evaluative adjective + *that*-clause or *to*-infinitive clause (8 and 12 above).

4.6 Style

This section discusses a formal style of written academic discourse. There is surprisingly little research into student problems with academic style, possibly because stylistic issues are less frequent in student writing than lexico-grammatical errors (Cutting 2012). Nevertheless, style is an area of academic language that EAP students need to master, as formality is a commonly accepted convention in academic writing.

Academic style is formal, objective, concise and precise (Bennett 2009), fitting the purposes of academic genres, such as to inform and to persuade the reader. These qualities are achieved by providing relevant, adequate and accurate evidence as well as by suitable linguistic devices. Previous research (Chang & Swales 1999; Cutting 2012; Hyland & Jiang 2017) has identified a number of language features often considered informal, which I will now discuss one by one.

To begin with, **contractions**, e.g. *don't*, are a way of increasing economy in language while keeping the text clear. Although they can be increasingly encountered in the writing of soft disciplines (Hyland & Jiang 2017: 45), avoiding contractions remains the standard and students should therefore be advised to follow this convention.

Although **exclamations** (19) marginally occur in expert academic writing, especially in soft sciences (Hyland & Jiang 2017: 45), they carry a highly subjective tone since they emphasize the writer's feelings and, as raising one's voice in speech, they can be potentially face-threatening (see Chapter 2.3). For these reasons, students should be strongly discouraged from using exclamations in writing.

(19) This is remarkable, given how little evidence he really had for his theory and how much of the evidence he had was wrong! (BNC CMH 116)

Informal lexis, including colloquial vocabulary, slang and overuse of phrasal verbs (cf. Bennett 2009), is a particular problem for students (20), as EAP practitioners will know from experience. Nevertheless, research tells us little about the specific challenges students face or how to address them. Therefore, future research is needed to explore informal lexis in student writing.

(20) From my perspective, I think both reading and practice are important in our daily life, we should combine them together , because practice just like the catalyst, the information of books is *pretty* thin *stuff* unless mixed with practice. (TECCL 08066)

Vague language is another informal feature of academic writing. Vague vocabulary includes general nouns and verbs with little semantic content, e.g. *thing, people, place, do, happen*; vague classifiers, e.g. *kind of, some sort of*; indefinite prepositional phrases, e.g. *in a way*; indefinite pronouns used for general reference, e.g. *everybody, something*; general extenders used to complete lists, e.g. *etc., and so on and the like*; and metadiscourse particles, e.g. *so to say* (Cutting 2012; Metsä-Ketelä 2012). The problem with vague lexis is that it removes specificity needed in formal writing, e.g. *people* instead of *students*. Expert writers occasionally exploit this vagueness to hedge claims or to deliberately withhold information for various reasons (Cutting 2012). Lower-level L2 English learners, in contrast, are more likely to use vague language due to their limited lexical range (Hinkel 2002a: 83) rather than strategically. Therefore, EAP pedagogy should help learners increase their range of formal academic vocabulary.

Sentence fragments are syntactically incomplete sentences that lack either the subject or the verb. They very rarely occur in the writing of experts (Hyland & Jiang 2017: 44), who use them for a particular rhetorical effect (21); in learner writing, however, sentence fragments are typically a product of grammatical inaccuracy, or using spoken-like utterances in writing (22). Therefore, EAP pedagogy should help learners rewrite sentence fragments into full, grammatically well-formed sentences (23).

(21) From the former, they emulate its dense informativity. From the latter, its chatty tone favouring fluency over accuracy. From both, the profusion of metadiscursive items. (Sancho Guinda 2012: 180)

(22) Disadvantages: First, a large gap between materials and photos. Second, can not be tried. (TECCL 01490)

(23) The first disadvantage is a large gap between materials and photos. (constructed on the basis of Example 22)

Preposition stranding is the use of prepositions in a sentence-final position after its complement, e.g. 24 instead of 25. Research shows that sentence-final prepositions are only marginal in academic writing, especially in hard sciences (Hyland & Jiang 2017: 45). Nevertheless, in some cases postponing a preposition creates desirable rhetorical effects: thus, 26 uses the passive voice (*is being searched for*) to maintain focus on the subject (*the information/it*) and to remain impersonal while specifying concurrency of two processes (*testing* and *being searched for*).

(24) It is exactly this latter view of the nature of reference which the discourse analyst has to appeal *to*. (BNC F9V 423)

(25) It is exactly this latter view of the nature of reference *to* which the discourse analyst has to appeal. (constructed on the basis of Example 24)

(26) The information needs to be stored in such a form that will facilitate fast testing of whether it matches what is being searched *for*. (BNC CHF 1540)

Some **sentence-initial transition markers** (see Chapter 5.5) are generally considered informal, yet understanding to what extent this applies to individual transition markers varies. Thus, for instance, *however* and *thus* in a sentence-initial position have been traditionally considered informal (Chang & Swales 1999) but as Hyland and Jiang (2017) show, they are particularly common in contemporary academic texts across disciplines, and therefore do not need to be taught as informal. In contrast, other transition markers, particularly *and*, *but*, *or* and *so*, are felt less formal in sentence-initial positions than others. Nevertheless, Bell (2007) shows that expert writers use sentence-initial *and* and *but* for strategic rhetorical purposes, such as to build a complex argument (27) and to signal topic shift. In learner writing, however, transition markers in sentence-initial positions might be used at the expense of syntactic complexity (28). EAP classes should therefore teach more formal alternatives, including joining short sentences with sentence-initial *and, but, or* and *so* with the previous sentence, or replacing these transitions with more formal ones, e.g. *in addition, however, alternatively* and *therefore*, respectively.

(27) Designing, implementing and understanding a brand new architecture, such as the blackboard system, is complicated enough without trying to solve the problems of speech processing at the same time. *And* we would like the architecture to be as simple as possible, the idea being that such a self-effacing architecture would help lay bare the problems of speech processing. (BNC HX9 590–591)

(28) Just answering those questions. *And* this brings the problem on. (TECCL 04148)

Direct questions marginally occur in expert academic writing across disciplines (Hyland & Jiang 2017: 45). Questions enable the writer to engage the reader in a dialogue and to establish a niche (Hyland 2001a), e.g. (29). While expert writers use questions as engagement features (see Chapter 6.7), learners tend to use questions as discourse markers (Hyland 2012), e.g. (30). Therefore, I suggest that EAP classes advise students to use direct questions for the formulation of research questions only.

(29) Is time alone the criterion? (BNC CG9 530)
(30) How does that happen? Because when one breaks, others follow. (TECCL 07056)

Unattended *this* is the use of *this/these* as a pronoun rather than as a demonstrative determiner, i.e. without being followed by a noun or a noun phrase (31). Of all the instances of *this/these* in expert writing, about one-quarter to one-third is unattended (Gray 2010; Swales 2005). According to Gray (2010: 176), unattended *this/these* anaphorically refers to clauses 'that may not be easily summarized in a single noun or noun phrase', e.g. (31). It is typically followed by a verb that interprets findings, e.g. *suggest, imply, indicate, explain*, or a verb with little semantic content, e.g. *be, mean*, followed by an explanation, e.g. *this means that, this is because*, or an adjective, e.g. *this is surprising* (Gray 2010; Swales 2005; Wulff, Römer & Swales 2012).

Attended and unattended *this/these* share some common characteristics. Both can be used to show stance (see Chapter 6.3): with unattended *this*, stance can be shown by an adjective in the structure *this is* + stance adjective (Gray 2010), e.g. (32). With attended *this*, stance is signalled by the noun following *this* (Geisler, Kaufer & Steinberg 1985; Gray 2010; Swales 2005), e.g. (33). More generally, both attended and unattended *this/these* in sentence-initial position are used to show criticality by the writer, namely to move from description to explanation and interpretation, e.g. *this explains, this difference is due to* (Gray 2010; Wulff, Römer & Swales 2012).

The difference between attended and unattended *this/these*, then, lies in the trade-off between economy and clarity – while unattended *this/these* is economical, attended *this/these* is unambiguous (Geisler, Kaufer & Steinberg 1985). Drawing on this discussion, I suggest EAP teachers do not advise the avoidance of unattended *this/these* by default. Instead, the focus should be on clarity and criticality – if unattended *this* is unambiguous in its reference and if it is used to show stance and criticality, there is no reason for the writer to be asked to insert a noun after *this*.

(31) Surface roughness also deepens the NBL, and results in a shallower θ profile. *This implies* that nocturnal radiative cooling of the air is less intense when surface roughness is increased. (BAWE 6172)
(32) *This is important* from an evolutionary biologists standpoint because often these syndromes are seen as an isolating mechanism in sympatry. (MICUSP BIO.G0.02.3)
(33) *This assumption* behind the question was not explicit. (BNC F9T 1200)

Split infinitive, i.e. an adverb positioned between *to* and its corresponding verb (35), is a rather controversial issue. According to Mitrasca (2009) and Perales-Escudero (2011), the prescriptivist rule that warns against the use of the split infinitive seems to have originated in the eighteenth century yet solid linguistic grounds for the rule do not exist, resulting in modern style guides being ambiguous about the use of the split infinitive. Perales-Escudero (2011) found that in expert academic texts, the infinitive is typically split by adverbials *effectively*, *fully* and *better*, and followed by longer noun phrases.

This finding can be explained by drawing on the FSP theory (see Chapter 2.3): as new information is placed towards the end of a sentence, a sentence element that is presented later in a sentence will receive more focus than one presented earlier. The split infinitive is thus often followed by long noun phrases because these are informationally heavy and need to receive end focus. In (34), the adverb cannot be moved after the noun phrase, as it would be too far from the verb it modifies, and placing it after the verb (*to understand fully human interventions*) could result in an unintended meaning in which the adverb modifies the adjective rather than the verb (*fully human* rather than *to understand fully*). The split infinitive thus clearly shows that the adverb modifies the verb.

The noun phrase following the split infinitive verb, however, does not have to be long to require focus. In (35), the infinitive is split to enable focus on *the dead*, which is new information in the clause, and to background *better*, which is less important than *understand*. These examples demonstrate that it might be rhetorically more effective to split infinitives, and therefore EAP teachers should not insist on avoiding split infinitives.

(34) We need *to fully understand* human interventions in natural systems, including climate and ecology. (BNC HJ1 18949)

(35) As one critic caustically observed, these early armchair anthropologists, who seldom had any direct acquaintance with the tribal customs that so intrigued them, appeared to be only interested in the living in order *to better understand* the dead. (BNC CS0 320)

Finally, the use of **personal pronouns** has aroused so much controversy that it deserves an elaborate discussion, which is reserved for Chapter 6.6. For now, suffice it to say that not all personal pronouns are equal, as they carry different rhetorical functions. The focus of EAP writing instruction should therefore be on specificity and evidence related to the use of personal pronouns.

To sum up the discussion of informal features, prescriptivist rules from style guides are not necessarily followed in expert writing. One reason for this might be that authors strive to make their texts more colloquial and as such more reader-friendly, as Bell (2007) suggests. However, the fact that prescriptive rules from style guides do not necessarily reflect how language is used by expert writers might perplex EAP students (Chang & Swales 1999: 146). When discussing issues around style, students often expect straightforward rules that they can follow in their writing, such as *Do not use split infinitive*. The expectation of clear rules might be based on their previous learning experience and might be motivated by the pressing need to master features of academic style quickly. However, unlike grammar, style is not based on rules but on conventions: while in grammar teaching there are clear rules on acceptable and non-acceptable forms, teaching academic style needs to go beyond rules-giving and needs to highlight desirable rhetorical effects that skilled use of informal features can achieve.

I therefore propose that an EAP class should make students aware that academic writing style is based on conventions rather than rules, and that unlike grammatical rules, conventions can be broken, but they should be broken sparingly and to good rhetorical effect rather than as a result of negligence or ignorance. Awareness-raising of formal conventions is presented in Teaching activity 4.8.

Teaching activity 4.8. Formal academic style

Read a transcript extract from the talk you watched and an extract from the article you read and for each, answer the following questions. How does the language differ in the two extracts? Why?

1. Are questions used?
2. Are any sentences incomplete (i.e. not having both a subject and a verb)? If yes, give an example.
3. Do any sentences start with *And, But, So* or *Or*?
4. Are contractions (e.g. *don't, it's*) used? If yes, give an example.
5. Are informal words and phrases used? If yes, give an example.

Commentary

This activity is designed for lower-level learners who tend to use features of spoken register in their writing. It should follow up on listening to a (semi-academic public) talk and reading an academic article (preferably on the same topic). The extracts should be selected in such a way that they demonstrate the presence (spoken talk) or absence (written article) of informal features under focus. This inductive learning activity enables students to discover conventions of formality from authentic texts.

4.7 Summary

This chapter has discussed language and content, proposing several pedagogical approaches. First, teaching criticality should be embedded within the context of discipline and/or genre. Second, as argument is more than taking a side for or against a case, its development involves several critical cognitive processes. Their selection for a particular argument, however, depends on the context of the genre and on disciplinary epistemology. Third, effective paraphrasing should recognize the primacy of content and help students select content from a source for a particular purpose in writing instead of promoting formalism by paraphrasing (preselected) sentences. Fourth, I have proposed that language teaching should include both corrective intervention to increase learners' accuracy and/or appropriateness to conventions and developmental instruction to increase learners' range of expression. This should be based on the selection of language devices relevant to target genres. Language selected for teaching should include grammatical structures, lexical items and bundles, collocations, as well as syntactic and word formation patterns. Finally, stylistic conventions should be seen as different from grammatical rules – unlike the latter, the former can be flouted by skilled writers to achieve particular rhetorical effects.

This chapter introduced some of the lexico-grammatical devices identified as relevant for the academic genres presented in Chapter 3. The remaining language devices will be explored in the following two chapters: Having discussed content and language as building blocks of text in this chapter, the next chapter explores how content is ordered in text and how language is used to organize academic texts.

CHAPTER 5

Structuring the text

5.1 Introduction

After focusing on content and language in the previous chapter, this chapter turns to organizing the content of text by means of language and by ordering information. Overall textual organization will be, of course, determined by the given genre, as discussed in Chapter 3. This chapter therefore focuses on local organization, at the level of paragraph and sentence, and on respective linguistic devices. I first discuss paragraph structure and the role of topic sentences in authentic expert texts and in EAP pedagogy (Section 5.2). I then turn to discussing coherence (Section 5.3) and cohesion (Section 5.4). I argue these are two interrelated yet distinct concepts, and I present the conceptualization of coherence based on information structure and of cohesion based on lexico-grammatical devices. The next two sections review metadiscourse devices that serve to organize text (Hyland 2019a), namely transition markers (Section 5.5), frame markers, endophoric markers and code glosses (Section 5.6). In Hyland's (2019a: 59) model these devices represent interactive metadiscourse 'used to organize propositional information in ways that a projected target audience is likely to find coherent and convincing'. Contra Hyland, I do not include evidentials in interactive metadiscourse, as these, I argue, are markers of stance towards academic community (see Chapter 6). Section 5.7 turns to clarity and conciseness, discussing informativity and the use of language to create balanced texts, before concluding in Section 5.8.

5.2 Paragraph development

Paragraph development has received scant research attention since the 1980s, so research interest in this area needs to be revived. In absence of recent relevant studies, regrettably this section has to rely on outdated references. Broadly, the available research focuses on two areas: paragraph types and topic sentences.

Research focusing on paragraph types investigated types of paragraph development in authentic academic writing. For example, Meade and Ellis (1971) analysed paragraphs in expert writing in the field of English language teaching to see if authentic paragraphs by expert writers reflected the pedagogical models of types of paragraphs presented in writing manuals. They found that less than half of all paragraphs were of the types described by writing manuals. These included *exemplification paragraph* as the most frequent type, followed by *chronological paragraph* and *paragraph giving reasons for a central idea*. Paragraphs presenting *definition*, *contrast* or *repetition of a central idea* were marginal, while the remaining three types of paragraphs found in writing textbooks – *description*, *comparison* and *cause and effect* paragraphs – did not occur in the authors' sample at all. On the other hand, the sample contained types of paragraphs typically not taught: paragraph providing *additional comments*, paragraph using *mixed types of development*, *paragraph presenting two central ideas*, *one-statement paragraph*, *opposition* paragraph and paragraph with a *question* related to the central idea.

Unfortunately, Meade and Ellis (1971) do not provide sufficient description or exemplification of the new paragraph types to enable their application in pedagogy.[1] For instance, *additional comment* paragraph, although being the second most frequent paragraph type overall, is rather vaguely described.[2] Nonetheless, what Meade and Ellis's study demonstrates is discrepancy between pedagogical models of paragraph and authentic expert practices.

Weissberg (1984) arrived at a similar conclusion, using texts of different disciplines (biology, agriculture and engineering) and a different classification of paragraph types (Daneš's 1974 thematic progression, see Section 5.3). Weissberg found that just over half of all paragraphs followed the three patterns described by Daneš (1974), with *linear pattern* being the most frequent, followed by *hypertheme* and *constant topic*. About a fifth of the paragraphs in the sample used *mixed patterns* and another fifth used none of the patterns. Weissberg concluded that while Daneš's classification of paragraphs is useful, it should not be taught as a rigid formula, as shown by frequent occurrence of paragraphs that do not fit any of the three categories.

Taken together, these two studies (as already mentioned, more recent research on paragraph types is lacking) suggest that paragraphs can be analysed and accordingly classified in different ways, yet each classification is an oversimplification of the complexity found in authentic expert writing. As Meade and Ellis (1971: 76) put it, it is likely that 'writers determine no method at all prior to writing but merely use a method which naturally follows from the main thesis of a paragraph'. This suggests that a classification of paragraph types is not very useful: In the context of EAP as defined in this book (see Chapter 1.2), the complexity of student writing will often call for mixed-pattern paragraphs or paragraphs with no previously identified pattern. In a similar vein, Eden and Mitchell (1986) argue that learners need to be flexible in their paragraph development rather than choose from an inventory of paragraph types which is not, and cannot be, exhaustive. I propose that rather than focusing on paragraph types, EAP pedagogy should focus on teaching general principles of logical and coherent organization of texts (see Section 5.3).

The second area of research into paragraph development is the topic sentence – 'a sentence which describes the topic, purpose or main idea of a paragraph' (Richards & Schmidt 2010: 605). The topic sentence is another pedagogical concept whose validity has been questioned for its limited occurrence in authentic writing. A study by Braddock (1974), in particular, seemed to discourage teaching topic sentences, as he found that less than half of all 889 paragraphs in professional magazine writing (not academic writing) contained a topic sentence.

Braddock's (1974) findings were contradicted by Popken (1987), who analysed academic journal articles (1,477 paragraphs) from seven disciplines (including hard and soft disciplines) and broadened the concept of the topic sentence by increasing its scope over more than one paragraph. Popken showed that when the topic sentence is understood narrowly as having scope over one paragraph, only about half of paragraphs can be said to have a topic sentence (thus confirming Braddock's 1974 findings), yet when it is understood to have scope over a stretch of several paragraphs, then most paragraphs (between 60 and 88 per cent, depending on the discipline) can be said to have a topic sentence. In Popken's (1987) framework, such a topic sentence can be of three types: One type is a proposition on a topic (Example 1), followed by exemplification or elaboration in the following sentences. Another type presents a topic but no proposition (2). Finally, some topic sentences have a metadiscoursal function, organizing the upcoming text (3).

(1) There several reasons for which I believe a fetus is not entitled to Constitutional rights. (MICUSP PHI.G0.14.1)

(2) In this paper, I am going to focus on aspects governing natal dispersal, specifically regarding active emigration from a site. (MICUSP BIO.G1.03.1)

(3) This section details the equipment setup and the methodology we used for testing. (MICUSP MEC.G0.02.1)

What follows from the comparison of Braddock's (1974) and Popken's (1987) studies is that the conclusions about to what extent topic sentences are used in authentic expert writing will largely depend on one's definition of topic sentence. Indeed, it seems that definitions of topic sentence need to be extended in order to encompass a majority of authentic paragraphs, and some conceptualizations go as far as to suggest that a topic sentence 'may be unstated but implied' (Richards & Schmidt 2010: 559). Obviously, it would be circular to reason that all paragraphs have a topic sentence, and if a topic sentence is not expressed, then it is implied. Dissatisfaction with 'the vague topic-sentence concept', as Harris (1990: 81) puts it, has led scholars to introduce other, similar concepts.

For instance, Harris (1990) uses the concept of *the organizing sentence*, which relies on rhetorical functional criteria: The organizing sentence defines or describes facts or concepts or reports previous research (4), announces a topic rather than presents a proposition (5), makes a list or comparison (6) or introduces a lack of understanding of an issue (7).

(4) Confirmed seasonal influenza is reported to affect between 483 to 1097 pregnant women per 10,000 and between 3 to 91 infants per 10,000 [4, 5]. (Vousden et al. 2021: 2)

(5) Maternal and perinatal outcomes are shown in Table 2. (Vousden et al. 2021: 7)

(6) The most commonly cited reasons for not being immunised include perceptions of risk of influenza and concern over effectiveness or safety of the immunization [33–35]. (Vousden et al. 2021: 3)

(7) However, there is insufficient evidence to describe the impact of seasonal influenza on pregnancy outcomes, the characteristics of those at greatest risk and therefore the associated influence of prior immunization. (Vousden et al. 2021: 3)

Harris (1990) shows that about half of paragraphs in science university textbooks have one organizing sentence (similar to Braddock's 1974 findings for professional writing and to Popken's 1987 findings for research articles), yet the other half of paragraphs have more than one organizing sentence, with the second organizing sentence serving either to narrow down the topic of the paragraph or to signal topic shift.

Giora (1985: 116) uses the concept *discourse topic*, which she defines as 'the element relative to which the whole set of propositions (of [the paragraph]) is taken to be "about"'. In this approach, the discourse topic must be a proposition rather than a noun phrase only (contra Popken 1987 and Harris 1990, see Examples 2 and 5), it must be a generalization and it must be followed by propositions which are relevant to the discourse topic. In Giora's sample of forty paragraphs from an English language textbook, a large majority (88 per cent) of paragraphs contained a discourse topic.

Ravelli (2004), working in the SFL framework (see Chapter 2.3), draws on the concept of *hyper-Theme*, which is defined by discoursal functional criteria. Namely, the hyper-Theme has two discourse functions. One is linking back to the previous paragraph or to the overall argument, which makes paragraph a building block of macrostructure rather than a stand-alone unit. This function can be linguistically realized through the use of nominalizations, transition markers and verbs expressing a relation, e.g. *tendency, also* and *is (apparent)*, respectively, in Example (8):

(8) The tendency of sociologists to equate agency and an active subject is also apparent in Herbert Blumer's outline of the methodology of symbolic interactionism. (MICUSP SOC.G0.09.1)

The second discourse function of the hyper-Theme is indicating the content of the following sentences by adding information to the overall argument (*Herbert Blumer's* work in Example 8). Analysing student writing, Ravelli does not quantify how many paragraphs contain a hyper-Theme; rather, she shows how the use of hyper-Themes improves writing. Nevertheless, Ravelli (2004: 116) points out that '[e]ven the clearest of hyper-Themes does not necessarily fulfil its promises' when a good hyper-Theme is followed by irrelevant sentences.

To sum up the discussion so far, there are several approaches to the topic sentence and its alternatives (I will continue using the term *topic sentence* for consistency), but none of the approaches seems to be able to account for authentic paragraphs exhaustively. From the above studies of authentic expert writing, three points emerge which have not informed pedagogical models of paragraph development. First, a paragraph can have more than one topic sentence (Harris 1990). Second, a topic sentence can have scope over more than one paragraph (Popken 1987). Third, not every paragraph has a topic sentence (Braddock 1974; Giora 1985; Popken 1987).

More recent research, scarce as it is, has explored learner problems with paragraph development in L2 English academic writing. These include underdeveloped or incoherent paragraphs, absence of topic sentences, topic sentences being too general and vague or too specific, topic sentence being placed too late in the paragraph or divided into two, mismatch between the topic sentence and the paragraph or the argument, and absence or misuse of transition markers (Liu & Wang 2011; Miller & Pessoa 2016). These studies clearly show that paragraph development is often challenging for learners. However, in light of the studies cited above, some of the issues identified are not necessarily problematic as they appear in expert writing too, such as paragraphs with two topic sentences or missing topic sentences.

Popken (1987) offers two reasons why some paragraphs do not have topic sentences: one is the use of subheadings rather than topic sentences to signal topic shifts, and the other is drawing on the reader's knowledge of the conventional organization of (sub)genres. An example of the latter is (9), an introductory paragraph which shows that available research (on formal learning) does not adequately address reality (informal learning). The first sentence thus provides a background against which a different view will be presented in the following sentences. As such, the first sentence is not a topic sentence, as it does not express the main idea of the paragraph and the following sentences do not provide further details on *the prior research*. The following sentences then list instances of informal learning, which are not generalized into a topic sentence such as *However, both youth and adults learn about science informally through leisure activities*. Duncan (2007) even warns against paragraphs which are simplistic and over-predictable because of unnecessary use of topic sentences.

(9) Much of the prior research on science interest and learning has centered on experiences in formal educational settings – classrooms and schools [1, 2]. However, youth spend the majority of their time outside of formal school environments [3]. Often youth have the opportunity during out of school time to engage in activities that might foster science interest and learning, with prior research demonstrating that these out-of-school-time science experiences lead to science interest and engagement [4, 5]. Likewise, adults frequently engage in science learning after their formal schooling ends, for instance through hobbies [6]. Museums, zoos, aquariums and other informal science learning sites (ISLS) function as rich sources of science content and as engaging spaces where learning might occur outside of the formal classroom environment [7]. (Mulvey et al. 2020: 1–2)

One implication of the absence of topic sentences in expert texts is that it might be difficult to find good models of topic sentence in authentic writing. For instance, some candidates for topic sentence include simply too much information to serve as general topic sentences (cf. Giora 1985): In Example (10), the subject of the first sentence (*The difference in word use frequency during discussions of the different chocolate bars*) introduces the main idea of the paragraph, yet the rest of the sentence gives very detailed information on the main idea.

(10) The difference in word use frequency during discussions of the different chocolate bars illustrate that when tasting the mainstream, and only milk chocolate bar in the group, the emphasis was on the sweet taste and creamy, smooth melt of the Hershey bar, whereas with the Lindt, Green & Black's and Endangered Species bars, the focus was on packaging elements, such as cacao percentage, organic and GMO [free] certifications. When the Dandelion craft chocolate bar was tasted, participants focused on flavor. Several participants were curious how the fruit flavor got into the chocolate and could not believe that the ingredients statement did not include raspberry. (Brown, Bakke & Hopfer 2020: 8–10)

Consider now Example (11). In this paragraph, the first sentence looks like a good candidate for a topic sentence. It is a generalization (cf. Giora 1985) of appropriate length, it links back to the previous text with transition marker *so* (cf. Ravelli 2004) and puts forward a proposition (*impersonality is constantly transgressed*). The following sentence further develops the proposition by giving a reason (*This is because*). The rest of the paragraph, however, is not about transgression of impersonality, but about *authorial identity and authority*, introduced in the last clause of the second sentence. However, the second sentence cannot be considered a topic sentence either, since it develops the previous sentence in addition to introducing the topic of the paragraph (but not making a proposition about it).

(11) So while impersonality may often be institutionally sanctified, it is constantly transgressed. This is generally because the choices which realise explicit writer presence also contribute to a high degree of ego-involvement (Chafe 1985), and are closely associated with authorial identity and authority. All writing carries information about the writer, and the conventions of personal projection, particularly the use of first-person pronouns, are powerful means for self-representation (Ivanic 1998; Ivanic & Simpson 1992). Authority, as I noted above, is partly accomplished by speaking as an insider, using the codes and the identity of a community member (e.g. Bartholomae 1986: 156). But it also relates to the writer's convictions, engagement with the reader, and personal presentation of 'self'. Cherry (1988) uses the traditional rhetorical concepts of *ethos* and *persona* to represent persuasiveness as a balance between these two dimensions of authority: the credibility gained from representing oneself as a competent member of the discipline, and from rhetorically displaying the personal qualities of a reliable, trustworthy person. (Hyland 2001: 209)

As can be seen from the examples and discussion above, good writing does not necessarily need topic sentences. Nevertheless, the use of topic sentences increases readability of text, as shown by a number of readability studies reviewed in, e.g. D'Angelo (1986) and Duncan (2007). Giora (1985) found that topic sentences improve text processing especially if the text is otherwise difficult to process due to a lack of subject knowledge on the part of the reader or due to a lack of explicit cohesive ties in the text. What follows from Giora's findings is that in L2 texts with limited linguistic accuracy, topic sentences might improve readability, and EAP teachers might therefore encourage their use. This does not mean, however, that topic sentences need to be used in every paragraph.

As presented in (9–11), students will get little exposure to topic sentences in expert writing they read (see the EAP genre paradox in Chapter 3.3), and I strongly advise against modelling topic sentences on constructed paragraphs due to inauthenticity of such writing. Therefore, I propose that topic sentences are not taught as a default writing strategy through analysing model paragraphs but as a remedial strategy for ineffective paragraphs. Such an approach starts with exploring reasons for the ineffectiveness of a sample paragraph and ways to improve it, as presented in Teaching activity 5.1. It is my belief, however, that the writing of such ineffective paragraphs can be largely prevented by pedagogy focusing on coherence, to which I turn next.

> ### Teaching activity 5.1. Topic sentence
>
> Read the paragraph below and answer the following questions:
>
> 1. What is the paragraph about?
> 2. Does it read well? Why (not)?
> 3. What makes the paragraph ineffective?
> 4. How could the paragraph be improved? Try to rewrite it.
>
> The Velvet revolution resembles the American Revolution in that Czechoslovak citizens could not really elect suitable representatives as the elections in communism were forced and one-party elections. From the economical point of view, there was no free trade with western countries, the private ownership was abolished and property was nationalized. Freedom of speech and press were unknown. There was massive censure and the unwanted and critics of communism were persecuted. Intelligentsia and the artists refusing to praise the communist regime were suppressed. Media were manipulated; religious belief was subdued; travelling abroad was restricted.
>
> **Commentary**
>
> The paragraph is taken from my own unpublished student writing from many years ago. The first sentence attempts a comparison in terms of election between two revolutions, one in British America in the eighteenth century and one in communist Czechoslovakia in 1989. The rest of the paragraph, however, discusses only Czechoslovakia without comparison with British America and turns to elements of public life other than election. The questions in the activity help students discover this disconnect between the first sentence and the remaining sentences. To improve the paragraph, students could decide to focus either on the comparison between the two countries, using the first sentence as the topic sentence and completely re-writing the rest of the paragraph, or on the description of public life in communist Czechoslovakia, removing the first sentence and replacing it with a relevant topic sentence.
>
> As re-writing this particular paragraph requires background knowledge, it would be more appropriate to use students' own sample paragraphs and evaluate their effectiveness. This requires identifying sub-topics in a paragraph (e.g. revolution in two countries; elections, economy and

> freedom in the sample paragraph) and seeing if these can be joined and generalized into one topic sentence or if the ideas need to be divided into several paragraphs (hence two possibilities for a rewrite of the sample paragraph).

5.3 Coherence

Coherence is an important feature of texts which is typically part of assessment criteria (e.g. Knoch 2007). It has nevertheless received relatively little attention in EAP research (Basturkmen & von Radow 2014) and teaching (Chen 2019), with the latter sometimes reduced to simplistic advice to *write logically*. Obviously, every student wants to write logically but what is logical to the novice writer is not necessarily logical to the reader (cf. Flower's 1979 psychological subject in Chapter 2.2). For this reason, it is important that EAP instruction explain to students what is meant by writing logically or coherence.

The task of teaching coherence is complicated by the theoretical disagreements over the conceptualization of coherence and its relationship to cohesion. In some frameworks, coherence is a superordinate concept that includes cohesion and other aspects, such as information structure, relations between propositions, macrostructure, metadiscourse and consideration of purpose and audience (e.g. Lee 2002). Some support for understanding cohesion as part of coherence comes from the finding that in academic essays coherence and cohesion are highly correlated (Meurer 2003).

In some other frameworks, coherence and cohesion are two different aspects of textual *connectedness* (Todd, Khongput & Darasawang 2007). For instance, the title of Carrel's (1982) paper decisively argues that *Cohesion is not coherence*. Likewise, for Kuo (1995: 48) coherence means 'links derived from thematic development, organization of information, or communicative purpose of the particular discourse', while cohesion involves only surface textual links. The difference between the two concepts is well illustrated by the following constructed example from Thornbury (2006: 31), which exemplifies a text that is cohesive yet incoherent: 'If there is a fault with the toilet please call extn 1071. Place in water halfway up basin. That's where all the salty water comes from.' In this short text, cohesive links are made through lexical repetition (*water*) and lexical chains (*toilet – basin – water*), through grammatical repetition (the use of the imperative in *call* and *place*) and grammatical reference (*that's where*), yet the text is not coherent. As Thornbury (2006: 31, original emphasis) puts it: 'If a **text** is *coherent*, it makes sense.'

This book considers coherence and cohesion as interrelated yet different concepts which enhance the structure of a text, along with paragraph development, metadiscourse and conciseness. Coherence is understood here in terms of information structure at sentence level, as proposed in the FSP (see Chapter 2.3) theory. With a pedagogical application in mind, this book uses student-friendly terms *known* and *new information* to refer, respectively, to information that the reader already knows (*theme* in FSP) and to information that is introduced to the reader (*rheme* in FSP). According to Lovejoy and Lance (1991), the information can become known to the reader through background knowledge shared with the writer (e.g. *The current interest in the economic impacts of neighbourhood effects* in Example (12) assumes the audience is aware of current research on the topic), through contextual relation in the text (e.g. in 12, *The field* is indirectly related to the research interest mentioned in the previous sentence) or through a direct mention in the preceding text (e.g. *The research focus on poorer neighbourhoods* in 12 refers back to the newly introduced information on *poverty* in the preceding sentence). Known information is typically realized as the sentence subject (Schneider & Connor 1990), which might be preceded by various metadiscourse devices, e.g. *Moreover* in (12).

(12) The current interest in the economic impacts of neighbourhood effects was ignited by W.J. Wilson's book *The Truly Disadvantaged* [1]. The field has been dominated by a 'poverty paradigm' ever since [2] as studies on a wide range of individual outcomes focussed almost exclusively on the presumed negative effects of living in poverty concentration neighbourhoods. The research focus on poorer neighbourhoods is understandable, as these are the places where a variety of problems accumulate and restrict individual life chances. Moreover, poor neighbourhoods are highly relevant from the perspective of public policy interventions aimed at reducing poverty and related problems. (Troost, van Ham & Manley 2023: 1)

The normal progression in English is from known to new information (see Chapter 2.3),[3] e.g. from *the current interest in* to *W. J. Wilson's book The Truly Disadvantaged* in (12). According to Daneš (1974), the known-to-new progression can take three different forms. One is *simple linear progression*, in which the new information introduced in one sentence then becomes the given information in the following sentence, e.g. the definition introduced in the first sentence of (13) becomes the given information referred to in *this definition* in the second sentence. Another type is *constant theme*, where the given information of every sentence in a sequence is the same, e.g. *it* referring to *this method* in (14). Finally, in *hypertheme*, each theme is related to an overarching hypertheme, e.g. *the roots, the leaves and the flowering stem* in (15) are all related to *the morphological characteristics of this genus*. Knoch (2007) adds another type of progression, *superstructure*, in which a metadiscourse device, rather than information structure, is used to achieve coherence, e.g. *For example* in (16).

(13) 'Fake news' can be defined as 'fabricated information that mimics news media content in form but not in organizational process or intent' [15]. While this definition may be straightforward, the everyday task confronting citizens of distinguishing between false and true can be daunting. (Mazepus et al. 2023: 3)

(14) There are many merits to this method. It teaches patients how to prevent themselves from being in situations that they fear or feel anxious about. It also arms patients with the knowledge of what to expect. (BAWE 0017)

(15) The morphological characteristics of this genus are as follows: the roots are fibrous and there is no rhizome. The leaves are linear to ovate, often with dull purple dots; the apex is usually cuspidate with a white and cartilaginous appendage that is softly obtuse or acuminate. In the first year, the leaves stand together in solitary, basal, and dense rosettes. The flowering stem arises from the center of the rosette in the second year. (Lee et al. 2022: 2)

(16) The materialist/neo-materialist perspective holds that it is the social differences in material circumstances that lead to health inequalities 7. For example, poor housing tends to be damp, cold and mouldy and is linked to a greater incidence of asthma and respiratory diseases, particularly in children. (BAWE 0182)

Research (Schneider & Connor 1990; Knoch 2007) shows that poor and strong writing tend to use different types of progression. High-scoring student writing frequently employs simple linear progression and superstructure, making a case for teaching these types of progression to students. In contrast, low-scoring essays rely on constant theme progression or exhibit a lack of coherence. The literature has identified several types of incoherent progression in low-scoring writing. One is *unrelated progression*, in which the known information in a sentence is not related to either the overall topic of the text or to the given or new information in a previous sentence (Schneider & Connor 1990). An example of unrelated progression is (17), the opening to a text, where *athletes* is not clearly related to any information in the previous sentence. Second, *connection between rhemes* involves repetition of the same new information (Mauranen 1996). For instance, in (18), both finite clauses present the same information (*convenience*) as new, the result being that the text does not advance communication of information. The last type of incoherent progression is *unmotivated theme* or a sudden shift in topic (Wikborg 1985; Mauranen

1996). This is presented in (19), in which the first two sentences focus on a book (*The Lost World/It*) and the third sentence suddenly shifts focus to its author (*Coan Doyle*). Coherence could be improved here by re-writing the third sentence into a passive one: *It was written by Coan Doyle in 1935*. An example of teaching the known-to-new progression is presented in Teaching activity 5.2.

(17) There are lots of gentlemen in the past. Athletes put a high value on the sportsmanship. (TECCL 09495)

(18) Originally, the phone is only for the convenience of communication between person, undoubtedly, the phone provides us with considerable convenience, making many things possible. (TECCL 09549)

(19) The Lost World is a great book. It is more than an adventure story. Coan Doyle wrote it in 1935. (TECCL 00283)

In sum, this section has focused on local coherence as information structure proceeding from information known to the reader to information presented as new to the reader. In the examples given above, the known information can be recognized as known due to cohesive devices such as grammatical reference, e.g. *this* in (13), *it* in (14) and *the* in (15) and lexical cohesion, e.g. *poverty – poorer – poor* in (12) and *defined – definition* in (13). Cohesion is the subject of the following section.

Teaching activity 5.2. Known-to-new progression

Look at the following pairs of short extracts and for each pair, decide which alternative is better and why.

1. In this section the types of written teacher feedback preferred by students are discussed.
2. In this section we discuss the types of written teacher feedback preferred by students.
3. Most students commit plagiarism unintentionally. One example of unintentional plagiarism is patchwriting.
4. Most students commit plagiarism unintentionally. Patchwriting is an example of unintentional plagiarism.
5. For this study, 60 student participants were recruited. A questionnaire with 10 questions was completed by each participant.
6. For this study, 60 student participants were recruited. Each participant completed a questionnaire with 10 questions.

> **Answers**
> Extract 2 is better than 1 because it places the information-heavy noun phrase at the end of the sentence, making it easier to process the information. Similarly, 3 is better than 4 and 6 is better than 5 because they introduce new information (patchwriting; questionnaire) gradually by placing it at the end of the sentence, thus avoiding sudden topic shifts.
>
> **Commentary**
> This activity is designed to illustrate how the known-to-new progression improves writing. When deciding which option is better, students might rely on other, often formalistic and unsubstantiated rules and actually prefer a less effective option. Thus, for instance, they might choose 1 over 2 because it avoids the use of *we* and 5 over 6 because it uses the passive rather than the active voice (*was completed – completed*). This can lead to the discussion of the relative merit of such rules.

5.4 Cohesion

As mentioned in the previous section, this book sees coherence and cohesion as separate concepts, with the former concerning information structure and the latter linguistic links between parts of text. Most research into cohesion is based on the seminal framework by Halliday and Hasan (1976), who distinguish between grammatical and lexical cohesion and their interface. **Grammatical cohesion** includes (i) grammatical reference through personal and possessive pronouns, comparison and demonstratives, e.g. *this (definition)*; (ii) substitution, e.g. *one* to refer to a previously used noun and (iii) ellipsis, e.g. *one group received corrective feedback and the other* [group] *received no feedback*. **Lexical cohesion** includes (i) general nouns, e.g. *result*; (ii) reiteration, i.e. repetition of the same word, synonymy and hypernymy, e.g. *essay – genre* and (iii) collocational cohesion, i.e. the use of lexical chains, e.g. *root – leave – stem – flower*. (Collocational cohesion thus does not include collocations discussed in Chapter 4.5.) Some studies (e.g. Lovejoy 1991) add antonymy, e.g. *poor – affluent*, and word families, e.g. *define – definition*, to the original Halliday and Hasan's framework of lexical cohesion. Finally, on the **borderline** between grammatical and lexical cohesion is conjunction, which involves conjunctions, adverbs and prepositional phrases to express additive, adversative, causal and temporal relations, e.g. *and, in spite of, therefore* and *subsequently*, respectively. (See Teaching activity 5.3 for an awareness-raising activity of a variety of cohesive devices.)

> ### Teaching activity 5.3. Cohesion
>
> Read the following extract from Bryan and Moriano (2023: 1) and underline all the cohesive devices you can find.
>
> The increasing complexity of today's software requires the contribution of thousands of developers. This complex collaboration structure makes developers more likely to introduce defect-prone changes that lead to software faults. Determining when these defect-prone changes are introduced has proven challenging, and using traditional machine learning (ML) methods to make these determinations seems to have reached a plateau.
> (Bryan & Moriano 2023: 1)
>
> **Answers**
> Grammatical cohesion: determiners *this, these*.
> Although there are also two instances of article *the*, these are not used as cohesive devices: rather, the first indicates known information (see Section 5.3) and the second is used to refer to the following (*of thousand of developers*) rather than preceding text. Similarly, the comparative form *more likely* is used as a hedge (see Chapter 6.5) rather than a comparison (*more likely than*).
> Lexical cohesion: lexical chain *developers – software – machine learning*, word families *complexity – complex* and *determining – determinations*, repetition of *developers, software, defect-prone changes* and *to introduce – are introduced*, synonyms *contribution – collaboration* and *defect – faults*
> Conjunction: *and*
>
> **Commentary**
> It can be seen that even such a short extract contains a range of cohesive devices, and lexical ones in particular. The use of word families indicates the need to teach word formation patterns (see Chapter 4.5).

Halliday and Hasan's (1976) framework is useful for classifying learner issues with cohesion. In terms of grammatical cohesion, ellipsis and substitution are relatively rare in academic texts (Tangkiengsirisin 2010), so it is grammatical reference that poses a problem for learners. The issues identified in the literature (Liu & Braine 2005; Dastjerdi & Samian 2011; Meisuo 2000) include unclear reference due to shifts in number and person of pronouns (20), problems with articles, including use of the wrong article, omission of obligatory articles and insertion of unnecessary articles (21), double comparative forms (22) and overuse of *more and more* (23).

(20) Above all, *we* cannot lose hope. *You* will find life is always meaningful. (TECCL 06569)

(21) Death and birth can not be a circle of only one person but, can be that of all *the* creature, making *the* immortality *the* perpetual theme of *the* nature. (TECCL 04609)

(22) Fizz 's sales were much *more higher* than Solo 's. (TECCL 02595)

(23) In modern society, English is becoming *more and more important* than before. (TECCL 02986)

Turning now to lexical cohesion, L2 English student texts tend to over-rely on lexical repetition, e.g. *convenience* in (18) above, suggesting a limited range of vocabulary (Liu & Braine 2005; Dastjerdi & Samian 2011; Meisuo 2000). L2 English student writers also tend to rely on more common and more concrete vocabulary (e.g. listing hyponyms rather than using a hypernym), resulting in more context-dependent writing (Crossley & McNamara 2009; Green 2012). An example is given in (24), which uses *natural gas* and *solar energy* instead of more abstract *alternative fuels*. These learner issues with lexical cohesion suggest the need for EAP classes to focus on increasing the range of abstract topic-related vocabulary.

(24) We can use natural gas, solar energy, etc. instead of gasoline to reduce carbon dioxide emissions. (TECCL 09504)

Finally, problems with conjunctive ties include their limited range, overuse (especially of additive devices), misuse (especially of adversative and temporal devices) and the use of stylistically inappropriate devices such as *besides* and *what's more* (Liu & Braine 2005; Dastjerdi & Samian 2011; Meisuo 2000). Conjunctive cohesion is discussed in detail in the following two sections as transition markers (which include additive, adversative and causal conjunction) and frame markers (including temporal conjunction), following Hyland's (2019a) metadiscourse model.

5.5 Transition markers

This and the following section draw on Hyland's (2019a) model of interactive metadiscourse (see Chapter 2.3), discussing transition markers, frame markers, endophoric markers and code glosses as language devices which enhance the structure of text. (Evidentials will be discussed in Chapter 6, as these do not help organize text.) Transition markers, also known as *linking words* in pedagogical literature (e.g. Harrison, Jakeman & Paterson 2016), function as discourse markers (Maschler & Schiffrin 2015), organizing the text and 'helping the reader interpret links between ideas' (Hyland 2019a: 59).

Formally, transition markers include conjunctions, e.g. *while*; adverbs, e.g. *equally*; and prepositional phrases, e.g. *in contrast* (cf. Liu 2008). Gardner and Han (2018) show that the distinction between conjunctions on the one hand and adverbs and prepositional phrases on the other has syntactic implications, since unlike the latter, conjunctions can only appear in complex sentences and only in clause-initial positions, e.g. *This area of inquiry has, however/*while, received little attention so far*. Semantically, transition markers in Hyland's (2019a) framework express addition, e.g. *in addition*; comparison, e.g. *similarly*; and consequence, e.g. *therefore*. Looking at these semantic categories more closely, it can be seen that comparison involves both similarity, e.g. *likewise*, and contrast, e.g. *in contrast*, and that consequence involves both cause, e.g. *for this reason*, and effect, e.g. *as a result*. Transition markers which indicate causal relations and contrast express criticality (Bruce 2020, see Chapter 4.2), and therefore should be paid particular attention in EAP pedagogy.

The frequency of transition markers in expert writing varies according to discipline, type of research and type of writing: transition markers are more frequent in soft than in hard sciences (Peacock 2010; Gao 2016; Gardner & Han 2018), in quantitative than in qualitative research (Cao & Hu 2014) and in argumentative than in factual writing (Gardner & Han 2018). Compared to expert writers, novice writers and L2 English writers tend to overuse transition markers overall (Chen 2006; Lei 2012). This results in student texts in which a large proportion of sentences start with a transition marker (25). In terms of semantic categories, learners overuse transition markers of addition but underuse transition markers of contrast and consequence (Elahi & Badeleh 2013; Granger & Tyson 1996; Narita, Sato & Sugiura 2004; Lei 2012), as presented in Example (25). Since transition markers of contrast and consequence are devices of criticality, as mentioned above, their underuse indicates a lack of criticality in learner writing. This may be due to, among other things, intercultural rhetoric (see Chapter 2.5): Mur Dueñas (2009), for instance, shows that argument is developed cumulatively in Spanish academic writing but antithetically in Anglophone academic writing.

(25) There is no doubt that taking part-time job would bring plenty of benefits. Above all, part-time job can make our life more enjoyable and meaningful; that is to say, it can add more color to the same day in and day out of the life. *What's more*, part-time job can make we college students get in touch with the society earlier. We would know what the real world is. *And* some college students live an extravagant life with a pocket money given by their parents, which keeps them from the hardship of earning money in the real world. More importantly, part-time job can help students gain some useful experience to approach the society and establish some connections in advance. *Besides*, because not every family is wealthy, getting a part-time job can lighten their burden. (TECCL 09536)

Apart from frequency, L2 English learner issues with transition markers include semantic and stylistic misuse. Semantic misuse concerns two problems. One is the use of transition markers with the wrong meaning, i.e. using a transition marker from one sematic class with the intended meaning of another semantic class (Gardner & Han 2018), e.g. *on the other hand* instead of *in addition* in (26). This type of misuse might be an unintended effect of encouraging learners to use consequence and contrastive rather than additive transition markers in order to show criticality. Another type of semantic misuse is the use of transition markers to establish links between ideas which are not inherently connected (Crewe 1990: 320), e.g. (27). In other words, this type of misuse attempts to establish cohesion without coherence – which is why the distinction between the two concepts is vital (see Section 5.3).

(26) With the rapid development of tourism, more and more cities have benefited from this. On the one hand, the tourism itself could expand quickly, and *on the other hand*, it will create more chances to make profits for the city. (TECCL 03645)

(27) For one thing, electricity is regarded as one of the "green fuels." As we all know, when burning petrol, it will release some poisonous gases. *Besides*, carbon dioxide gas is the largest greenhouse gas. (TECCL 09475)

Stylistic misuse encompasses three problems. The first concerns the use of informal transition markers, such as *besides, what's more* and *though* (Chen 2006; Lei 2012; Shaw 2009), e.g. (25) above. Another stylistic problem is the use of *and, so, but* and *or* informally, in a sentence-initial position (Granger & Tyson 1996; see also Chapter 4.6), e.g. (28). Lastly, novice writers might use conjunctive transition markers in simple rather than complex sentences (29). This can be considered a syntactic problem, as in Gardner and Han (2018), but I include it under stylistic misuse, as such use is common in colloquial speech as an additional afterthought or an answer to a question.

(28) *So* it appears that tetrapods evolved in some sort of coastal wetland environment around the margins of the Euramerican plate during the Late Devonian. (MICUSP BIO.G1.04.1)

(29) *Because* the sun has always risen up until now. *And so* we assume that the sun will rise tomorrow as well. (BAWE 0055)

What follows from the above discussion is that EAP pedagogy should discourage learners from overusing additive transition markers and instead encourage the use of transition markers of contrast and consequence to present ideas critically. When doing so, emphasis should be placed on semantically accurate and stylistically appropriate use. This can be done by analysing the frequency, syntax, semantics and rhetorical effects of transition markers in authentic texts, as presented in Teaching activity 5.4.

Teaching activity 5.4. Transition markers

Read the extract below from Weber et al. (2023: 1–2) and answer the following questions about transition markers highlighted:

1. Do the highlighted transition markers express (i) addition, (ii) comparison and contrast or (iii) cause and effect?
2. Which two ideas does each transition marker link?
3. How are the transition markers used to show criticality?
4. Which transition markers are (i) conjunctions, (ii) adverbs and (iii) complex prepositions?
5. Where and how in the sentence is each transition marker used? Could it be used in a different position? Why (not)?

Slugs can both positively and negatively affect plant biomass production depending on a myriad of environmental and biological factors [14–16] and can alter overall plant species composition of vegetative stands through highly selective foraging [17]. For example, in pasture and grassland settings, gastropods have been reported to selectively graze seedlings [16], **although** this depends on plant species [18], seedling age [18], and nitrogen (N) content [19]. Plant N content is an important factor determining grazing preference for gastropods, with plant material containing greater N preferred when all else is equal [19]. **However**, as shown by Mattson [19], seedling age appears to be the dominant factor governing palatability for gastropods, **due**, in part, **to** young shoots having fewer physical barriers (e.g. production of plant defense compounds) to herbivory **in addition to** increased N availability. **While** seedling age may govern grazing selection in monocultures, species identity and abundance can be greater drivers of grazing selection in polycultures [18].

(Weber et al. 2023: 1–2)

Answers

1. a) *in addition to*; b) contrast *although, however, while*; c) cause *due to*.
2. *although*: gastropods selectively graze – factors upon which the selection depends; *however*: factors – the most important factor; *due to*: the most important factor – reason; *in addition to*: reason 1 – reason 2; *while*: the most important factor in one type of environment – factors in another type of environment.
3. The transition markers of contrast are used to progressively narrow down the argument from gastropods being selective to factors which influence this selection in different environments. The transition marker of consequence is used to explain a particular factor.

> 4. a) *although, while*; b) *however*; c) *due to, in addition to.*
> 5. *Although* and *while* have to be used at the beginning of a clause but not at the beginning of a sentence – they have to be used in a complex sentence, as they are conjunctions. In contrast, *however* can be moved to a later position in the sentence (just before *seedling age*) and it can be used in a simple sentence because it is an adverb. *Due to* and *in addition to* have to precede a noun phrase because they are complex prepositions.
>
> **Commentary**
> This activity raises awareness of the semantics and syntax of transition markers, as well as their use for writing critically. This can be juxtaposed with a sample of student writing that overuses additive transition markers.

5.6 Frame markers, endophoric markers and code glosses

This section discusses three types of interactive metadiscourse that help structure text: frame markers, endophoric markers and code glosses. They are treated together here as they are less frequent in academic writing than transition markers, and consequently there is also less research available on their use in learner writing.

To start with, **frame markers** organize text through 'references to rhetorical elements of text structure' (Hyland & Zhou 2020: 31). In Hyland's (Hyland 2019a; Hyland & Zhou 2020) framework, they fall into four functional categories. First, the most frequent type of frame markers in expert writing are labellers (Hyland & Zhou's 2020 term) or discourse labels (Cao & Hu's 2014 term), which label text's stages and summarize preceding text, e.g. *to conclude, in short*. The second most frequent type of frame markers are sequencers, which sequence parts of text. Hyland and Zhou (2020) classify sequencers into numerical (*firstly*), temporal (*to start with*) and listing (*i, ii, iii*) and show that they are often preceded by a structure that introduces a sequence, e.g. *a few reasons* in Example 30. The third type of frame markers are goal announcers, which announce the overall aims of a text at its beginning, typically by using an inanimate noun (31). Finally, the least frequent type are topic shifters (Hyland & Zhou's 2020 term) or topicalizers (Cao & Hu's 2014 term), which signal topic shifts, e.g. *with regard to, turning now to*.

(30) These findings are important for *a few reasons. Firstly*, the fact that the effects were only modest is important to note. (MICUSP EDU. G1.12.1)

(31) *This paper aims to* review the associations between SES and race with social development. (MICUSP PSY.G1.08.1)

Although individual disciplines vary in the overall frequency of use of frame markers, there is no clear divide between hard and soft disciplines (Hyland 2004a). Rather, what seems to influence the frequency of frame markers is type of research: quantitative research has been found to use more sequencers than qualitative research (Cao & Hu 2014).

Research investigating frame markers in learner writing is limited and inconclusive. Some studies have not found any statistically significant difference in the frequency of frame markers in L1 and L2 English student and expert writing (Akbas 2012; Gao 2016). In contrast, other studies indicate overuse (Faghih & Rahimpour 2009 for Iranian L2 English expert writers; Atasever Belli 2019 for Turkish L2 English student writers and Pavičić Takač & Vakanjac Ivezić 2019 for Croatian Turkish L2 English student writers) or underuse of frame markers (Sultan 2011 for Arabic L2 English expert writers). However, it is unclear if this overuse or underuse is detrimental to the quality of the text (as is the case of overuse of transition markers, see Section 5.5) or if it is a mere quantitative difference which has no impact on the overall textual quality or which is a result of other factors. For instance, Pavičić Takač and Vakanjac Ivezić (2019) found no relation between the frequency of frame markers and overall text quality.

I suggest, therefore, that research on frame markers in student writing should focus on issues of quality rather than quantity. For instance, in my experience, learners tend to overuse additive transition markers, as discussed in the previous section, at the expense of frame markers. Thus, Example (25) in Section 5.5 could be improved by re-writing *plenty of benefits* into *several benefits* to clearly indicate a forthcoming sequence and by replacing the additive transition markers (*what's more, and, besides*) as well as the other discourse markers (*above all, more importantly*) with numerical sequencers (*first, second*). Another learner issue I have seen in my practice is the use of noun phrases only rather than full sentences with numerical sequencers (32). Students can practice re-writing such sentence fragments into full sentences, e.g. *The first element of a healthy family is a system of sharing responsibility.*

(32) First, a system of sharing responsibility. (TECCL 05898)

Endophoric markers make reference to other parts of the given text (Hyland 2019a: 60). This reference may be anaphoric, referring backward to preceding discourse, e.g. *as discussed previously*, or cataphoric, referring forward to upcoming discourse, e.g. *see below*. Cao and Hu (2014) distinguish between linear endophoric markers, which refer to the text itself, e.g. *the following section will demonstrate*, and non-linear endophoric markers, which refer to visuals or free-standing examples, e.g. *see Figure 1*. Hard sciences use more endophoric markers than soft sciences (Hyland 2004a) and quantitative research uses more non-linear endophoric markers than qualitative research (Cao & Hu 2014).

L2 English student writers have been found to underuse endophoric markers, especially those referring to the whole text, chapter or section, e.g. *the next chapter* (Burneikaitė 2009; Akbas 2012). Moreover, L2 English students frequently misuse some endophoric markers, using *part* and *paragraph* for *chapter* and *section,* or *bachelor work* and *dissertation thesis* for *thesis* (Burneikaitė 2009; Walková 2014). These learner issues suggest that EAP pedagogy should draw students' attention to effective use of endophoric markers as cohesive devices, and teach the vocabulary of referring to texts and their parts. The latter is presented in Teaching activity 5.5.

Teaching activity 5.5. Referring to text and its parts

Match the following definitions to the right words below.

1. An extended research report written by a student for a university degree
2. A large part of a dissertation or book that can be read as a stand-alone text
3. A part of a text composed of a number of paragraphs, not intended as a stand-alone text
4. A visual representation of content in academic genres, such as a graph or a diagram
5. Supplementary material at the end of a research report

A. Chapter
B. Figure
C. Thesis
D. Appendix
E. Section

Answers
1C, 2A, 3E, 4B, 5D

> **Commentary**
> This activity proceeds from definitions to words, i.e. from meaning to form, rather than the other way round, in order to simulate students' cognitive processes during the selection of appropriate vocabulary for writing. The activity can be made more difficult by having students retrieve appropriate words themselves rather than providing the vocabulary to choose from.

Finally, **code glosses** signal the writer's elaboration of the text's content in order to clarify it to the reader (Hyland 2019a: 61). Hyland (2007) recognizes two categories of code glosses. First, exemplifiers provide an example for illustration, e.g. *e.g.*, *such as* and *say*. Second, reformulators, e.g. *in other words, namely* and *which means*, reformulate a previous statement by either expanding its original meaning or narrowing it down. Hyland points out that the equivalence between the original proposition and the reformulated one is discoursal rather than logical, so the two formulations do not have identical meanings. Reformulators occur more frequently in quantitative than in qualitative research papers (Cao & Hu 2014) and in hard sciences, whereas soft sciences use more exemplifiers (Hyland 2007).

With regard to pedagogical issues, low-scoring student writing contains fewer code glosses than high-scoring student writing (Intaraprawat & Steffensen 1995; Noble 2010), and L2 English students tend to overuse *for example* and *for instance* at the expense of other exemplifiers (Narita, Sato & Sugiura 2004; Tapper 2005). Another problem, which I frequently encounter in my teaching practice, is the use of exemplifiers in sentence fragments (33, see also Chapter 4.6), similarly to numerical sequencers discussed above.

(33) For example received pronunciation forms. (BAWE 6174)

To sum up this section, research into EAP learner writing has paid relatively little attention to frame markers, endophoric markers and code glosses. Although endophoric markers and code glosses are not part of Halliday and Hasan's (1976) framework of cohesion (see Section 5.3), both serve cohesive functions by linking parts of text and helping the reader navigate the structure of the text. For this reason, EAP classes should raise students' awareness of these and other cohesive devices.

5.7 Clarity and conciseness

This last section is devoted to two textual features that are commonly considered necessary for good writing, yet that have received scant research attention – clarity and conciseness. I present these two features together because I consider them two sides of the same coin: a text which is made more concise than is appropriate will become unclear, and adding too much detail will make a text not only wordy but also unclear in terms of its focus and purpose. Both clarity and conciseness can be accounted for by three of Grice's (1975) maxims of his Co-operative Principle: maxim of quantity (being appropriately informative, not less or more), maxim of manner (being brief and orderly, avoiding ambiguity and obscurity of expression) and maxim of relevance (including only relevant content). For further discussion and examples of application of Grice's maxims to academic writing, see Wyatt (2024).

There is surprisingly little research on clarity of academic writing. One exception is Maxwell (2020), who introduces a framework of clarity composed of (i) understanding of content (concepts, sources) clearly demonstrated by the writer; (ii) purpose of text explicitly spelled out in the text; (iii) clarity of expression involving language accuracy and appropriate level of complexity and (iv) explicit links between parts of text, achieved by appropriate use of interactive metadiscourse and cohesion. It can thus be seen that content, language and structure all combine in the production of a clearly written text.

As can be seen from Maxwell's (2020) framework, part of clarity is explicitness or adding sufficient detail. Crossley and McNamara (2016) demonstrate that student writing improves when extra content is added, if this goes hand in hand with increasing coherence and cohesion. Crossley and McNamara conclude that asking students to write longer texts can improve their writing. I would argue, however, that adding more words does not necessarily result in quality enhancement, if writers repeat already existing content or add irrelevant content. The question therefore arises what content is informative and relevant. Giora (1988) distinguishes between *redundant* content, which represents information shared between the writer and the reader, and *informative* content, which reduces ambiguity and uncertainty. It follows that for writers to write appropriately informative texts, they need to be able to gauge their audience's knowledge of the topic. This can be particularly problematic for student writers with limited subject-specific knowledge (see Chapter 4.2) whose actual (rather than imagined) audience has more subject-specific knowledge than them (see Chapter 3.3).

It can be seen from the discussion so far that achieving clarity and conciseness is a matter of finding an appropriate balance: a lack of detail can result in obscurity; adding too much detail can result in redundancy. Obscurity can be a result of a lack of cohesive links or syntactically complex language as well as a result of overuse of cohesion and of overcomplicated language (Maxwell 2020). Taken this into consideration, I suggest that EAP classes should help students navigate the continuum of explicitness, gauging the appropriate level of explicitness for the given audience and avoiding writing wordy texts lacking in conciseness.

Wordiness is an issue for learners who 'focus on length, not content', in Sloane's (2003: 429) words. Yet conciseness is grossly neglected in EAP literature. Consequently, we do not know how wordiness is demonstrated in academic texts of L2 English writers and how best to teach conciseness. In my own teaching practice, I see the following issues with conciseness that some L2 English writers have. One is inclusion of irrelevant content, which can be a result of stating the obvious, i.e. inclusion of an unnecessary amount of shared knowledge in a text (Giora 1988). Another type of wordiness is unnecessary repetition of the same idea, same words or synonyms. Yet another type of wordiness is syntactic. This includes, for instance, using long post-modifying phrases instead of shorter pre-modifying ones, e.g. *a method according to one's preferences* instead of *a preferred method*, unnecessary transition markers and frequently starting sentences with linguistic material other than the sentence subject. Based on these observations, I have developed Teaching activity 5.6. Future research, however, needs to confirm and complete these informal observations.

Teaching activity 5.6. Conciseness

Read the following text and rewrite it to make it more concise.

> One of the features of good academic and scientific writing is a concept that is known as conciseness. All academics need to be able to write in a concise way. Conciseness means being concise, succinct, brief and to the point. The opposite of conciseness is wordiness. Wordiness is using many words and these words impart little meaning.
>
> To avoid wordiness in texts, two steps should be followed by writers. The first step is that only information which is relevant should be included in any text, which is the first step of conciseness. This means that any unnecessary pieces of information which are not needed should be avoided in writing. Any information that is not relevant should be left out. Second, words should be used judiciously, so that no unnecessary words are used by writers. As for unnecessary repetitions of words, they can be deleted or replaced with pronouns during the process of writing. In addition, lengthy phrases should be re-written if it is possible that the same meaning can be conveyed in fewer words.
>
> Concerning students, according to Sloane (2003), students sometimes focus on word count more than they focus on text quality when writing. When students reach the required word count, however, it does not make their text automatically good. On the contrary, a wordy text will contain relatively little information expressed in many words. Moreover, a wordy text

might fail content requirements. Nevertheless, writing concisely does not mean writing in underdeveloped paragraphs or grammatically incomplete sentences. Furthermore, it does not mean writing in an informal style. It could be said that any good academic writing, therefore, expresses content which is relevant in language which is concise yet formal.

(280 words)

A sample answer

One feature of good academic writing is conciseness, which means being brief and to the point. The opposite of conciseness is wordiness, i.e. using many words which impart little meaning. To avoid wordiness, two steps should be followed. First, only relevant information should be included in a text; any unnecessary information should be avoided. Second, words should be used judiciously, so that no unnecessary words are used. Unnecessary repetitions of words can be deleted or replaced with pronouns. Lengthy phrases should be re-written if the same meaning can be conveyed in fewer words. According to Sloane (2003), students sometimes focus on word count more than on text quality. Reaching the required word count, however, does not make a text automatically good. On the contrary, a wordy text will contain relatively little information and might fail content requirements. Nevertheless, writing concisely does not mean writing in underdeveloped paragraphs, grammatically incomplete sentences or an informal style. Good academic writing, therefore, expresses relevant content in concise yet formal language.

(167 words)

Commentary

The text presented here is constructed but authentic student text can be used as well. The original text is shared with students, who individually notice where and why the text is wordy before comparing their findings. The text is then re-written through joint construction: students propose suggestions for improvements, including deletion, reordering and re-writing of phrases. The teacher incorporates the suggestions in the text projected on screen, invites students to critique the suggestions and to propose further improvements, and gives feedback. During the activity, students are led to see that there may be a certain trade-off between clarity and amount of detail and to consider what information adds to the ongoing discourse and which information merely repeats what has been presented before.

5.8 Summary

This chapter has explored local organization of academic texts. I have argued in favour of a distinction between coherence as information structuring and cohesion as linguistic devices connecting parts of text. I have proposed that the concept of topic sentence be taught as a remedial rather than a default writing strategy and advocated the teaching of known-to-new progression in order to achieve coherence. The chapter has illustrated learner issues with cohesive devices and presented sample teaching activities focusing on structure. Given that existing research on structure is limited and often outdated, the chapter has also called for more research into frame markers, endophoric markers, code glosses, paragraph structure, clarity and conciseness. The next chapter focuses on the interaction between the writer, the reader and the academic community.

CHAPTER 6

Writer, reader, community

6.1 Introduction

While the previous two chapters were concerned with text's content, language and structure, this chapter focuses on academic writing as interaction between the writer and others. These others include not only the reader – a direct participant of the interaction, but also members of the larger academic community, who participate in the communicative exchange indirectly, by being referred to through the intertextual character of academic discourse. The chapter starts with the consideration of the writer as manifested through the writer's voice (Section 6.2) and stance (Section 6.3). I will argue that stance has four components. The first component includes attitudinal and epistemic stance towards the text realized by attitude markers (Section 6.4) and hedging and boosting (Section 6.5), respectively. The second aspect includes the writer's stance towards self and is manifested as self-mention (Section 6.6). The third aspect is stance towards the reader, realized by engagement markers (Section 6.7). The final aspect is stance towards the academic community manifested as attribution and realized by evidentials (Section 6.8). By considering the academic community to be an indirect participant of the communicative exchange established by academic discourse, this chapter considers evidentials to be interactional rather than interactive metadiscourse devices, contra Hyland (2019a) (see Chapter 2.3).

6.2 The writer's voice

This section focuses on a feature of discourse that most obviously represents the writer – the writer's voice. A comprehensive definition of voice is offered by Matsuda (2001: 40), who defines it as 'the amalgamative effect of the use of discursive and non-discursive features that language users choose, deliberately or otherwise, from socially available yet ever-changing repertoires'. The non-discursive features might involve formatting of the text,[1] while discursive features encompass, for instance, lexical choice, syntactic patterns, organization, transition markers, topic and argumentation (Matsuda & Tardy 2007). Ivanič and Camps (2001) illustrate discursive features of voice with the choices between nominalizations and verbs to denote processes, between personal and impersonal language and between the active and the passive voice and optional realization of the agent. To them, such choices reflect the writer's authority, relationship with the reader, interests and beliefs, including beliefs about how texts should be constructed.

One example of how the writer's beliefs are reflected in a text is the choice of third person singular pronouns for generic reference. This may include the now outdated gender-biased choice of masculine pronouns by default (1), a feminist response to that stereotype by choosing feminine pronouns by default (2), gender-balanced combinations of masculine and feminine pronouns (3), gender-neutral pronouns (4) or pronouns acknowledging that gender is not necessarily binary, such as *zie* and *hir*, which have not yet made their way into academic writing.[2]

(1) A graduate chartered *librarian* with a full teaching qualification and working in schools is a teacher when *he* is engaged with a class, and mostly a librarian when *he* is devising an alphabetical subject index, and so on. (BNC EW7 929)

(2) Considerable variations in format are possible, depending on what the *teacher* wants *her* students to achieve as a result of *her* teaching. (BNC B33 816)

(3) If a constable reasonably suspects that an arrestable offence has been committed, *he or she* may detain anyone whom *he or she* reasonably suspects to be guilty of it. (BNC ASB 383)

(4) Bearing that in mind, we find ourselves setting whole group dramas on spaceships or sailing ships, in medieval castles, on expeditions; and what all these have in common is that within the setting it is comparatively easy to ensure that each participant has an essential role; we can easily create a chain of dependency, to ensure that each *child* feels *they* have a stake in the drama. (BNC HYA 772)

The concept of the writer's voice has been interpreted variously in the literature (see, e.g. the 2001 special issue of *Journal of Second Language Writing* 10(1–2) edited by Diane Belcher and Alan Hirvela): these interpretations include an individual one that sees voice as an expression of the writer's individuality (cf. Ramanathan & Atkinson 1999), a collective or social one that understands voice as a manifestation of the writer's membership to a particular group (Ivanič & Camps 2001; Prior 2001), one that sees voice as an effect on the reader (Tardy & Matsuda 2009) and one that views voice simply as authorial presence (Stapleton 2002). As will be shown below, practitioners' conceptualization of voice determines their view of student issues with voice and respective teaching approaches.

To start with, the **individualist approach** considers voice to be a unique personal expression (Ramanathan & Atkinson 1999). In this view, voice is either present or absent in a text, and good writing should display a strong voice (Hashimoto 1987). Teaching, then, focuses on helping students develop a strong voice. Stock and Eik-Nes (2016) equate this approach with the study skills approach in EAP (see Chapter 2.5), seeing voice as a skill transferrable across different contexts. However, research suggests that writers do not develop a single voice that they would apply consistently in different writing situations. Rather, depending on the context in which s/he writes, a writer can have many voices (Hirvela & Belcher 2001), and even several voices in a single text (Ivanič & Camps 2001).

Thus, for instance, multilingual scholars often develop different voices in English depending on whether they write for a regional or international audience (Belcher & Yang 2020), and teachers simultaneously adopt the voice of an authoritative expert and the voice of a reader reacting to a text in their written feedback on student writing (Hyland & Hyland 2006). In alignment with the view of multiplicity of writer's voices, Hirvela and Belcher (2001) argue that L2 English novice writers do not lack voice completely – instead, they often have a voice in their L1 writing and only need to develop an additional L2 voice. Matsuda (2001) suggests that students might struggle expressing their own voice for a want of linguistic resources to express voice in the given L2, and EAP teaching should therefore focus on discursive features of voice.

Another approach sees **voice as self-representation**, and thus always present in writing (Ivanič & Camps 2001). In this sense, voice can be unintentional, as expressed in Matsuda's (2001: 40) definition quoted above, and the voice that the writer aims to present might not be the same voice as the one the reader constructs (Tardy & Matsuda 2009). Thus, a novice writer might unknowingly project a voice that s/he does not necessarily identify with; for instance, s/he might use informal features in his/her text not because s/he believes academic texts with a certain degree of informality are more reader-friendly (as a skilled writer might) but because s/he is unaware that the linguistic features s/he has selected are considered stylistically inappropriate in formal writing.

In this approach, teaching focuses on enabling writers to make informed and intentional choices related to voice, in the spirit of Academic Literacies approach (Stock & Eik-Nes 2016; see also Chapter 2.5). Furthermore, as Ivanič and Camps (2001) point out, certain voice features might be privileged in a given social context, and the writer might decide to conform to these conventions or resist them. By implication, EAP students might at times choose features that are valued in the context of assessment, even if these do not reflect their beliefs. An example might be a student avoiding first-person singular pronouns in writing reluctantly but believing it will result in a higher mark.

Finally, an approach aligned with academic socialization (Stock & Eik-Nes 2016; see also Chapter 2.5) sees **voice as signalling membership** to a particular social group (Ivanič & Camps 2001; Prior 2001), and selection of an appropriate voice is determined by context, such as discipline, genre and culture. This perspective is similar to the view discussed above that a writer might have multiple voices. Teaching, then, focuses on enabling writers to follow the voice conventions in a given context. Helping writers to develop multiple voices depending on the context might empower them to resist privileged voice features in low-stakes contexts while observing conventions in high-stakes contexts.

What follows from the above discussion is that the choice of a teaching approach will be determined by the teacher's understanding of the concept of voice. When asking students to display their voice in writing, therefore, it is imperative for a teacher to clarify what s/he means by voice and how students can demonstrate their voice in a text, both discursively and non-discursively. Discrepancies in interpreting the notion of voice seem to lie at the heart of the controversy in the literature as to the pedagogical usefulness of the concept of voice. For instance, Helms-Park and Stapleton (2003) found no correlation between the measure of voice and the overall quality of a text (i.e. unless voice is already incorporated in the marking criteria, as shown in Zhao & Llosa 2008), arriving at the conclusion that voice need not be taught to novice writers. Similarly, Stapleton (2002) doubts the value of teaching voice, pointing out that content, argument and critical thinking are more important.

Paul Matsuda and Christine Tardy (Matsuda & Tardy 2007; Tardy & Matsuda 2009) respond by showing that voice is a relevant concept in academic writing since readers construct an identity of the writer in terms of gender, race, breadth of content knowledge and linguistic background. As the 'same process may occur in . . . classroom assessment and written placement tests' (Tardy & Matsuda 2009: 47), the authors believe voice is of value in pedagogy. It is hard to imagine, however, how teaching voice in this sense would be realized in practice: Would the point be in teaching students to mask their identity for blind peer review or for assessment purposes? And after all, can, say intermediate English learners new to academic writing in English in their subject area project a voice other than that of a novice L2 English writer (and why should they want to project a different voice)? To project a voice of an expert writer, one has to become an experienced, fluent and confident writer, and this is best done by attending to the content, well-supported argumentation, criticality and linguistic features of academic texts. Moreover, it is not just readers who construct a representation of the writer but also vice versa: Wong (2005) shows that writers construct a representation of their audience and adjust their writing accordingly. I would argue that it is the latter type of construction of an identity that is more important in academic writing, as it directly influences the writing process.

In the sense of positioning oneself as a knowledgeable and skilful writer, then, voice is more than discursive and non-discursive features, and as Stock and Eik-Nes (2016: 97) propose, voice includes also content features such as 'reasoning and argumentative strategies, breadth of knowledge, clarity, or uniqueness of a central point, or how writers use others' voices to create their own disciplinary voice'. Teaching voice, then, is a rather broad issue that includes other concepts, such as argument, criticality, using sources and metadiscourse (see Chapters 4 and 5). The rest of this chapter explores one aspect of voice, namely stance. Voice and stance are often treated together in the literature, as both 'are central to ways of looking at written texts as social interactions, where readers and writers negotiate meanings, and to how students can be taught to convey their personal attitudes and assessments and appropriately connect with their readers' (Guinda & Hyland 2012: 1).

6.3 Stance and evaluation

While stance has been shown to play a minor role in academic writing compared to other registers (Gray & Biber 2012), it is considered an important part of social interaction that occurs via academic texts (Guinda & Hyland 2012). Hyland (2012: 134) defines stance as 'a writer's rhetorically expressed attitude to the propositions in a text'. But stance, like voice, is a fuzzy concept that has been variously interpreted and labelled with various terms, e.g. evidentiality, affect, evaluation and appraisal (Hyland & Guinda 2012), depending on one's theoretical framework.

Working within the framework of SFL, Hood (2012) discusses stance and voice under the term **appraisal**. Appraisal is a complex notion composed of attitude, graduation and engagement, each in turn composed of further notions. Thus, attitude involves affect, e.g. commenting on something as being *interesting*; appreciation, e.g. recognizing something as *complex* or *important*; and judgement, e.g. judging someone as being *honest*. Graduation, in turn, includes focus, e.g. *this study attempts to show*, and force, which stresses a degree, e.g. *well-documented*. Finally, engagement refers to the ways of integrating other voices and includes projection, e.g. reporting verbs such as *suggests*; modality, e.g. *might*; negation, e.g. *not*; and counter-expectancy, e.g. *however*. While this classification feels too fine-graded to be used in class as is, the examples can be used to illustrate to students a range of what stance means and how they can show criticality at a word/phrase level. Stance markers are explored in *Teaching activity 6.1*.

> ### Teaching activity 6.1. Stance markers
>
> The following text below is an extract from Li et al. (2023: 2). Which word classes are the stance markers highlighted in **bold**? Put them in the correct column in the table below.
>
> The **success** of modern architecture does not depend **entirely** on the creation of modern artistry but on the development of the material foundation. That is, more **powerful** industrial production technology is due to the **improvement** of material productivity brought about by the development of industrial technology [1–3]. Similarly, the **rapid** development of prefabricated buildings **largely** depends on technological **progress** in the entire assembly process. In other words, the progress of architectural design **often** depends on some **innovative** development outside of architecture. At present, the combination of Artificial Intelligence (AI) and the computer field is a **huge leap**. However, the intersection of neural networks and architecture design is not much, and they are **basically** focused on the engineering technology of architecture. This provides an **opportunity** for the combination of AI and architectural design. Thus, combining **traditional** architectural design with **advanced** AI will provide a new development opportunity.
>
> In the era of AI, communication and discussion between architectural designers are **essential** sources to stimulate **innovation**, which is **crucial** to increase the **necessary** architectural intelligence space [4, 5]. **Expanding** the flexible space division according to the designer's intention is necessary. There is a need to organize the space in an **orderly** form and **maximize** the Research and Development (R&D) space to adapt to the development of the AI industry. The common architectural intelligent space of the R&D office can meet the **uncertain needs** of industries and enterprises related to AI. Thus, it **improves** the operation **efficiency** of the park and **promotes** regional economic development. The current technical development background **shows** that the **effective** combination of AI and architectural space design can meet different individuals' architectural space design needs [6].
>
> (Li et al. 2023: 2)

Stance nouns	Stance adjectives	Stance verbs	Stance adverbs

Answers

Stance nouns	Stance adjectives	Stance verbs	Stance adverbs
success	powerful	expanding	entirely
improvement	rapid	maximize	largely
progress	innovative	improves	often
leap	huge	promotes	basically
opportunity	traditional	shows	
innovation	advanced		
needs	essential		
efficiency	crucial		
	necessary		
	orderly		
	uncertain		
	effective		

Commentary

The text contains a great number of various stance markers, and as such lends itself to illustrating stance. Stance markers are highlighted for the learners. To make the activity more challenging, the teacher might choose not to highlight the stance markers in the text, and might instead ask students to identify stance markers before classifying them. This may open discussions as to the degree of evaluation in individual words, the value added by them (e.g. *the development* vs. *the rapid development*) and contrast with more neutral counterparts (e.g. *provides an opportunity for* vs. *provides a space for*).

In considering whether certain words are stance markers, degrees of evaluation need to be pointed out. Thus, for instance, *modern* and *intelligent* are not highlighted in the teaching activity as they are used as part of a term rather than evaluatively.

The activity can be followed by students (a) adding more stance markers to each column, (b) using some of the stance markers in sentences of their own and (c) improving their writing by revising and adding stance markers.

Hood's (2012) model demonstrates that stance is realized by various linguistic means. Gray and Biber (2012) list the following devices for expressing stance:

- modal verbs, e.g. *may*,
- stance complement clauses, e.g. *it is clear that*,
- stance adverbs, e.g. *clearly*,
- stance adjectives, e.g. *important*, and
- lexical verbs, often used with personal pronouns, e.g. *we propose*.

To this list, Jiang and Hyland (2015) add stance nouns, e.g. *suggestion* or *belief*, which head complement clauses:

- starting with *that*, e.g. *assumption that*,
- *to*-infinitive, e.g. *reason to*,
- or preposition *of*, e.g. *danger of*.[3]

It can be seen that these stance markers can function as hedges (e.g. *may*), boosters (e.g. *it is clear that*) and attitude markers (e.g. *important*).

According to Gray and Biber (2012), there are two basic types of stance, with some scholars adding a third type. One type is epistemic stance, or evidentiality, which evaluates the status of knowledge, e.g. *obviously*. In contrast, attitudinal stance, or affect, expresses the writer's personal attitude, e.g. *unfortunately*. Finally, the writer's presence, sometimes included under the umbrella of stance, is expressed by the use of first-person pronouns referring to the writer, e.g. *I*. For Hyland (1999b), stance is composed of evidentiality, affect and relation, the last one comprising both writer presence and reader engagement. In yet another understanding, Aull and Lancaster (2014) suggest that stance has three aspects – author's stance towards the text, towards the reader and towards the discourse community.

Drawing on these models and relating them to Hyland's (2019a et passim) metadiscourse model (see Chapter 2.3), I propose a model of stance as having four main components: stance towards the text, the writer, the reader and the academic community (see Figure 6.1). First, the textual component involves attitudinal stance realized by attitude markers (Section 6.4), and epistemic stance involving assertiveness by using boosters and toning claims down by hedges (Section 6.5). Second, the component of the writer is the writer's explicit presence in the text, realized by self-mention (Section 6.6). Third, the component of the reader is direct engagement of the audience, realized by engagement markers (Section 6.7). Finally, the component of the community refers to attribution realized by citation and evidentials (Section 6.8). The selection of particular stance markers thus mirrors the writer's position towards the content of his/her text (textual component),

```
                    Attitudinal stance:        Epistemic stance:
                     attitude markers         hedging and boosting
                                   \       /
                                    TEXT
                                     ▲
                                     │
   Attribution:                                                      Presence:
citation and evidentials — COMMUNITY ◄── STANCE ──► WRITER —        self-mention
                                     │
                                     ▼
                                   READER
                                     │
                                Engagement:
                             engagement markers
```

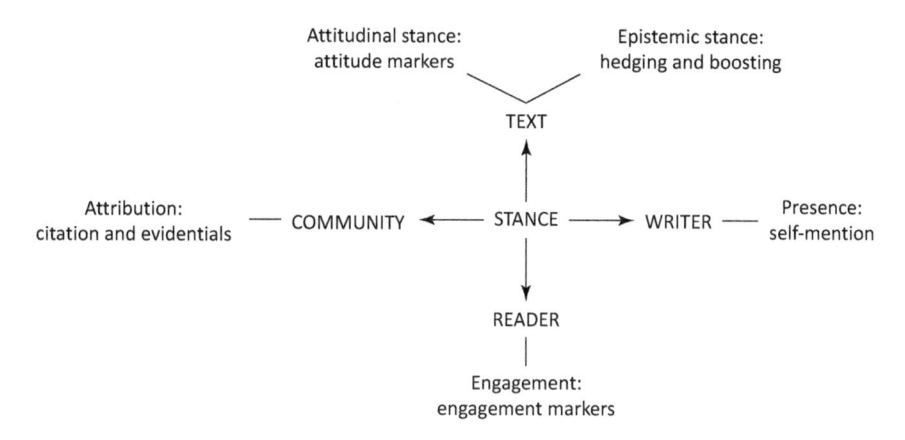

FIGURE 6.1 *Stance.*

towards self as a decision to remain largely visible or invisible in the text (the writer component), towards the reader as a decision to address the audience directly or not (the reader component) and towards the academic community by acknowledging other scholars and agreeing or disagreeing with them (community component).

Two aspects have to be pointed out before discussing these individual stance markers in the following sections. The first aspect is a certain overlap of types of stance in some metadiscourse devices. For instance, hedges and boosters express not only epistemic but also attitudinal stance (Hyland, K. 1998). More specifically, hedging and boosting express attitude through 'deference, humility, and respect for colleagues [*sic*] views' (Hyland, K. 1998: 351) and 'involvement and solidarity with an audience, stressing shared information, group membership, and direct engagement with readers' (Hyland, K. 1998: 350). It follows, then, that hedging and boosting express not only the textual component of stance but also the reader and community components. However, what appears to be primary in hedging and boosting is epistemic stance, with the other components of stance being only secondary.

Similarly, certain verbs can be used for attribution when used as reporting verbs to refer to others' findings and claims, e.g. *suggest* in (5), and for expression of epistemic stance when used as stance verbs to hedge or boost one's own findings and claims, e.g. *suggest* in (6).

(5) As *Foresman (1986) suggests*, we might expect remote sensing technology to play a major role. (BNC B1G 1414)

(6) *Our results suggest* that oxygen supplementation decreased the intensity of dyspnoea in patients with terminal cancer. (BNC HWU 453)

Crompton (1997) considers only the latter, but not the former, use of these verbs to be hedging/boosting. In other words, for Crompton hedging is used with ideational but not with interpersonal functions (cf. Chapter 2.3). However, Thompson and Ye (1991) show that the writer's choice of reporting verb can show his/her stance to the work of the cited author, e.g. *demonstrate* (the writer presents cited information as a fact) – *disregard* (the writer presents cited information as false) – *explore* (the writer's stance is neutral). Equally, the writer's choice of a reporting verb might impart a stance to the cited author, e.g. *point out* (information is presented positively) – *question* (information is presented negatively) – *focus on* (information is presented in a neutral way). It follows, then, that epistemic stance and attribution overlap in these verbs, although one or the other function might be primary in a particular context.

Another aspect that needs to be pointed out is interconnectedness of the stance components, meaning that various stance markers tend to go hand in hand in certain contexts. One example is frequency levels of stance markers in soft disciplines in contrast to hard disciplines: Soft disciplines show a higher frequency of interactional metadiscourse (Hyland 1999b), as well as integral citations (Ädel & Garretson 2006; Samraj 2008) and verbs of cognition (Hyland, K. 1998) than hard disciplines. Hyland, K. (1998) relates these disciplinary differences to the level of (im)personality: soft sciences, being more personal, feature more writer presence through self-mention and cognition verbs; more reader engagement and citations focusing on cited authors; and more subjective evaluation through hedges, boosters and attitude markers. In contrast, hard sciences, being less personal, contain fewer stance markers overall. The following sections discuss individual stance components and respective stance markers in detail.

6.4 Attitudinal stance: Attitude markers

Attitudinal stance, or the writer's personal stance towards the content of his/her text, involves the writer's appraisal (Hyland 2010b), affect, appreciation and judgement (cf. Hood 2012, see Section 6.3). It is expressed with attitude markers indicating (dis)agreement, interest, importance, necessity and feelings such as surprise (Hyland 1999b, 2019a). Attitudinal stance in academic writing is less frequent than epistemic stance (e.g. Gray & Biber 2012), and it is particularly infrequent in hard sciences (Hyland 1999b, 2010b; Jiang & Hyland 2015; Çakır 2016).

It might seem, then, that as a relatively marginal issue, attitudinal stance is of limited pedagogical value. It can, however, pose a problem for learners, as the literature shows. For instance, L2 English expert writers, when compared to L1 English expert writers, have been found to underuse attitude markers (Abdollahzadeh 2011 and Çakır 2016 for Iranian and Turkish writers, respectively), thus limiting the writer's voice. In contrast, student writers, when compared to expert writers, have been found to overuse attitude markers (Hewings & Hewings 2002). Moreover, student writers sometimes use attitude markers that are qualitatively inappropriate due to their force, such as *strange, pointless, amazing* and *wise* (Hewings & Hewings 2002). It might be therefore beneficial to EAP students to be directed to typical attitude markers in academic writing.

Attitudinal stance is typically expressed by adjectives, e.g. *difficult, essential*; verbs, e.g. *indicate, propose*; nouns, e.g. *assumption, limitation*; and adverbs, e.g. *importantly, simply* (Charles 2007; Hewings & Hewings 2002; Hyland 1999b; Hyland & Tse 2005a, 2005b; Koutsantoni 2004; Mur Dueñas 2010). By choosing one attitude marker over another the writer conveys his/her attitude. For instance, by labelling something as *danger* rather than *possibility* the writer shows his/her negative rather than neutral evaluation. An activity that asks learners to use attitude markers appropriate in a particular context and to draw on a variety of forms is presented in Teaching activity 6.2.

Teaching activity 6.2. Attitude markers in context

The text below is a gapped extract from Amez and Baert (2020: 2). Some words have been taken out from the text. What word class are they? Can you suggest which words might be used in their place?

> The present review is the first to compile the existing literature on the impact of general smartphone use (and addiction) on performance in tertiary education.[1]
>
> We (1) _____ that a synthesis of this literature is (2) _____ to both academics and policy makers. Firstly, as we focus on divergences in the empirical findings – ergo, aspects in which there is no consensus in the literature – and (methodological) (3) _____ of existing studies, we (4) _____ provide scholars with directions for (5) _____ future research. Secondly, while in several countries interventions have been developed to discourage heavy smartphone use in class because it is (6) _____ to obstruct knowledge acquisition (e.g. in France, a smartphone ban was introduced into schools in 2017; Samuel 2017), it is (7) _____ whether these popular perceptions correspond with a consensus in the related scientific literature.
>
> (Amez & Baert 2020: 2)

Answers

The following is a list of the words originally used in the text. Of course, many other attitude markers are equally possible. One alternative is given for each gap in the brackets in the list below. Students will undoubtedly suggest further possibilities, thus opening the discussion as to the appropriateness and force of the alternative: Notice how the original and the alternative word sometimes impart a very different stance.

1. verb: believe (argue)
2. adjective: valuable (important)
3. noun: limitations (deficiencies)
4. adverb: explicitly (tentatively)
5. adjective: fruitful (possible)
6. adjective/past participle: believed (known)
7. adjective: unclear (questionable)

Commentary
This short extract provides a range of attitude markers. The students' attention is first drawn to the word classes, as the words proposed must fit both syntactically and semantically. To make the activity less challenging, the teacher can provide three options, with two suitable alternatives and one plausible but less suitable distractor, e.g. *think* for (1) and *precious* for (2), and ask students to decide which alternative is least suitable and to justify their decision.

Attitude markers can appear in a number of linguistic patterns, both at phrasal and clausal level. The simplest one is the use of determiner *this* with a stance noun, e.g. (7). This structure functions both as a cohesive device by referring back to the preceding content (italicized in Example 7) and as a stance marker (cf. Charles 2003). In contrast, the use of unattended *this* (i.e. the use of *this* as a pronoun without a stance noun) has only the former, but not the latter, function (see Chapter 4.6) and thus does not convey the writer's attitude.

(7) Based on the experiences of traditional, residential students, Tinto describes *college-going as an either/or proposition: Individuals go to college or they do something else.* This assumption weakens his model's explanatory power for understanding commuting students. (MICUSP EDU.G1.04.1)

Another simple structure is modification of a stance adjective with an adverb (Hewings & Hewings 2002), e.g. (8). As the adverb typically indicates degree (cf. Hood 2012, see Section 6.3), e.g. *equally, particularly, increasingly,* it adds further stance to the attitudinal adjective.

(8) Evaluating charges of 'underfunding' is *extremely difficult.* (BNC HXT 829)

The last phrasal structure is the use of a stance noun with a post-modifying prepositional phrase (Jiang & Hyland 2015). As presented in Example (9), this structure enables construction of complex noun phrases, a typical grammatical structure of academic writing (see Chapter 4.5).

(9)   These examples of programs and courses that bring together a variety of perspectives highlight *the importance of diversity in ideas and problem solving methods for students' intellectual growth*. (MICUSP EDU.G2.03.1)

More frequent than phrasal structures, clausal structures with attitude markers include *to-* and *that-* clauses. *To-* clauses can be preceded by a stance noun (Jiang & Hyland 2015), e.g. *chance* in (10), or anticipatory *it* and stance adjective (Hewings & Hewings 2002), e.g. *it + essential* in (11).

(10) For example, the decline in numbers of young people could be *a chance to improve educational standards*, thus making Britain better prepared to enter the next century and to manage the demands of an ageing population. (BNC FP4 236)

(11) While *it is essential to study the stability of pilot batches*, it is imperative that the stability of production scale batches also be studied. (BNC ARY 281)

Stance *that-* clauses are more frequent than stance *to-* clauses and produce a greater variety of structures, including one headed by a stance verb (Hyland & Tse 2005a), e.g. *agree* in (12); a stance noun (Hyland & Tse 2005a; Jiang & Hyland 2015), e.g. *assumption* in (13); anticipatory *it* with a stance adjective (Hewings & Hewings 2002), e.g. *it + clear* in (14); and anticipatory *it* with a stance verb in the passive voice (Hewings & Hewings 2002), e.g. *it + be noted* in (15).

(12) Although I *agree that* a number of sexual positions would have been employed, I find it very unlikely that sex manuals would have existed. (BAWE 6109)

(13) However Ross' statement also needs to be qualified, particularly in *its assumption that these processes of modernization were ever unambiguously completed and finalized*. (MICUSP HIS.G3.02.1)

(14) However, *it is clear that a strategy must be put into place soon* before snow leopard populations become so degraded that they cannot re-establish themselves. (MICUSP RE.G1.23.1)

(15) Before analyzing the various content theories, *it should be noted that human incentive is intricately linked with human nature*. (BAWE 0271)

When looking at the above examples, it can be observed that attitude markers tend to cluster together, as mentioned in Section 6.3; notice for instance *weakens* in (7) and *imperative* in (11).

One pedagogical consideration that needs to be taken into account is that attitude markers of the same word class are not freely interchangeable within the structures; rather, there are collocational restrictions. For example, the noun *limitation* cannot be followed by a *to-* clause, and the adjective *clear* will be typically followed by a *that-* clause rather than a *to-* clause. Teaching activity 6.3 raises awareness of some of the structures in which attitude markers occur.

Teaching activity 6.3. Using attitude markers

Complete the following sentences:

1. The issue of . . . is particularly difficult for international students.
2. The danger of . . . lies in the fact that . . .
3. It is important to . . .
4. It is possible that . . .
5. It should be emphasized that . . .

Commentary

The sentence frames used in this activity are general enough so that they can be used by students in a variety of contexts. Before students attempt to complete them, it might be useful to check what structure is needed for each gap, i.e. noun or clause.

6.5 Epistemic stance: Hedging and boosting

Epistemic stance is more central to academic writing than attitudinal stance, as Gray and Biber (2012) point out. Epistemic stance is related to epistemic modality, defined by Holmes (1982: 12) as 'the speaker's judgement of the likelihood that something is true or not'. Epistemic stance thus reflects the writer's commitment to the truthfulness of the propositions in his/her text. It involves boosting and hedging, which are 'communicative strategies for increasing or reducing the force of statements' (Hyland, K. 1998: 350), respectively.

Hedging has, according to Hyland (1995, 1996), three overlapping functions. The first one is **proposition oriented** and involves toning claims down by expressing tentativeness and doubt due to the writer's real uncertainty. As claims of 100 per cent validity can be rarely made, hedging allows writers to make their statements more precise. The second function is **writer oriented**. It involves cautiousness and reducing the writer's responsibility for the claims, thus shielding him/her from criticism should these claims be proved wrong. The third function of hedging is **reader oriented**. Acknowledging that the reader might disagree with the writer, hedging opens negotiation with the reader to enable the writer to gain acceptance for his/her claims. To these three functions Vold (2006) adds a fourth one, namely using hedges to cautiously criticize previous research. As such, it can be considered a **community oriented** function. As criticism of others is a potentially face-threatening act, writers use hedges for politeness reasons, as Myers (1989) argues. Hyland, K. (1998) points out, however, that seeing hedging as a mere politeness strategy ignores gatekeeping and consequent pressure for conformity in academia.

In contrast to hedging, boosting underlines claims by expressing the writer's confidence and conviction in his/her claims (Hyland, K. 1998). While boosting and hedging have opposite functions, both strategies need to be balanced in academic text to persuade the reader. Research shows that while some readers might perceive a lack of hedging negatively (Burrough-Boenisch 2005), others feel it is up to the writer to express the intended level of certainty, which will partially depend on the knowledge of the field (Mauranen 1997). The right balance of hedging and boosting, therefore, draws on shared knowledge and anticipates the reader's reactions. Taken together, hedging and boosting are used 'to balance objective information, subjective evaluation and interpersonal negotiation', as Hyland, K. (1998: 354) puts it.

Semantically, epistemic stance markers might express the following (Holmes 1982; Hyland and Milton 1997):

- certainty, e.g. *inevitably, in fact, will*,
- probability, e.g. *probably, would, seem*,
- possibility, e.g. *possible, might, perhaps*,
- frequency, e.g. *usually, often*, and
- approximation, e.g. *almost, around*.

Formally, hedges and boosters include a range of lexico-grammatical means (Hyland 1996; Crompton 1997; Hyland & Milton 1997), including:

- verbs, including performative verbs (e.g. *suggest, propose, claim*), cognitive verbs (e.g. *assume, think, know, believe*) and sensory verbs (e.g. *appear, seem*). These can be used with human subjects, inanimate subjects or the passive voice (e.g. *we propose, the results suggest, it seems that, it is believed that*) as appropriate;
- adverbs, including approximators (e.g. *quite, almost, usually*) and disjuncts (e.g. *probably, generally, evidently*);

- adjectives, e.g. *likely, possible, clear*;
- modal verbs, e.g. *would, may, could*;
- nouns, e.g. *possibility, assumption, estimate*;
- phrases pointing out limitations of research and gaps in knowledge, e.g. *it is not known whether*.

It should be noted that the forms that function as hedges and boosters might have another, non-metadiscourse function (Hyland & Milton 1997), cf. e.g. *could* be used as a hedge in (16) and used to express (in)ability in (17). What follows is that the function and the context are paramount in determining whether a word is used as a hedge/booster or not in a particular sentence. Vold (2006) compares frequencies of forms used as hedges and non-hedges in research articles and finds that while *seem, perhaps, probably, suggest* and *appear* are typically used as hedges, other forms such as *could* and *possible* are typically used to express meanings other than epistemic.

(16) For example, hoverflies appear to compute their interception paths with conspecifics according to a simply specifiable rule, one which *could* plausibly be 'hard-wired' into the flies' brains (Collett & Land 1978). (BNC CM2 1122)

(17) The Spanish admitted their guilt but no agreement *could* be reached and the two sides moved apart. (BNC A6U 125)

Hedges tend to cluster in writing (Crompton 1997; Hyland 1998), e.g. *could plausibly* in (16) and *seem to suggest* and *can* in (18), not only within a sentence but also across text (Mauranen 1997). At the same time, hedges and boosters are combined in text to achieve balance of certainty (Hyland, K. 1998), as in (19), which combines booster *obviously* with hedges *slightly* and *indicate*. Hedging and boosting occur most frequently in the results and discussion sections and in conclusions (Hyland 1995; Farrokhi & Emami 2008; Yang 2013; Dontcheva-Navratilova 2016a), suggesting a strong tendency to hedge and/or boost the writers' own findings.

(18) While this finding cannot directly rule out the ego-depletion model, it does *seem to suggest* that the feeling of difficulty *can* affect responses to the first question in a series. (MISUCP PSY.G0.09.1)

(19) The levels of H3K4me3 at the chromatins of five MAFs were *obviously* decreased. While, the levels of H3K4me2 were *slightly* decreased at MAF4, MAF5 but not MAF1, MAF2 and MAF3 (Figure 9D, 9E). These results *indicate* that JMJ18 demethylates H3K4me3 and H3K4me2 within the FLC and MAFs loci in vivo. (Yang et al. 2012: 8)

As with other metadiscourse, disciplines differ in the extent to which they employ hedges and boosters. While hedging is about three times as frequent as boosting across disciplines (Hyland 1999b), soft fields tend to employ hedging and boosting more than hard fields, with hedging being one and a half times and boosting three times more frequent in soft fields than in hard fields (Hyland, K. 1998). Hyland, K. (1998) explains this difference by epistemology: In hard sciences, knowledge is built cumulatively and the level of shared knowledge is relatively high. At the same time, writing in hard sciences is expected to be rather impersonal. Using fewer hedges and boosters, then, is one way how hard science writers reduce their presence in texts. In contrast, knowledge in soft sciences is based on interpretation and subjectivity, resulting in higher level of personality. Claims are therefore presented with greater caution and more reader acknowledgement through more frequent use of hedges and boosters.

Another way in which epistemology affects the amount of hedging and boosting is type of research: Hu and Cao (2011) compared the frequency of hedging and boosting in empirical and non-empirical research article abstracts in applied linguistics and found that while there was no difference in the use of hedges, boosters were used more frequently in empirical articles. Hu and Cao explain the higher occurrence of boosters in empirical articles by primary data giving writers an opportunity to put claims forward with greater confidence. Similarly, Liu and Tseng (2021) found that the use of different qualitative methods impacts the relative frequency of hedging and boosting in journal articles in education.

Turning to issues with epistemic stance in learner writing, L2 English writers typically overstate (rather than understate) their claims compared to L1 English writers, especially at lower proficiency levels (Hyland & Milton 1997). Overstatement is a result of underuse of hedging on the one hand and/or overuse of boosting on the other hand. A number of studies have found that both student and expert L2 English writers of various first languages underuse hedging (Hyland & Milton 1997; Vassileva 2001; Hinkel 2002a, 2005; Burrough-Boenisch 2005; Vázquez Orta 2010; Hu & Cao 2011; Yang 2013; Dontcheva-Navratilova 2016a). The research on the use of boosters in L2 English, however, is inconclusive. Some studies have found both student and expert L2 English writers to overuse boosting (Hyland & Milton 1997 for Chinese students; Hinkel 2002a, 2005 for Chinese, Japanese, Korean and Vietnamese students; Vassileva 2001 for Bulgarian expert writers; Vázquez Orta 2010 for Spanish experts). Contrary to this, other studies have found L2 English writers to underuse boosting (McEnery & Kifle 2002 for Eritrean students; Abdollahzadeh 2011 for Iranian experts; Dontcheva-Navratilova 2016a for Czech experts). Still other studies have found no statistical difference between boosting in L1 English and L2 English academic writing (Farrokhi & Emami 2008 for Iranian experts; Hinkel 2002a and 2005 for Arabic and Indonesian students; Hu & Cao 2011 for Chinese experts; Çandarlı, Bayyurt & Martı 2015 for Turkish students).

These conflicting results seem to indicate that what plays a role in the use of boosting in L2 English, rather than writing experience, is the influence of the writers' L1 rhetorical style, as suggested by Hinkel (2002a) and Hu and Cao (2011). For instance, L1 Chinese, L1 French and L1 Bulgarian writing tends to be more assertive than L1 English writing (Vold 2006; Hu & Cao 2011). However, writers might not apply the same level of (un)certainty in L2 English as in their L1: Writing in L2 English might be more assertive than in one's L1, as shown by Vassileva (2001) and Yang (2013). In sum, it can be seen that while hedging clearly presents a learner issue, boosting in L2 English writing is a more complex phenomenon. This might explain why boosting tends to receive much less attention in EAP classes than hedging. EAP teachers should therefore carefully gauge the appropriacy of boosting in their students' writing and help them to use more or less boosting, as appropriate.

Another factor which plays a role in the use of epistemic markers in L2 English is learners' language proficiency, or, more specifically, limited lexical range of epistemic markers appropriate for formal academic writing (Hyland & Milton 1997; McEnery & Kifle 2002; Hinkel 2005; Hu & Cao 2011). Some forms that are typically overused by learners include *think*, *know* (as in Example 20); modal verbs such as *can* and *will*; *some-* and *any-* pronouns, *in fact*, *always*, *never* and *about* (Hyland & Milton 1997; Hinkel 2005; Vázquez Orta 2010; Walková 2019), at the expense of *appear*, *apparent(ly)*, *perhaps*, *possible*, *certainly*, *indeed*, *might*, *often*, *usually*, *generally* and *frequently* (Hyland & Milton 1997). Some such overuse is related to learners' overreliance on hedges and boosters found typically in spoken rather than written registers, e.g. *completely*, *really*, *totally*, *no way* (Hinkel 2005). Hyland and Milton (1997: 200, their example) also show that lower-level L2 students combine boosters inappropriately, e.g. *I can tell with confidence it is definitely true*. This results in a kind of writing which is, in Hinkel's (2005: 46) words, 'more incredible than persuasive'.

(20) As *we all know*, the life has changed a lot in the recent years.
(TECCL 10050)

The discussion of available research into epistemic stance has several pedagogical implications. First, both teachers and students need to be aware that there is no one-to-one mapping between form and function: Forms used to hedge and boost statements can have other meanings, such as possibility in (17). This needs to be borne in mind when analysing model texts. Second, hedging and boosting need to be clearly distinguished, so as not to mislead students into thinking that, for instance, all modal verbs are hedges. Third, both hedging and boosting should be seen as legitimate. While learners tend to overuse boosting, boosters should not be completely 'banned' from student writing, since they are used also in expert writing. Rather, students need to learn to balance their claims, avoiding both over-assertion and under-assertion (Hyland & Milton 1997). One way of finding balance is avoiding categorical assertions, i.e. avoiding boosters which express extremes, such as *absolutely* and *never*. Fourth, students should not insert hedging into their writing randomly but instead its use should be a result of conscious rhetorical choices. In deciding whether to use hedging or boosting, available evidence needs to be considered. Finally, EAP classes should aim to increase the range of hedges in student writing. The last three points are presented in Teaching activities 6.4, 6.5 and 6.6.

Teaching activity 6.4. To hedge or not to hedge?

For each of the following sentences, decide if hedging should be used (✓) or not (☒).

1. All international students struggle at the beginning of their study abroad.
2. More than 9,000 international students study at the University of Leeds every year.
3. International students do not benefit from this programme.
4. This essay discusses the economic impact of the Covid-19 pandemic on the UK.
5. The Covid-19 pandemic was caused by a virus identified in 2019.
6. The virus that caused the Covid-19 pandemic originated in bats.

Now add hedges to the sentences that need hedging.

Answers
Sentences 2, 4 and 5 should not be hedged, as these simply report facts. In contrast, Sentences 1 and 3 are overstatements, and thus need to be hedged, e.g. by using *many* instead of *all* in Sentence 1 and by using a modal verb such as *might* instead of *do* in 3. The answer for Sentence 6 is not straightforward, which will hopefully open up a discussion around using available evidence to decide whether a statement needs to be hedged or not.

Commentary
This activity targets students who, after learning about hedging, start overusing hedges and hedge factual statements. Note how criticality plays a role in deciding whether a statement needs to be hedged: For Sentence 1, students need to consider whether there is evidence that all international students struggle. More specific topics will require subject knowledge: Sentence 6 might or might not need to be hedged depending on the currently available evidence.

Teaching activity 6.5. Hedging and boosting

Read the sentences below. How certain is the writer that the strategies improve academic writing skills? Order the sentences from the most to the least certain. When would you use more certain and when less certain sentences?

1. The strategies described above improve academic writing skills.
2. The strategies described above evidently improve academic writing skills.
3. The strategies described above improve academic writing skills of some students.
4. The strategies described above improve academic writing skills of many students.
5. The strategies described above might improve academic writing skills of some students.
6. There is no doubt that the strategies described above improve academic writing skills of all students.

Answers
With decreasing certainty: 6 – 2 – 1 – 4 – 3 – 5

Sentence 6 is an overstatement and thus inappropriate in an academic text. Sentence 2 is acceptable assuming that adequate evidence is provided. Sentence 1 is neither boosted nor hedged. The choice among Sentences 4, 3 and 5 will depend on the strength of evidence available.

Commentary
This activity juxtaposes hedging and boosting and invites students to see the choice of epistemic markers as a result of considering available evidence.

Teaching activity 6.6. Hedges

Hedge the following sentence by re-writing it into several sentences, each one using one of the phrases below.
Second language writers underuse hedging in academic writing.

- *appear to*
- *generally*

- *likely to*
- *tend to*
- *research suggests that*

Answers
Second language writers *appear to* underuse hedging in academic writing.
  Second language writers *generally* underuse hedging in academic writing.
  Second language writers *are likely to* underuse hedging in academic writing.
  Second language writers *tend to* underuse hedging in academic writing.
  Research suggests that second language writers underuse hedging in academic writing.

Commentary
This simple activity attempts to introduce students to specific hedges which they might not be using themselves. As a follow-up activity, students can be asked to use these hedges in their own writing.

6.6 Presence: Self-mention

The writer's stance towards self is represented by a choice of a particular degree of his/her own explicit presence in text via self-mention. Self-mention is 'explicit reference to author(s)' (Hyland 2019a: 58), typically realized as first-person singular and plural personal and possessive pronouns, e.g. *I, me, my/mine*, and reader-exclusive *we, us, our(s)*. Self-mention pronouns used to be considered inappropriate in academic writing (Chang & Swales 1999), as it was felt that academic texts need to be impersonal to be objective and persuasive. Gradually, the convention has lost its rigidity and today, self-mention pronouns are a legitimate part of written academic discourse (Hyland 2001b, 2002b; Harwood 2005a; Zapletalová 2009; Walková 2019). Defying the convention, however, has not made its way with such a success into the teaching of academic writing, and EAP tutors and writing guides might still routinely advise students against using 'personal pronouns':[4]

(21) Generally, in order to write objectively you need to avoid using words like 'I', 'me' and 'you'. (Gillet, Hammond & Martala 2009: 95)

This mismatch between expert texts with self-mention pronouns that students read and texts without self-mention pronouns that students are asked to produce is a manifestation of the EAP genre paradox (see Chapter 3.3). Take for instance the use of the phrase *I think*. Although students are advised not to use it (e.g. Bailey 2011: 151), its instances can be encountered in expert writing, e.g. (22). I would argue that the problem with *I think* lies not in its form but rather in the rhetorical function for which it is used. For instance, students might use *I think* – and other self-mention phrases, as *in my opinion*, to present a claim without adequate evidence, as in (23). Simply removing the phrase *I think* from the sentence, however, would not remedy the problem.

(22) Such syntactic formulae are not confined to elephant-jokes, and their pervasiveness warrants further consideration and analysis, *I think*, especially in projects for foreign students of English. (BNC J88 64)

(23) A report from the World Health Organization says that nearly 18 million children under the age of five around the world are overweight. *I think* that the reason for our fat is eating too much. Also, not enough exercise is important. (TECCL 05128)

Indeed, Aull (2015) shows that self-mention pronouns in student writing are associated with personal evidence, which tends to be used by students at the expense of source-based evidence. Similarly, Hinkel (2002a) found correlation between the frequency of self-mention pronouns in student writing and the prompt for writing – more personal prompts lead to more frequent use of self-mention pronouns by student writers. It follows, then, that self-mention pronouns in student writing might be a sign of a lack of appropriate evidence rather than a sign of authorial presence as used in expert writing. As Hyland and Milton (1997: 192) point out, academic writing presents a challenge for students because of its conflicting demands for impersonality on the one hand and for criticality on the other hand. Therefore, as a result of trying to avoid *I* in their writing, novice student writers might completely eliminate their presence from their text, possibly removing also their stance and/or criticality. In contrast, skilled student writers can use self-mention effectively to advance claims (24).

(24) *I think* that there is a rather serious problem for traditional intentionalism that has been overlooked: it cannot properly account for certain features of pleasure and pain qualia. (MICUSP PHI. G3.02.1)

For Hyland and Milton (1997: 198), the problem with self-mention pronouns in learner writing is 'their frequency, incongruity and relatively [*sic*] informality'. To attempt to solve this issue by advising students to never use self-mention pronouns is, in Aull's (2015: n.p.) words, 'prescriptive and simplistic', and I agree with Aull that toning the rule down to avoidance as in Example (21) is not helpful, either.

I propose, therefore, that students should be shown how expert writers use self-mention pronouns and encouraged to imitate expert writing in this respect. This will involve several important considerations. One is disciplinary differences in the frequency of self-mention pronouns. As a general rule, hard sciences use fewer self-mention pronouns than soft sciences (Hyland 1999b; Lafuente Millán 2010), which, however, is not meant to imply that hard sciences do not use self-mention pronouns at all (Harwood 2005a). In addition to this, some disciplines, such as chemistry, are typically collaborative, so their research articles contain plural self-mention pronouns to refer to a team of authors but not singular, as sole authorship is rare.

Another major consideration is the fact that self-mention pronouns can serve a variety of rhetorical functions, as determined by their immediate linguistic context. The literature presents several taxonomies of rhetorical functions with a degree of overlap (Tang & John 1999; Hyland 2002b; Mur Dueñas 2007; Sheldon 2009; Lafuente Millán 2010; McGrath 2016; Walková 2019). The taxonomy presented here is an attempt to generalize from several of these taxonomies.

Strong writer presence is achieved by using self-mention pronouns with two functions: **stressing one's contribution by presenting results and findings** (25) and **presenting one's argument, opinion or knowledge** (26). Expert writers employ self-mention pronouns with this function to a greater degree than student writers, who feel they lack the authority required and resort to impersonal linguistic devices instead (Tang & John 1999; Hyland 2002b). This suggests that students do not see themselves as full-fledged members of academic community. Therefore, it might be beneficial to discuss with students their role and status in academic community and to encourage them to contribute to the existing knowledge.

(25) Based on this *we propose* that two genes (orange eyes, a, and brown eyes, b) are involved in the expression of eye color, because with the simplifying assumption that each mutant gene has two alleles, at least two genes are needed to produce four phenotypes. (MICUSP BIO.G0.04.2)

(26) In this paper, however, *I argue* that Marx and Hobbes actually complement each other in surprising ways. (MICUSP SOC. G1.05.1)

A somewhat weaker writer presence is achieved by foregrounding the research process in the function of **describing research methods** (27) or by foregrounding the text by **stating a purpose, intention or focus** (28). Student writers use these two functions to a larger extent than the stronger functions discussed above, and the function of stating a purpose, intention or focus even to a greater degree than expert writers (Tang & John 1999; Hyland 2002b).

(27)   *We analyzed* the sodium spectrum for evidence of nuclear screening and electron spin. (MICUSP PHY.G0.04.2)

(28)   In this essay *I examine* Popper's criterion of falsification contrasted against Kuhn's puzzle-solving criterion. (BAWE 0311)

A rhetorical function of self-mention pronouns which is less frequent in both student and expert writing is **acknowledging others** (Hyland 2002b; Walková 2019), e.g. (29). Writer presence is weak here, as this function turns attention away from the writer to other members of the academic community, to research participants or to members of the writer's social circle. In contrast, the last two functions are writer focused. One is the **reflexive** function (Sheldon 2009; McGrath 2016) of **expressing self-benefits**, which is typical of student writing but not of expert writing (Hyland 2002b), e.g. (30). Another function sometimes present in writing is **narrative**, i.e. **personal recounts** without reflection (McGrath 2016), e.g. (31).

(29)   *I would like to thank* the headteacher and staff of the school and the local advisers for making this study possible. (BNC HNW 6)

(30)   There was much to learn from this project. Not only did *I learn* about the process of change, but also learned the process of developing a data-collecting tool. (MICUSP NUR.G0.07.1)

(31)   Some fifty years ago, when *I was an undergraduate* at a small liberal arts college, *I was asked* one day by the then Dean of Students whether *I would mind* rooming with the institution's first three foreign students – a Czech, a Frenchman, and a German. (Kaplan in Hinkel 2002a: ix)

When discussing self-mention in class, students' attention should be drawn to the variety of functions self-mention pronouns can serve. An example of an awareness-raising activity using students' own corpus is shown in Teaching activity 6.7. The preferred rhetorical functions might differ across rhetorical cultures (see, e.g. Vassileva 1998 for L1 Bulgarian, Russian, French and German; Mur Dueñas 2007 and Sheldon 2009 for L1 Spanish; Molino 2010 for L1 Italian; Walková 2019 for L1 Slovak) and disciplines, although intra-disciplinary variation has been pointed out as well (Hyland 2003b; Lafuente Millán 2010; McGrath 2016). The use of particular rhetorical functions is also related to genre (see Chapter 3.4 for an overview of university genres). For instance, self-mention pronouns describing research methods or presenting results and findings will be found in methodology recounts and research reports while an essay will lend itself to self-mention pronouns presenting an argument. Reflective, narrative recounts will in turn rely on self-mention pronouns with narrative and reflexive functions, and pronouns that acknowledge others will be suitable in dedicated sections of longer student genres such as dissertations but not in term papers. Finally, self-mention pronouns for stating a purpose, intention or focus will be suitable for most genres, apart from explanations and exercises, which are likely (and rightly so) to be devoid of self-mention pronouns completely.

Teaching activity 6.7. Self-mention pronouns

How are personal pronouns used in your discipline? Search for instances of *we* in the concordancer. Look at the concordances. Can you find instances where *we* refers to:

- the writers (e.g. *we present the results*),
- academics in the discipline or in general (e.g. *demands we make on students*),
- people in general (e.g. *how we make sense of the world*).

Which type is the most frequent?

Now search for *I* (capital letter), using a case-sensitive search to exclude instances of *i* as in *i.e.* Look at the concordances. Are all the hits instances of personal pronoun?

Find instances where *I* refers to the author's:

- findings and conclusions (e.g. *I have argued*),
- opinions and beliefs (e.g. *I believe*),
- research methods (e.g. *I calculated*),
- structure of the paper (e.g. *I will show in Chapter 3*).

Which tenses are used in the above instances?
How will this inform your own writing?

Commentary

The activity assumes that students have built their own corpus of discipline-specific research articles and that they know how to use concordancing software. If students' corpora represent a variety of disciplines, disciplinary differences might be explored in class in terms of frequency of individual

> uses of personal pronouns. If students find no instances of *I*, this might be due to multiple authorship of the texts: they can analyse instead instances of *we* referring to writers for the same rhetorical functions. Only selected rhetorical functions have been chosen for this activity, as these are most likely to occur in a corpus of research articles.
>
> If corpus tools are unavailable to students, the teacher might provide students with a limited number of selected concordance lines instead.
>
> The activity might be followed by students comparing and contrasting the findings with the use of self-mention pronouns in their own writing.

The last aspect that teaching authorial presence should consider is a discussion of a variety of linguistic means to foreground or obscure the writer's presence in a text, as first-person singular pronouns are just one means of self-mention. Another is authorial *we*, i.e. the use of the first-person plural by a single author instead of first-person singular. Authorial *we* is preferred in some rhetorical cultures, including L1 Spanish, German, French, Russian, Bulgarian and Lithuanian (see Mur-Dueñas & Šinkūnienė 2016 and references therein). This may be in some cases an influence of collectivist national cultures and ideologies (Vassileva 1998; Khoutyz 2013; Walková 2018). In English, authorial plural used by sole authors might be preferred to singular in some disciplines, such as mathematics (McGrath & Kuteeva 2012), physics and computer science (Harwood 2005a).

Another linguistic device for self-mention is the use of the third person. According to Walková (2018), the third person involves the use of (i) self-citations,[5] e.g. *according to Walková (2018)* in a text written by Walková herself; (ii) initials, e.g. *translated by M.W.* for 'my translation' and (iii) self-mention terms, e.g. *the (present) author* as in Example (32):

(32) *The author* must confess that the inflectional decomposition of particular words was not done thoroughly for all the inflected items in all the languages sampled. (Janigová 2016: 77)

There are various reasons for the use of the third rather than the first person. One may be the decision to present one's own work seemingly impartially and thus to claim the position for one's own work as equal with the work of others. Thus, for instance, the writer might choose to reference his/her own work using the third person, as I have done at the beginning of this paragraph (*according to Walková*), rather than using the first person, e.g. *as I argue in Walková (2018)*, where s/he directly acknowledges that s/he is the author of the cited work. This decision might be culturally determined: in some rhetorical cultures, such as L1 Persian, the third person is preferred to the first person (Taki & Jafarpour 2012; cited in Mur-Dueñas & Šinkūnienė 2016), as it is felt it makes the text more objective. Equally, the use of the third person might be a result of anonymizing the author for the purposes of a blind review process before publication. Finally, in the case of multiple authorship, the third person can be used to differentiate the roles of individual authors in the research process (Walková 2018), e.g. (33).

(33) It is the problematic outcome of this misinterpretation that *the first author* navigates in her professional life every day, and that this article seeks to address. (Williams & Condon 2016: 1)

In sum, influenced by their L1 rhetorical cultures, L2 English writers might use authorial *we* or the third person to make their writing less personal. However, as these are not the default choices in most disciplines in English academic writing, the pedagogical implication is that L2 English learners will benefit from the presentation and practice of impersonal structures which might be used instead of personal pronouns and which feel natural in contemporary English academic writing. One such structure is the use of the passive voice (34). If the patient of the passive verb is realized as a clause, the subject is anticipatory *it* (35). Another impersonal structure is the use of inanimate subjects – following the terminology of Master (1991) – or abstract rhetors in Hyland's (1996) terms (36). These are often used in a *that-* clause construction with a demonstrative pronoun or definite article to show reference to the given text and with a stance verb typically in the present simple tense (cf. Charles 2006): *The/This/These* + *inanimate subject* + *stance verb* + *that* (37). An activity based on re-writing sentences, using personal pronouns, passive voice and inanimate subjects, is presented in Teaching activity 6.8.

(34) There are many wild reservoir hosts of plague, but only a few *will be discussed* here. (MICUSP BIO.G0.01.1)

(35) In this dissertation *it is argued* that the development of critical realism by Roy Bhaskar is a positive development for sociology. (BAWE 0004)

(36) *This essay will* first *examine* the assumptions of both men on the innate characteristics of individuals and the ideal organization of the state. (MICUSP SOC.G2.03.2)

(37) *The findings suggest that* in the management of pregnant women phenylalanine control needs to be, if anything, even stricter than in children with phenylketonuria. (BNC EA0 1154)

Teaching activity 6.8. Personal and impersonal self-mention structures

Teaching activity 6.8a. Personal and impersonal self-mention structures

The text below is the abstract of Jordan, Yekani and Sheen's (2020) journal article. In the abstract, find examples of the following structures:

a. personal pronoun *I/we* referring to the writer(s) + verb, e.g. *we analyse*,
b. the passive voice referring to the writers' activity, e.g. *a survey was conducted*,
c. inanimate subject + verb referring to the writers' research and/or text, e.g. *the results show*.

The hijab is central to the lives of Muslim women across the world but little is known about the actual effects exerted by this garment on perceptions of the wearer. Indeed, while previous research has suggested that wearing the hijab may affect the physical attractiveness of women, the actual effect of wearing the hijab on perceptions of female facial attractiveness by Muslim men in a Muslim country is largely unknown. Accordingly, this study investigated the effects of the hijab on female facial attractiveness perceived by practising Muslim men living in their native Muslim country (the United Arab Emirates). Participants were presented with frontal-head images of women shown in three conditions: in the *fully covered* condition, heads were completely covered by the hijab except for the face; in the *partially covered* condition, heads were completely covered by the hijab except for the face and areas around the forehead and each side of the face and head; in the *uncovered* condition, heads had no covering at all. The findings revealed that faces where heads were uncovered or partially covered were rated as equally attractive, and both were rated as substantially more attractive than faces where heads were fully covered. Thus, while wearing the hijab can suppress female facial attractiveness to men, these findings suggest that not all hijab wearing has this effect, and female facial attractiveness for practising Muslim men living in their native Muslim country may not be reduced simply by wearing this garment. Indeed, from the findings we report, slight changes to the positioning of the hijab (the *partially covered* condition) produce perceptions of facial attractiveness that are no lower than when no hijab is worn, and this may have important implications for wearing the hijab in Muslim societies. Finally, we argue that the pattern of effects we observed is not explained by anti-Islamic feeling or cultural endogamy, and that a major contributory factor is that being fully covered by the hijab occludes external features, especially the hair and lateral parts of the head and face, which, when normally visible, provide a substantial perceptual contribution to human facial attractiveness.

(Jordan et al. 2020: 1)

Answers

The hijab is central to the lives of Muslim women across the world but little is known about the actual effects exerted by this garment on perceptions of the wearer. Indeed, while previous research has suggested that wearing the hijab may affect the physical attractiveness of women, the actual effect of wearing the hijab on perceptions of female facial attractiveness by Muslim men in a Muslim country is largely unknown. Accordingly, **this study investigated (C)** the effects of the hijab on female facial attractiveness perceived by practising Muslim men living in their native Muslim country (the United Arab Emirates). **Participants were presented with (B)** frontal-head images of women shown in three conditions: in the *fully covered* condition, heads were completely covered by the hijab except for the face; in the *partially covered* condition, heads were completely covered by the hijab except for the face and areas around the forehead and each side of the face and head; in the *uncovered* condition, heads had no covering at all. **The findings revealed (C)** that faces where heads were uncovered or partially covered were rated as equally attractive, and both were rated as substantially more attractive than faces where heads were fully covered. Thus, while wearing the hijab can suppress female facial attractiveness to men, **these findings suggest (C)** that not all hijab wearing has this effect, and female facial attractiveness for practising Muslim men living in their native Muslim country may not be reduced simply by wearing this garment. Indeed, from the findings **we report (A)**, slight changes to the positioning of the hijab (the *partially covered* condition) produce perceptions of facial attractiveness that are no lower than when no hijab is worn, and this may have important implications for wearing the hijab in Muslim societies. Finally, **we argue (A)** that the pattern of effects **we observed (A)** is not explained by anti-Islamic feeling or cultural endogamy, and that a major contributory factor is that being fully covered by the hijab occludes external features, especially the hair and lateral parts of the head and face, which, when normally visible, provide a substantial perceptual contribution to human facial attractiveness.

Commentary

I selected this text because it contains all the three target structures. Alternatively, two or three texts can be analysed, possibly from different disciplines. Note that students might find instances of the same structures with functions other than self-mention, e.g. *previous research has suggested, heads were . . . covered, both were rated.* This can be used to discuss the potential ambiguity of impersonal structures. A follow-up class discussion can compare the degree of (im)personality and ambiguity of the three structures, and discuss why writer might choose a particular form over others or a combination of structures. The use of tenses might also be discussed.

Teaching activity 6.8b. Personal and impersonal self-mention structures

The examples from the abstract in Teaching activity 6.8a have been simplified below. Rewrite each sentence using two alternative structures:

Personal pronoun + verb	The passive voice	Inanimate subject + verb
		This study investigated the effects of the hijab.
	Participants were presented with frontal-head images of women.	
		These findings suggest that not all hijab wearing has this effect.
We argue that the pattern is not explained by anti-Islamic feeling or cultural endogamy.		

Answers

Personal pronoun + verb	The passive voice	Inanimate subject + verb
We investigated the effects of the hijab.	The effects of the hijab were investigated.	**This study investigated** the effects of the hijab.

We presented participants with frontal-head images of women.	**Participants were presented with** frontal-head images of women.	This study presented participants with frontal-head images of women.
We suggest that not all hijab wearing has this effect.	It is suggested that not all hijab wearing has this effect.	**These findings suggest** that not all hijab wearing has this effect.
We argue that the pattern is not explained by anti-Islamic feeling or cultural endogamy.	It is argued that the pattern is not explained by anti-Islamic feeling or cultural endogamy.	This paper argues that the pattern is not explained by anti-Islamic feeling or cultural endogamy.

Commentary

As the sentences in the original text are syntactically rather complex, they have been simplified in order to enable learners to manipulate the structures more easily. This might or might not be necessary, depending on the structural complexity of the text used and on students' language level. The clausal complexity of the last two sentences requires the use of anticipatory *it* in the passive voice structure. The inanimate subjects in the third structure can vary, referring to research activity (e.g. *these findings*) or the text (e.g. *this paper*). Note that tense should be maintained the same across the three syntactic alternatives.

6.7 Engagement: Engagement markers

The writer's stance towards the reader is realized through engagement markers – a type of interactive metadiscourse that serves to engage and persuade the reader (Hyland 2001a). In Hyland's metadiscourse model (2001a, 2019a), there are five categories of engagement markers: reader references, directives, questions, references to shared knowledge and personal asides. I will discuss each of these in turn.

Reader references are the most frequent type of engagement markers in expert writing and contain several classes – first-person plural inclusive pronouns, second-person pronouns, indefinite pronouns and items referring to the reader (Hyland 2001a). **First-person plural inclusive pronouns** refer to both the writer(s) and the reader (and possibly others), e.g. (38). Writers use them in ways similar to exclusive first-person pronouns (see Section 6.6), namely to describe research methods, to elaborate arguments, to organize text and to describe and critique disciplinary practices and to suggest further research (Harwood 2005a).

In themselves, first-person plural pronouns are ambiguous between inclusive and exclusive readings, which, as Harwood (2005a) shows, writers exploit to make their writing more persuasive. Inclusive pronouns, however, are also ambiguous as to their reference (Vladimirou 2007; Walková 2018): First, they can refer to the writer and reader only, which is the most frequent type of inclusive pronouns in expert English and which is typically used with verbs of perception and modality to organize text (38). Second, inclusive pronouns can involve the whole academic community to which the writer and the reader belong (39). Lastly, inclusive pronouns can be used as universal, referring to a large group of people, such as a nation, or to people in general (40). The last use of *we*, called *impersonal we* in Kitagawa and Lehrer (1990), can be substituted with indefinite pronouns such as *everyone* and *anybody*. While in English expert writing this impersonal use of first-person plural pronouns is relatively rare, it can be much more common in academic writing of collective cultures, and as a consequence, some L2 English writers might overuse it (Walková 2018).

(38)   *As we can see* from Figure 5.1, the physical schema represents a mapping from the logical view. (BNC HRK 1805)

(39)   *As anthropologists we* tend to regard the larger society from the local community's viewpoint and to see events in terms of the impact that outside influences have upon known individuals. (BNC BMP 89)

(40)   *We all know that* the best way to stop crimes is education. (TECCL 00017)

Turning now to **second-person pronouns**, *you/r(s)* is infrequent in expert writing, since it implies detachment of the writer from the reader (Hyland 2001a), in contrast to inclusive pronouns, which stress solidarity. L2 English expert writers are typically aware of the informal nature and power relations that second-person pronouns imply, and therefore avoid them in their writing (Hyland 2005; Lafuente-Millán 2014). L2 English students new to academic writing, however, tend to overuse second-person pronouns as impersonal pronouns with general reference (41).

(41)   If *you* kill others or commit a serious crime, *you* would be a sentence to death. (TECCL 00027)

Another class of reader references is **indefinite pronouns**: While expert writers use the indefinite pronoun *one* (Hyland 2001a), e.g. (42), novice student writers overuse indefinite pronouns such as *everyone* and *nobody* (Aull, Bandarage & Miller 2017), e.g. (43). The problem with these generalizing indefinite pronouns, as well as with impersonal *we* and impersonal *you* discussed above, is that they increase vagueness and generality in learner writing, which is undesirable (Aull, Bandarage & Miller 2017).

In fact, student writers tend to use impersonal *we* to put forward unsupported claims (Kwon, Staples & Partridge 2018), as presented in (40) above.

(42)   If microalbuminuria is an appropriate surrogate end point that could replace glomerular filtration rate changes in clinical trials, *one* can anticipate that enalapril will protect glomerular filtration rate better than hydrochlorothiazide in the long term. (BNC EA1 680)

(43)   *Nobody* can deny the fact that the appearance of money makes the trade become justice and equity. (TECCL 09943)

More marginally, reader references in expert academic writing include **nouns explicitly referring to the reader** (44). These are rare in current expert writing (Hyland 2010a), and the literature does not indicate any learner problems in this respect.

(44)   To justify the use of parametric methods we refer *the reader* to the LP for paper recycling discussed in Section 1.1. (BNC CA4 81)

What follows from the discussion so far is that expert writers tend to use reader references to address the reader directly, in contrast to student writers, who tend to use similar linguistic devices to refer not just to the reader but to people more generally. It is this general use of reader references that should be discouraged in EAP classes.

Another category of engagement markers is **directives**, which are 'utterances which instruct the reader to perform an action or to see things in a way determined by the writer', as defined by Hyland (2002c: 215–16). Formally, directives include imperatives, obligation modals and *to-* clauses complementing modal adjectives used to instruct the reader (Hyland 2002c), e.g. (45)–(47), respectively. Imperatives are the most frequent type of directives, yet their range is typically limited, with *see, consider, note, suppose, let (us)* and *cf./compare* being the most common (Hyland 2002c). Although they are potentially face-threatening (see Chapter 2.3), they are economical, which is why they are rather common in hard sciences (Hyland 2001a, 2002c), unlike most other metadiscourse devices.

(45)   The distinction between second language learning and second language acquisition is one that has been proposed by Krashen; *see* for example Krashen (1981). (BNC K93 1868)

(46)   The spot size *should* be at least 3 mm and energy density 5–8 J/cm to ensure deep injury of ectatic vessels. (BNC CNA 140)

(47)   First *it is necessary to consider the arguments used in the public debates*. (BNC A07 1458)

Hyland (2002c) divides directives pragmatically, into textual, physical and cognitive acts. Textual acts serve to navigate the reader through the text itself (internal references to parts of the text) or through a network of related texts (external references to literature), e.g. (45) above. Physical acts direct the reader in the physical world, even if just hypothetically (46). Finally, cognitive acts attempt to influence the reader's thinking (47). Cognitive acts are common in expert writing, but students are wary of the authority that cognitive acts exert, and consequently rely on directives expressing physical acts to demonstrate their mastery of research procedures (Hyland 2002c). Lower-level learners, however, might use directives in a general way, similarly to impersonal *we* and impersonal *you*, as presented in (48).

(48) *Keep* your heart healthy and *reduce* your heart attack risk with 10 simple tips. *Call* someone that you walk 30 minutes everyday and *do* whatever to keep you blood pressure number to 115/75. *Eat* an ounce of nuts a day. (TECCL 00061)

Another category of engagement markers are **questions**. They are more common in soft disciplines, especially philosophy, than hard disciplines (Hyland 2002d). Rhetorical questions (questions followed by the writer's answer or questions whose answer is too obvious to be given) are more common than real questions (Hyland 2001a). The purpose of a particular question seems to determine its location in text: Blagojević and Mišić Ilić (2012) found that in expert writing, rhetorical questions followed by an answer typically occur at the beginning or middle of a paragraph, while rhetorical questions serving to announce the aim of the article, attract the reader's attention, engage and persuade the reader are used at the end of paragraphs. In contrast, real questions typically occur in conclusion sections to suggest further research (Hyland 2002d) or in the methods sections as research questions.

Turning now to learner issues, Hyland (2002d) found that while expert writers use questions for a variety of rhetorical purposes, including indicating a research gap, supporting claims and evaluating (49), students overuse questions to organize their text (50). Students tend to overuse yes/no questions at the expense of Wh-questions, and the questions they use are rather informal (Hyland 2005). According to the findings of Paquot, Hasselgård and Ebeling (2013), L2 English student writers use more questions than L1 English student writers, and EGAP essays use more questions than ESAP essays in linguistics, suggesting that more skilled language users limit their use of questions in academic text.

(49) What does it mean to specify, for instance, the indicated object co-ordinate? (BNC F9V 924)

(50) Why some people did not think so? Because they paid attention to the heavy traffic jams. What causes traffic jams? (TECCL 04295)

The problem with some of the questions learner writers use is, in my experience, that students might use questions, typically in subheadings, to compensate for an absence of complex sentence statements. Such a question might be followed by a sentence fragment (50), suggesting the writer's lack of ability to write sentences stylistically appropriate for formal academic texts.

The last two categories of engagement markers are **references to shared knowledge** (51) and **personal asides** (52). These have attracted less research attention, possibly because they are the least frequent types of engagement markers (Hyland 2009). Nevertheless, available findings suggest that these engagement markers do not pose particular problems for students (Hyland 2005). Both types are more common in soft than in hard disciplines (Hyland 2001a). References to shared knowledge seem to overlap, to some extent, with other categories of metadiscourse: for instance, references to shared knowledge *obviously* and *of course* function also as boosters, and *usually* and *typically* function also as hedges.

(51) However, at a longer time scale, the rooms of the building will come to an equilibrium temperature despite the thicker walls between them, and this will, *of course* affect the temperature of the cubicles in those rooms. (MICUSP BIO.G2.02.1)

(52) In October 1988 the report and its recommendations was considered *(as is required by the complaints procedure)* by the relevant Commander of the Metropolitan Police. (BNC FBT 112)

To conclude this section, it can be seen that only some types of engagement markers, namely reader references and questions, might be an issue for EAP students, especially for lower-level learners, as they tend to use reader references and questions in a stylistically inappropriate way (see Chapter 4.6). A teaching activity focusing on these engagement markers is presented in Teaching activity 6.9.

Teaching activity 6.9. Engagement markers

Rewrite the following sentences into more formal by removing questions, imperatives and second-person pronouns *you* and *your*.

1. What is one of the most common problems students have with academic writing? Using formal academic style.
2. When you are reviewing literature, you should evaluate your sources.
3. Why do students often feel stressed at the beginning of their postgraduate study? Because it is demanding.
4. Lantsoght (2018) gives recommendations for you to improve your writing. First, plan your writing. Second, write daily.

> **Suggested answers**
> 1. One of the most common problems students have with academic writing is using formal academic style.
> 2. When reviewing literature, sources should be evaluated.
> 3. Students often feel stressed at the beginning of their postgraduate study due to the demands of the study.
> 4. Lantsoght (2018) gives recommendations for improving writing, including planning writing and writing daily.
>
> **Commentary**
> The activity as presented here uses constructed examples. For classroom use, however, I would recommend using authentic examples from students' work.

6.8 Attribution: Evidentials

The writer's stance towards the academic community is realized as citation practice and the use of evidentials – language used to introduce citations explicitly, e.g. *according to* and reporting verbs (Hyland 2019a). I consider both citation practice and evidentials as stance markers because they enable the writer to foreground or background cited members of the academic community and to evaluate their work. This section starts with discussing functions of citations (Section 6.8.1), then distinguishes between citations and references (6.8.2) and finally discusses various types of citations – by formal type (6.8.3), by type of rephrasing (6.8.4) and by language structures (6.8.5).

6.8.1 Functions of citations

Citations serve to attribute ideas to their respective originators, which is one of the basic tenets of academic text. In Tadros's (1993) framework, **attribution**, or providing a source of information, may be citational, i.e. including an explicit citation in any form, or non-citational, i.e. including a reference to a research group, school of thought or discipline without a specific citation, e.g. (53). In the absence of explicit attribution, the information presented in a text is by default attributed to the writer, which Tadros calls **averral**. Averral can be signalled negatively, by an absence of attribution, or positively, by an explicit commentary and evaluation, and possibly self-mention terms.

(53) Clearly *positivists*, and, as we shall see, *Marxists* as well, will feel unhappy about any approach to literature which, like that of *the Formalists* and *the Prague School*, concentrates on the analysis of

a text's structure rather than its genesis, and on the explanation of literary facts within a predominantly literary framework of reference. (BNC H8V 468)

The fact that without attribution, the ideas in a text are by default attributed to the writer, poses challenges for writers new to academic writing, as they might unknowingly claim authorship of ideas taken from sources, and thus commit plagiarism. Indeed, novice writers often struggle not only with signalling averral and attribution in their own writing but also with identifying averral and attribution in academic texts they read (Tadros 1993; Borg 2000; McCulloch 2012). This latter difficulty has implications for using secondary citations, as I discuss in Section 6.8.4. As novice writers learn to attribute ideas to sources, they might mask unsupported claims with references to unspecified sources (Kwon, Staples & Partridge 2018), as in *we all know* in Example (40) in Section 6.7. Example (54) is a more sophisticated variant of the same issue, purportedly referring to academic sources yet failing to provide a citation of a single one.

(54) *Many studies* show that people with a wide range of social contacts get sick less than those who don't. I always feel better when I am with friends than when I am alone. (TECCL 01646)

Avoiding plagiarism is but one – and rather superficial – reason for citing sources. Reasons for attribution are in fact multiple and as Thomson and Tribble (2001: 92) put it, '[s]ome of the reasons that academic writers are expected to make references are to integrate the ideas of others into their arguments, to indicate what is known about the subject of study already, or to point out the weaknesses in others' arguments, aligning themselves with a particular camp/school/grouping'. Research has proposed several complex taxonomies of rhetorical functions of citations: For instance, Petrić (2007) has eight main functions, Dontcheva-Navratilova (2016b) has nine functions, Harwood (2009) has eleven functions with additional sub-functions. Without going into detail here, what is relevant for EAP pedagogy is observations that L2 English student writers use citations for a limited range of functions, and typically for knowledge-telling rather than knowledge-transformation (Borg 2000; Petrić 2007; Mansourizadeh & Ahmad 2011; Lee, Hitchcock & Casal 2018), cf. Chapter 2.2. Of particular difficulty for L2 English writers are functions demonstrating criticality, such as using sources for one's own purposes and explicit evaluation of sources (Petrić 2007; Dontcheva-Navratilova 2016b). These functions are presented in Example (55), which contains both citing a source to support the writer's argument (*I draw on*) and evaluation of another source (*what I argue is missing*).

(55) However, *what I argue is missing from MacLaughlin's model* is an affective component, aspects of schooling that serve to develop an emotional attachment between the students and the nation. Here *I*

draw on William Damon's work on moral education and citizenship that asserts: (MICUSP EDU.G3.01.1)

The lack of critical use of sources is related to students often considering the information in sources as facts rather than arguments that can be questioned (Borg 2000; McCulloch 2012; Jomaa & Bidin 2017). These observations suggest a need for greater emphasis on criticality in teaching how to cite sources: as McCulloch (2012: 57) observes, '[t]he emphasis in much of the available guidance on referencing sources tends to lie on the mechanical aspects of citation rather than its role in constructing knowledge'. Another problem related to critical evaluation of sources is learners' lack of appropriate evaluative language (Thompson & Ye 1991; Jomaa & Bidin 2017; Lee, Hitchcock & Casal 2018). Nevertheless, it has to be acknowledged that the amount of criticality in student writing is to a large extent determined by subject knowledge (Mansourizadeh & Ahmad 2011; Jomaa & Bidin 2017) and affected by power relations between students as writers and their audience (Petrić 2007; Jomaa & Bidin 2017), see Chapter 4.2.

6.8.2 *Citations and references*

Let us now focus on options writers have for citational attribution. Each source used needs to be acknowledged with one or more in-text **citations** and a corresponding reference in the list of **references** at the end of the text. Although the terms citation and reference are often used interchangeably in academic jargon, they are technically different (see, e.g. American Psychological Association (APA) 2019: 257) and as EAP practitioners, being experts on academic writing, we should carefully distinguish between them. Both citations and references have to follow precise formatting guidelines, depending on the HE institution, journal or publisher. Among the best-known formatting styles are APA, Modern Language Association and Harvard styles. Accurate formatting of citations and references following a particular referencing style can be problematic for both L1 and L2 English student writers (Borg 2000). Referencing is the focus of Teaching activity 6.10 and various types of citations are presented in Teaching activity 6.11.

Teaching activity 6.10. Referencing

Work in a small group. The teacher will give you four sources. Determine the genre of each source (journal article, chapter in a book, book, website, newspaper article) and then write a full reference following your chosen referencing style.

Commentary

I use this activity to help students format the list of references correctly, following their target referencing style. I split the class into several groups, assign each group a source and then rotate the sources. The sources represent a variety of genres and they can be printed and/or digital copies.

Although the activity might seem straightforward, students find it rather challenging. To start with, many have problems identifying the genre, and thus miss details specific to a particular genre (e.g. volume and issue number for a journal article, publisher for a book, authors and editors for a book chapter). Some students find it difficult to distinguish authors' first names and surnames – particularly if in their first language the order is reverse to the English one. Finally, students sometimes do not pay attention to such details as the use of italics and bold, correct punctuation and capitalization in the target referencing style.

For these reasons, the activity is rather time consuming. If using print sources, it is better to select sources with short titles to save time for typing. Students typically need several instances of on-task feedback to get the references right.

Teaching activity 6.11. Citation

Scan read the following extract (Hulme 2021: 209) to find all the citations and then answer the questions below.

The development of EAP has been studied extensively in the literature of language teaching, ever since the term was first used by Tim Johns in 1974 as the title for the published proceedings of a conference held in 1975 (Ding & Bruce 2017; Hyland & Shaw 2016; Jordan 1997). The available literature provides a thorough historical overview of EAP from its origins in English for Specific Purposes (ESP), 'a practical affair concerned with local contexts and the needs of particular students' (Hyland & Shaw 2016: 1) to a view of EAP as a 'research-informed *academic field of study*' (Ding & Bruce 2017: 4). Many authors have written on this topic (see Basturkmen 2010; Ding & Bruce 2017; Dudley-Evans & St John 1998; Flowerdew & Peacock 2001; Hyland & Shaw 2016; Jordan 1997).

ESAP's beginnings in ESP were concerned with notions of specificity, understanding texts and 'communicative behaviors' as well as providing practical, pedagogic solutions to students' specific needs (Hyland 2007). Initially, the emphasis was on language/register analysis and meeting specific aims within specific academic disciplines (Swales 1985), in particular, the STEM subjects (science, technology, engineering and medicine) (Hutchinson & Waters 1987).

As ESP became more widely adopted across education, it developed to include different ideas about specificity. Hutchinson and Waters questioned its importance and advocated seeking a common ground between disciplines (Hyland 2016). Widdowson (1983 as cited in Basturkmen 2010) argued ESP courses could be plotted at either end of a continuum from 'narrow-angled', catering for students with specific needs for English, to 'wide-angled', more appropriate for students with general needs for English. The idea of varying degrees of specificity was further developed by Jordan, who presented Blue's (1998 as cited in Jordan 1997) view of specificity in EAP: English for general academic purposes (EGAP) and English for specific academic purposes. EGAP is concerned with study skills and 'a general academic English register', which applies to all disciplines, whereas ESAP's concern lies with 'language needed for a particular academic subject [. . .] together with its disciplinary culture' (Jordan 1997: 5). EAP practitioners were invited to choose between an EGAP or ESAP approach, creating what appeared to be opposing camps (Hyland 2016). Bodin-Galvez and Ding (2019) provide an overview of the arguments given in support of ESAP and the differences between ESAP and EGAP.

(Hulme 2021: 209)

1. Find examples of direct quotation. How do you know these are direct quotations? Why do you think the writer uses them instead of paraphrasing? How does she integrate them with her own words? What does the use of *[. . .]* mean?
2. Find examples of paraphrasing. How do they differ from direct quotations?
3. Find an example of generalization. Why does the writer use it?
4. Find examples of (a) integral citations and (b) non-integral citations. Why do you think the writer uses them?
5. Which reporting verbs are used with integral citations? In what tense, number and voice are they? Why do you think this is so?
6. Why do you think the writer uses *as cited in* with two citations?

Answers

1. There are three instances of direct quotation in the extract *(Hyland & Shaw 2016: 1; Ding & Bruce 2017: 4; Jordan 1997: 5)*, signalled by quotation marks and page numbers from which the quotations were taken. The quotations are not simply pasted into the text as stand-alone

sentences; rather, they are integrated into the writer's own sentences (e.g. *ESAP's concern lies with*). The author possibly chose to quote rather than paraphrase to highlight what language is used to talk about EAP in the literature and to highlight differences (e.g. *practical – research-informed, general – particular*). The author uses ellipsis *[. . .]* to indicate she omitted some words from the quoted original as these did not serve the purpose of her writing.
2. Using paraphrasing (all the other citations) enables the writer to express the cited ideas very selectively and succinctly and thus to better integrate them into her own writing.
3. There are two generalizations (*Ding & Bruce 2017; Hyland & Shaw 2016; Jordan 1997;* and *Basturkmen 2010; Ding & Bruce 2017; Dudley-Evans & St John 1998; Flowerdew & Peacock 2001; Hyland & Shaw 2016; Jordan 1997*) in the extract. The writer uses them to refer to a body of literature on the topic.
4. The writer uses both integral (*Hutchinson and Waters questioned and advocated; Widdowson argued; developed by Jordan; Blue's view; Bodin-Galvez and Ding provide*) and non-integral citations (all the other citations), with some use of the middle type (*has been studied extensively in the literature; the available literature provides; many authors have written*), thus creating rich variety. She uses the middle type to refer to a body of literature, integral citations to highlight cited authors' personal contributions to the debate and non-integral citations to foreground ideas rather than authors (e.g. *notions of, emphasis was on*).
5. Most reporting verbs are used in the past simple and active voice, thus not being marked for number (*questioned, advocated, argued*). One reporting verb is used in the past simple and passive voice in singular to refer to a single author (*was developed by Jordan*), and one reporting verb is used in the present simple and active voice in plural to refer to two authors of the same work (*Bodin-Galvez and Ding provide*). While the use of singular or plural is given by single or multiple authorship of works cited, the use of tense reflects the writer's choice to present older literature (from 1983, 1987 and 1997/8) in the past simple and more recent literature (2019) in the present simple in order to show different degrees of the literature's relevance for the present. The choice of the passive voice seems to be guided by coherence, as it enables the writer to start the clause with known information (*the idea of varying degrees of specificity* referring to the *continuum* mentioned in the previous sentence).
6. The use of *Widdowson (1983 as cited in Basturkmen 2010)* and *Blue's (1998 as cited in Jordan 1997) view* indicates that the writer did not have access to and thus did not read Widdowson's or Blue's works, only Basturkmen's and Jordan's works citing them. (The year 1998 is probably a typo, as it is illogical that a later work would be cited in an earlier one.)

> **Commentary**
> The activity can be expanded in the following ways:
>
> 1. Discussing whether italics in the Ding and Bruce quote appeared in the original source or whether it was added by the writer of the extract, and ways of preventing this ambiguity (e.g. *original emphasis – emphasis added*).
> 2. Questioning the use of quotation marks but no page number with the citation for terms used in the original source (e.g. *narrow-angled*).
> 3. Discussing why citations *Hutchinson and Waters questioned* and *developed by Jordan, who* do not use year of publication with the authors' names.
> 4. Analysing the reporting verbs used with the middle type of citations (*has been studied, provides, have written*).
>
> I am not suggesting that a text about the development of EAP would be useful for EAP students. Rather, this extract was selected here for illustrative purposes only, because it uses a variety of different types of citations in a small space. To do a similar activity with students, EAP teachers should select a text read on the course and analyse the type of citations that appear there. The variety of citations might be relatively limited, depending, among other things, on the discipline.

6.8.3 Formal types of citation: Integral and non-integral citations

Formally, citations can be divided into two types, integral and non-integral (Swales 1990). In **integral citations**, the cited authors' names are syntactically embedded within the main text (56), while in **non-integral citations**, they appear in brackets (57) or are merely signalled with numerical referencing (58). Between these two neat types sits a middle type of citation which appears to combine aspects of both types, presented in (59) and (60). Example (59) combines an indefinite noun (*several studies*) with a reporting verb (*report*) and numerical referencing. Example (60) combines a definite noun (*the Feringa group*) with a reporting verb (*demonstrate*) and numerical referencing. Swales (2014) considers only the former type and calls it a reporting subtype of non-integral citations, since it uses a reporting verb. Contrary to his account, Shaw (1992) distinguishes the two types and considers the former type a non-integral reporting citation and the latter type an integral reporting citation based on the (in)definiteness of the noun.

(56) *Lee* (1992) discusses the ways in which this might happen. (BNC F9T 1890)

(57) They had a strong incentive to ensure hospitals made efficient use of their money on behalf of their patients (*Glennerster* 1992). (BNC G1C 2188)

(58) Microarray time series gene expression experiments have essential applications in studying cell cycle development *[1, 2]*, immune response *[3]*, and other biological processes. (Tripto et al. 2020: 1)

(59) *Several studies have reported* that GPS2 participates in transcriptional regulation through acting as a transcriptional co-activator or co-repressor *[19], [20], [28], [29]*. (Xu, Zin & Zheng 2013: 7)

(60) Another synthetic application of dichloride 7 *has recently been demonstrated* by *the Feringa group.*[51] (Krayushkin, Kalik & Migulin 2009: 332)

Research into disciplinary variation in respect to one type of citations over the other is inconclusive. While Hyland's (2019a, 2002a) corpus contains more non-integral citations than integral ones across several disciplines with philosophy being the only exception, in Ädel and Garretson's (2006) corpus most soft disciplines use predominantly integral citations and hard disciplines use mostly non-integral citations. Moreover, subfields of the same discipline can vary in their use of citations (see Ädel & Garretson 2006 for engineering and Clugston 2008 for health science). Likewise, it remains unclear whether the type of referencing system used (i.e. numerical referencing or author–date referencing) affects the ratio of integral and non-integral citations in academic texts: It might be expected that non-integral citations will be more common with numerical referencing than with author–date referencing system. This prediction has been confirmed by Swales (2014) for student writing but not by Charles (2006) or Clugston (2008) for student and expert writing, respectively.

Student writers typically overuse integral citations at the expense of non-integral citations (Thompson & Tribble 2001; Jomaa & Bidin 2017; Lee, Hitchcock & Casal 2018). Swales (2014) suggests this might be a result of EAP instruction that gives great prominence to reporting verbs. EAP instruction should therefore highlight that variation in citation types is desirable and that preference of one type of citations over another is determined by complex factors. One is the intended focus of the writer: Hyland (2019a) explains that integral citations foreground cited authors, while non-integral citations foreground cited ideas.[6] Related to this is the fact that the decision to focus on either cited authors or the content of their work is affected by cohesion and information structure (see Chapter 5), as Shaw (1992) points out. At the same time, the choice of focus might be determined by the nature of a particular discipline: One can expect hard sciences characterized by exactitude and reproducibility to emphasize content and thus to use more non-integral citations, and argumentative and interpretative soft sciences to highlight originators of ideas and therefore to use more integral citations.

This explanation is supported by Ädel and Garretson's (2006) findings mentioned above. Finally, integral citations seem to better lend themselves to the use of citations extending over more than one sentence (61).

(61) For example, *Kimberger et al.* evaluated a TAT in 35 adult patients in a neurosurgical operating room and 35 patients in a neurosurgical ICU and concluded that it was not an adequate substitute for core temperature monitoring [15]. *The authors* found a low mean difference of 0.07°C, but high LOA −1.48°C to 1.62°C, which corresponds fairly to the mean difference and LOA of our study. (Cox et al. 2020: 6–8)

6.8.4 Types of citation by rephrasing: Direct quotation, paraphrase/summary, generalization and secondary citation

Another classification of citations is by their relation to the original wording of the source. One type is **direct quotation,** which presents the original wording of a source without any changes. Direct quotations are minimal in expert writing, especially in hard sciences where they are practically non-existent (Hyland 1999a, 2002a). Students use direct quotations more frequently than expert writers (Ädel & Garretson 2006; McCulloch 2012; Jabulani 2014), and L2 English students tend to use longer direct quotations than L1 English students (Borg 2000). This may be due to students considering information in sources as accepted facts (see above), due to L2 English writers showing respect towards cited authors in this way (Walková 2017), or due to difficulties with presenting information from sources in one's own words. Overusing quotations is problematic, for it restricts writers in using sources for knowledge-transformation rather than knowledge-telling (see Chapter 2.2): Research has found that less skilled writers tend to use direct quotations without any obvious purpose and as substitution for their own argument (McCulloch 2012; Brooke 2014). This is especially evident when a direct quotation is used without the writer's introduction, as in (62). In contrast, skilled writers use direct quotations when they find these to be 'most vivid and effective' (Hyland 1999a: 348).

(62) Facebook use indeed varied, depending on a student's psychological well-being. 'Facebook use may be helping to overcome barriers faced by students who have low satisfaction and low self-esteem' (Ellison et al. 2007: 1163). (Lee & Ranta 2014: 29)

Another problem related to using direct quotations is acknowledging them as such: Direct quotations need to be marked off with quotation marks and the citation must include the page from which the quotation was taken (62), and failure to do so is considered plagiarism. Interestingly, Pecorari (2006) found that acknowledging direct quotations is a challenge especially for hard science students: Not only do students in hard sciences use original wording of sources more often than students in soft sciences, but hard science students are also less likely to acknowledge that they use original wording. It seems, then, that student writers follow the overt practices of their disciplines by not using direct quotations, yet not understanding that information from sources needs to be reformulated in their own words. Overall, research into quoting suggests that teaching should focus on purposes of using quotations (see Teaching activity 6.11) and on preferred alternative ways of presenting information from sources.

Such alternative ways include **paraphrase** and **summary**.[7] The distinction between the two, to the best of my knowledge, dates back to Dubois (1988: 183), who characterizes them as follows: 'Paraphrase is restatement of an idea in different words but the same length. Summary is an abbreviated statement of a result or fact from a single source article.' It is common to see pedagogical literature drawing learners' attention to differences between paraphrase and summary (e.g. Bailey 2011). Ironically, however, Dubois (1988) found paraphrase to be much less common than summary in her corpus of expert writing and accordingly questioned the usefulness of the concept of paraphrase for student writers. Siding with Dubois, I feel the differences between the two are of limited pedagogical value, as overemphasizing these differences might take students' attention away from what really matters – effective reformulation of meaning in their own words.

If any differences exist between paraphrase and summary, then it is the level of abstraction in summary: If paraphrase retains the same approximate length as the original text, then it handles information at sentence level rather than at the level of ideas. It is this understanding of paraphrase that leads to learning activities in which any sentence from a source text, or even an entire paragraph, can be paraphrased (e.g. Bailey 2011, Section 1.6) – a practice that strips citing sources of its very purpose of supporting the writer's own argument and instead encourages the use of sources as a substitute for the writer's argument, as discussed above. In contrast, summary handles information at the level of ideas, since it involves selecting ideas from a source for the writer's own purpose and thus using citation for knowledge-transformation rather than knowledge-telling (see Chapter 2.2). For these reasons, the present book does not distinguish between paraphrase and summary and considers the two terms interchangeable. Nevertheless, to distinguish between summary as a type of citation and summary as a type of genre (see Chapter 3), I opt for the term paraphrase, which I use to refer to citation of any length that presents information from a single source in a reformulated form, e.g. (61) above.

Yet another type of citation, which requires a high level of abstraction, is **generalization**, or paraphrasing of ideas common to two or more sources

(63). While less common in expert writing than paraphrase (Hyland 2002a), generalization is typically underused by less skilled L2 English students (Brooke 2014; Lee, Hitchcock & Casal 2018), thus limiting the degree of synthesis of sources. It follows that EAP pedagogy should draw learners' attention to this type of citation and its effective and purposeful use (see Teaching activity 6.11).

(63)   Stance conventions influence the effectiveness of English language learner (L2) and native speaker (L1) student writers and the writing scores they receive *(Barton 1993; Coffin 2002; Hood 2004; Wu 2007)*. (Aull, Bandarage & Miller 2017: 29)

When discussing classification of citations based on relation of citations to the original source, a special kind of citation needs to be mentioned, namely **secondary citation**. Secondary citation is used when the writer refers to a source which s/he was not able to access directly and only relies on its citation in another source. This is exemplified in (64): The writer refers to Palmer's idea yet the writer learnt about this idea from Pascoe (1996) and did not read Palmer (1969). As the use of secondary citation might lead to a degree of misrepresentation of the original text or to misattribution of ideas to the wrong authors, it is preferable to use original texts and use secondary citation sparingly (APA 2019). In spite of this recommendation, Pecorari (2006) has found that while outwardly student texts contain few instances of secondary citation, unacknowledged secondary citations are in fact very common in student writing.

The reason why students rarely acknowledge secondary citation might be that they have difficulties in distinguishing attribution from averral in their source texts. This occasionally happens to expert writers as well, as I will illustrate with an example of a paper that cites my own work: In example (65), the authors attribute the observation that self-mention pronouns used to be unacceptable in academic writing to me, as indicated by the citation to my paper. However, as can be seen from my original text, shown in (66), the observation comes from other sources. Detection of unacknowledged secondary citation is possible only when one knows the source text well (as is my case presented in Examples 65 and 66) or upon careful comparison of every citation to its respective original text, as done by Pecorari (2006). It is therefore unlikely that an EAP teacher will be able to identify more than a few unacknowledged secondary citations. What follows is that teaching using secondary citation cannot be incidental, as a response to it being an issue for particular students, but should be pre-emptive and should include identification of attribution and averral in a source text.

(64)   According to *Palmer (1969, cited in Pascoe 1996)*, a student of Gadamer, Gadamer's view of understanding is that it is always an historical, dialectic, and linguistic event. (MICUSP NUR.G2.04.1)

(65) Although for a long time the use of first-person pronoun was discouraged among the academic community *(Walková 2019: 60)* ... (Grigoriev & Sokolova 2019: 424)

(66) About three decades ago, explicit self-reference through personal pronouns was discouraged in writing guides (*Chang & Swales 1999: 149*) and could even be a reason for editors to reject a research paper (*Webb 1992*). (Walková 2019: 60)

6.8.5 Linguistic types of citation: Language structures

The final classification of citations is linguistic, based on types of language structures in which citations can appear. Thompson and Tribble (2001) distinguish between **verb-controlling and naming citations**. Verb-controlling citations include the use of the cited authors' name with reporting verbs in the active or passive voice. Naming citations are nominal, as the names of cited authors form (part of) a noun phrase. Swales (2014) offers a finer classification, with five subtypes, according to the function of the cited author's name:

a) author as subject (67),
b) author as agent (68),
c) author as adjunct, either in a prepositional phrase (69) or in a subordinate clause (70),
d) author in a noun phrase (71),
e) and a small category of others (72).

(67) *Vernon* (1971) *argues* that over a period of time, and particularly as a new technology matures, host countries are more able to drive harder bargains with the TNCs that wish to invest in them. (BNC HTV 1166)

(68) A range of objectives for watershed experiments *was identified by Ward* (1971) and these extend from specific black box approaches to comprehensive studies in which there is an attempt to monitor many of the processes operating within a small area. (BNC GVW 619)

(69) *According to Porter* (1980 and 1985), the most important element is the industry in which the business competes. (BNC HRK 121)

(70) *As Richards* (1989) *discusses*, there are currently 26 out of 300 possible landfill sites in Britain which are producing energy on a commercial basis, and there is considerable scope for increased biogas production as there is in West Germany and the USA. (BNC B1E 1147)

(71) This was a clear example of *the phenomenon discussed by Pinker* (1971). (BNC G1C 1348)

(72) *In contrast to Chisholm*, Ayer argues that free will and determinism are compatible when the correct definition of freedom is employed. (MICUSP PHI.G0.18.2)

I believe Swales's labels to be technically imprecise, however, for two reasons. First, Swales mixes syntactic and semantic criteria when he proposes a difference between author as subject and author as agent: In fact, author's name has the semantic function of agent in both categories: The difference is syntactic, with author's name functioning as the sentence subject in the former category and as part of a *by-* prepositional phrase in the latter category. Second, what Swales calls adjuncts are, I believe, disjuncts, as these are not part of the basic sentence structure but rather a commentary on the rest of the sentence (see Quirk et al. 1985 for an exhaustive treatment of the subject, and note that on p. 623 they specifically mention *according to* as a disjunct). Nevertheless, I suggest simplifying the classification for pedagogical application as follows:

- citations with a reporting verb in the active voice, including those where the reporting verb occurs in the main clause (67) and those where it occurs in a subordinate clause (70),
- citations with a reporting verb in the past participle form, including those where it is part of the passive voice (68) and where it functions as a modifier in a noun phrase (71),
- and citations used as part of a prepositional phrase which is not used with a reporting verb (69 and 72). In addition to the examples in (69) and (72), prepositional phrases can include the use of prepositions in such structures as *beginning with, (the reader can) refer to, an example (taken) from, drawing on* and *(un)like,* among others.

We can thus see that there is a variety of linguistic options for presenting citations. Student writing, however, often lacks variety and tends to over-rely on structures with reporting verbs in the active voice in the main clause and on structures with *according to* (Thompson & Tribble 2001; Mansourizadeh & Ahmad 2011; Lee, Hitchcock & Casal 2018). This is not surprising given the emphasis on these structures in teaching citation, as Swales (2014) points out.

Even though students use reporting verbs frequently, this use does not come without issues. One issue is syntactic: less skilled learners make subject–verb agreement errors, especially with sources written by multiple authors (Jabulani 2014), e.g. (73), use reporting verbs in combination with *according to* (McCulloch 2012; Jabulani 2014; Lee, Hitchcock & Casal 2018), e.g. (74), or use reporting verbs in conflict with their selectional restrictions, e.g.

discuss about (Clugston 2008; Jabulani 2014). Another issue is stylistic: Some L2 English student writers use verbs common in speech but rare in formal academic writing, such as *think, imagine, know, say, talk* and *speak* (Loan & Pramoolsook 2015; Kwon, Staples & Partridge 2018; Lee, Hitchcock & Casal 2018), e.g. (73). Yet another issue is semantic, when writers use verbs whose meaning is different from the one intended by the writer, e.g. the use of *claim* for definitions (Thompson & Tribble 2001; Lee, Hitchcock & Casal 2018). What follows from this overview is that EAP pedagogy should place greater emphasis on syntactic range of evidentials, syntactic and semantic accuracy of reporting verbs, and their lexical range and stylistic appropriateness. Examples of respective teaching activities are given in Teaching activities 6.12 and 6.13.

(73) According to the HSBC report, as *JI YI, Meng Fang Yuan, Suresh Kumah says* (2013) 'China only consumed 5% Luxury product in 2007'. (TECCL 05417)

(74) *According to Will Durant* in his book 'History of Western Philosophy' in the records, *said* he had bald head, big round face, deep-set eyes, broad and upturned nose, like a porter. (TECCL 05295)

Teaching activity 6.12. Integral and non-integral citations

For the following sentences, decide whether an integral or a non-integral citation should be used and insert brackets (and possibly a comma) accordingly.

1. According to Dar and Gieve 2013, in exploratory practice practitioners should not take assumptions for granted.
2. In exploratory practice, practitioners should not take assumptions for granted Dar and Gieve 2013.
3. Dar and Gieve 2013 argue that in exploratory practice practitioners should not take assumptions for granted.
4. Previous research on exploratory practice has suggested that practitioners should not take assumptions for granted Dar and Gieve 2013.
5. In exploratory practice, practitioners should not take assumptions for granted, as argued by Dar and Gieve 2013.

Answers
1. According to Dar and Gieve (2013), in exploratory practice practitioners should not take assumptions for granted.

2. In exploratory practice, practitioners should not take assumptions for granted (Dar & Gieve 2013).
3. Dar and Gieve (2013) argue that in exploratory practice practitioners should not take assumptions for granted.
4. Previous research on exploratory practice has suggested that practitioners should not take assumptions for granted (Dar & Gieve 2013).
5. In exploratory practice, practitioners should not take assumptions for granted, as argued by Dar and Gieve (2013).

Commentary

This activity highlights to students that the same cited idea may be acknowledged with either an integral or a non-integral citation and how the choice is connected to syntax. It also illustrates several linguistic structures for integral citations. Note that the use of comma in non-integral citations depends on the referencing style used.

Teaching activity 6.13. Language of integral citations

Rewrite the following sentence with a non-integral citation into sentences with an integral citation, with each sentence using one of the structures below:

Critical use of sources requires extensive subject knowledge (Mansourizadeh & Ahmad 2011).

- *according to*,
- reporting verb in the active voice,
- reporting verb in the past participle form,
- phrase *in view*.

Sample answers

Several answers are possible, among them:

- *according to:*

According to Mansourizadeh and Ahmad (2011), critical use of sources requires extensive subject knowledge.

- reporting verb in the active voice:

Mansourizadeh and Ahmad (2011) argue that critical use of sources requires extensive subject knowledge.

As Mansourizadeh and Ahmad (2011) argue, critical use of sources requires extensive subject knowledge.

- reporting verb in the past participle form:

It has been argued by Mansourizadeh and Ahmad (2011) that critical use of sources requires extensive subject knowledge.

Critical use of sources requires extensive subject knowledge, as argued by Mansourizadeh and Ahmad (2011).

- phrase *in view*:

In Mansourizadeh and Ahmad's (2011) view, critical use of sources requires extensive subject knowledge.

In the view of Mansourizadeh and Ahmad (2011), critical use of sources requires extensive subject knowledge.

Commentary

This activity illustrates how language can be manipulated to achieve variety in the use of integral citations. A citation referring to a source written by two authors has been selected to address the issue of subject–verb agreement. It is expected that the activity will also lead to discussions around selecting an appropriate reporting verb. It might be useful to point out the use of comma and the possessive in these different types of language structures, and to explore how citations in subordinate clauses background the authors compared to citations in main clauses.

Focusing on lexical range, **reporting verbs** have both denotative and evaluative meanings (Thompson & Ye 1991; Hyland 1999a). According to their denotative meaning, reporting verbs can be divided into three, somewhat overlapping, types (Thompson & Ye 1991; Thomas & Hawes 1994; Hyland 1999a):

- research verbs which report on procedures and findings, e.g. *find, identify*,
- cognition verbs denoting mental processes, e.g. *believe, focus* and
- discourse verbs referring to expression in text, e.g. *argue, suggest*.

Hyland (2019a, 2002a) found that hard sciences use mostly research verbs, while soft sciences typically use discourse verbs, which is given by the experimental nature of the former and the argumentative nature of the latter type of sciences.

Evaluative meaning refers to the stance value of reporting verbs. In Hyland's (2019a) classification, reporting verbs can be

- factive, by which the writer shows agreement with the cited author, e.g. *confirm, point out*,

- counter-factive, by which the writer shows disagreement with the cited author, e.g. *overlook, not realize*, or

- non-factive, in which the writer does not evaluate the cited work.

In the last case, however, the stance may be attributed to the cited author. The cited author's stance can be shown to be

- positive, e.g. *argue, claim*,

- critical, e.g. *object, question*,

- tentative, e.g. *suggest, propose* or

- neutral, e.g. *state, report*.

Both expert writers (Hyland 1999a; Clugston 2008; Walková 2017) and student writers (Swales 2014; Loan & Pramoolsook 2015) most commonly use stance-neutral non-factive verbs, although soft sciences use more stance-marked verbs than hard sciences given the argumentative nature of the former (Hyland 1999a), and counter-factive and critical non-factive verbs are used rarely (Hyland 1999a; Walková 2017). This is not surprising given that such direct criticism of members of academic community is a face-threatening act (see Chapter 2.3). Although student writers use stance-marked verbs to a lesser extent than expert writers, L2 English students actually use more stance-marked verbs than L1 English students (Liardét & Black 2019). It seems, then, that stance marking as reflected in the choice of reporting verbs is not a particular issue in EAP, which questions the usefulness of presenting learners with long lists of reporting verbs with varying stance, as done in some learning materials (e.g. University of Technology Surrey, n.d.).

The final point related to the use of reporting verbs is the choice of tense. Interestingly, although citations are used with a specific point in the past – i.e. the year of publication – they are commonly used in the present simple tense (75); in my experience, this often confuses students new to using citations. Reporting verbs, nonetheless, can also be used in the present perfect (76) or the past simple (77). Swales (1990) explains that the continuum from the present to the past is that of a continuum from proximity to distance: By using past simple, the writer distances himself/herself from the cited work, for instance, in order to disagree with it or to show that its connection to the present is loose. The choice of tense of reporting verbs thus reflects the writer's stance towards previous work. The writer's stance is not the only factor influencing tense choice, however. Charles (2006) shows that discourse verbs are typically used in the present simple, e.g. (67) above, in contrast to research verbs, which tend to be used in the past simple, e.g. (68). EAP classes should therefore raise awareness of variations in tense choice in reporting verbs (see Teaching activity 6.11).

(75) Trilling (1972) *argues* that Diderot was a crucial influence on Hegel. (BNC CMS 36)

(76) As Crick (1976: 123) *has argued*, 'criminology (like anthropology), is largely concerned with systems of classification'. (BNC A0K 165)

(77) Crosland (1956) *argued* that economic growth was essential if the Fabian strategy of equality was to succeed. (BNC HXT 131)

To sum up the pedagogical implications discussed in this section, EAP classes should explore using sources critically and balancing integral and non-integral citations; introduce generalization and secondary citation; point out specific reasons for using quotations; and focus on reporting verbs' range, accuracy, appropriateness and use with tenses rather than with stance.

6.9 Summary

This chapter has proposed a model of stance composed of four aspects – stance to the text, to the writer's self, to the reader and to the wider academic community. Drawing on Hyland's (2019a) model of metadiscourse, I have shown that stance is signalled by interactional metadiscourse devices whose functions may be multiple and overlapping. Contra Hyland (2019a), I have argued that evidentials should also be considered interactional: Rather than merely organizing text, they indirectly engage members of the academic community in the dialogue that the text establishes. The chapter has also discussed EAP controversies concerning stance, such as teaching the writer's voice and the use of personal pronouns; questioned the pedagogical usefulness of some approaches, such as teaching stance through decontextualized lists of reporting verbs; and suggested which areas of academic writing need closer attention in EAP pedagogy, such as using sources critically.

CHAPTER 7

Formative feedback on writing

7.1 Introduction

This last chapter shifts attention to an aspect of teaching writing that occurs after learners have produced writing – formative feedback (summative assessment is not discussed here as it is beyond the scope of the book). The chapter first reviews general factors that impact on the effectiveness of teacher feedback, such as students' expectations; affect and engagement with feedback; and contextual constraints of feedback, such as power relations and institutional requirements (Section 7.2). The chapter then moves on to reviewing research on feedback within the areas of language acquisition and L2 writing (Section 7.3). Section 7.4 then offers recommendations arising from the research reviewed in the earlier sections. The last section concludes the chapter.

7.2 HE research on feedback

For students to improve their writing, it is necessary for them not only to receive instruction and to practise their skills but also to receive feedback on their performance. Formative feedback, defined by Shute (2008: 154) 'as information communicated to the learner that is intended to modify his or her thinking or behaviour for the purpose of improving learning', has attracted much research attention. This has been largely stimulated by reports of student dissatisfaction with teacher feedback in terms of its fairness, transparency and usefulness (Carless 2006; Price et al. 2010). This section reviews literature on individual student factors that impact the uptake of teacher feedback – students' expectations, affect and engagement, and contextual constraints related to feedback – considerations of power and institutional requirements. As the research on these factors both comes from and applies to HE more generally, including disciplines beyond language teaching, I call this strand of research HE research on feedback.

One factor that affects the uptake of teacher feedback is **students' expectations** of feedback. Since expectations tend to vary widely among students (Ferris & Kurzer 2019; Hyland, F. 1998), and since a discrepancy between student expectations and actual feedback received can negatively impact student engagement with feedback (Storch & Wigglesworth 2010), it is important that teachers and students build a shared understanding of feedback. This can be done, for example, through open discussions about students' and teachers' understanding of effective and useful feedback (Goldstein 2004; Green, S. 2019; Price et al. 2010).

The uptake of teacher feedback is also impacted by students' **affect**. Young (2000), for instance, shows that perceptions of feedback are related to students' confidence: while students with high confidence welcome negative feedback as an opportunity to learn, students with low confidence tend to disregard positive feedback and focus on negative comments only. At the same time, Young points out that students' confidence levels are independent of their actual achievement, which suggests that teachers should endeavour to get to know their students as individuals and tailor feedback accordingly. Students' affect plays a crucial role not only in their perception of feedback but also in their performance, as shown by Wingate (2010), who has found that students who succeed in academic writing tend to be confident and motivated, able to deal with anxiety and to attribute failure to internal rather than external causes. This suggests that it would be beneficial for university teachers to support students in developing strategies for handling affect.

For teacher feedback to be effective in improving the quality of writing, it is necessary that students engage with feedback. Although many university teachers feel that students are interested only in final marks, and that their time spent on giving detailed feedback is wasted (Bailey & Garner 2010; Tuck 2012), students typically report that they do read teacher feedback and expect to learn from it for future assignments (Carless 2006). It has to be acknowledged that students vary in the extent and form of their **engagement with feedback** (Hyland, F. 1998), yet as Goldstein (2004) points out, teachers cannot take for granted that students understand what teachers expect them to do with feedback, especially since these expectations may vary among institutions (Han & Hyland 2019). It follows that teachers need to encourage students to engage with feedback and train them to respond to it appropriately. This can be done, for instance, by students revising and resubmitting a piece of writing and reflecting on how they implemented teacher feedback in the revision stage.

Another factor that needs to be taken into account in discussion of feedback is **power relations** between teachers and students. In student writing, power typically rests with the teacher, who determines the topic, word count and deadlines of assignments and who evaluates student writing against criteria determined by the institution (Tardy 2019). This power imbalance can be, on the one hand, motivating for students when they appreciate receiving feedback from an expert, and discouraging on the other hand, when students do not seek further clarification of feedback from teachers whom they perceive as non-approachable (Small & Attree 2016). Ways to mitigate power imbalance can include, for instance, giving students a choice of topic for their assignment, assessing portfolios showcasing student-selected work, co-construction of marking criteria with students and giving students opportunities to give each other feedback in peer review. EAP practitioners can also work to empower students to discuss teacher feedback on their work with the subject lecturers.

Power relations generate particular tension in terms of text ownership: There is a danger that, when giving feedback, the teacher will take ownership of a student text and invest it with meanings not intended by the student writer – a phenomenon known as **appropriation** (Reid 1994). Following Bakhtin (1981, cited in Tardy 2019), Tardy (2019) distinguishes between feedback which is implemented by the writer because it is *internally persuasive*, i.e. the writer aligns with it, and feedback which is implemented by the writer because it is *externally authoritative*, i.e. the writer feels obliged to implement it due to the teacher's authority. Tardy shows that students' ability to resist externally authoritative feedback depends on their knowledge of relevant genres and of disciplinary practices. It follows that genre-based ESAP pedagogy can empower students to resist feedback, in the spirit of Critical Pragmatic EAP (see Chapter 2.5). Tardy (2019) proposes dialogic interactive feedback practice, in which the student is seen as a content expert and the EAP teacher as a language and writing expert and together they negotiate feedback. Thus, for instance, an EAP teacher can ask a student to clarify his/her intended meaning in a text and help him/her choose an appropriate language form to communicate this particular meaning (cf. SFL in Chapter 2.3 and grammaring in Chapter 2.4).

In an attempt to mitigate power imbalance when giving feedback, teachers draw on a variety of strategies, as Hyland and Hyland (2019) show. These include responding as a reader in feedback, using hedging and questions to formulate feedback and pairing a negative comment with a positive one and/or with a suggestion for improvement. Student responses in the Hyland and Hyland study, however, reveal that students might misinterpret mitigated negative feedback, especially when it is phrased as a question and without an accompanying suggestion for improvement. Hyland and Hyland (2019: 203) therefore point out that 'teachers may sometimes forget that students are reading their feedback in a foreign language and that being more indirect and "subtle" may actually result in significant misunderstandings'. It follows that, in order to be useful, feedback should be explicit, and mitigation of power relations might take place outside written feedback, in discussions of responding to feedback. Another implication is that EAP students might benefit from training on interpreting indirectly worded feedback.

The ability of teachers to meet student expectations, tailor feedback to individual students' needs, give detailed feedback and provide opportunities to discuss feedback individually is to a large extent determined by **institutional context**. Contexts with large student-to-teacher ratios, heavy teacher workloads and precarious contracts have a negative impact on the quality of teacher feedback and thus on students' learning. Massification of HE thus restricts the amount of formative feedback and opportunities for differentiation (Goldstein 2004; Guillen Solano 2016; Nicol 2010). Moreover, although providing feedback is time consuming, it tends to be unrecognized in terms of career progression, which can be demotivating for university teachers (Tuck 2012). As institutions may vary in what they value in feedback and writing, such as the relative importance of form and content, teachers on short-term contracts might find it difficult to realign with institutional values and practices in each new institution (Goldstein 2004). In institutional contexts suffering from the above predicaments, university writing loses its purpose to deepen students' knowledge (Hyland 2019b), and students might resort to passively receiving feedback instead of actively seeking and negotiating feedback (Green 2019).

Proposed solutions to the effects of HE massification on feedback practices include, for instance, collective in-class feedback (Bitchener 2008) and peer feedback (Nicol 2010). While these may alleviate the problem of limited amounts of feedback, they neither give students individual attention from teachers that they deserve, nor do they give teachers incentives to provide detailed feedback to students. In fact, conformity and uniformity of feedback resulting from institutional context and quality assurance processes can make teachers feel disempowered (Bailey & Garner 2010). Moreover, it has been shown that teacher feedback remains an invaluable component of feedback that integrates computer-generated automated feedback, peer feedback and teacher feedback (Zhang and Hyland 2022). I would therefore propose that, instead of teachers searching for ways of operating in unfavourable conditions, the results of research into feedback should be used to advocate for institutional conditions which make feedback a valuable activity inseparable from learning and which foster the development of feedback practices through collaboration between students and teachers. This would include time allocation for feedback for teachers and the development of feedback literacy (see Section 7.4) for students.

7.3 TESOL research on feedback

While the previous section was largely applicable to university students in general, across various student groups, this section focuses specifically on giving feedback to L2 English writer students, and thus on language issues related to writing. The research reviewed in this section is not exclusively EAP, and in fact, its applicability to EAP pedagogy can be quite limited, as I will argue. To recognize this fact, I call this strand of research TESOL research on feedback.

As pointed out by Ferris (2010), TESOL research on feedback is of **two types**: studies on SLA and studies on L2 writing. These two types differ in purpose, focus, research design and application. On the one hand, SLA studies use writing as a vehicle for investigating the acquisition of language structures and its translation into new pieces of writing rather than in revised texts. They are conducted in controlled experimental conditions, in which authenticity of writing tasks or conditions is not of concern. In contrast, L2 writing studies are pedagogically motivated with the goal of improving writing skills, and revision is considered an important part of the process. For these reasons, the research design of L2 writing studies aims to replicate authentic conditions of a writing class rather than to provide strictly controlled experimental conditions. Ferris concludes that there is much to learn from both strands of research and suggests ways for researchers to integrate the two approaches.

While I agree with Ferris that both strands of research are informative, I would suggest that EAP practitioners need to treat the results of both research strands with caution. The most serious limitation of TESOL research is its focus on genres that are hardly relevant to EAP: SLA studies explore the effect of feedback on such genres as picture description (Bitchener 2008; Bitchener & Knoch 2010) or picture narration (Ellis et al. 2008), a fable written from memory after it was read out to students (Sheen 2007) or an informal letter (Bitchener, Young & Cameron 2005). Similarly, L2 writing studies focus on genres that, in this book, are not considered academic (see Chapter 1) – autobiographical writing (Chandler 2003), personal essays (Ashwell 2000) or IELTS-like descriptions of a graph (Storch & Wigglesworth 2010). One exception appears to be a study by Ferris and Roberts (2001), since it relies on a reading-into-writing approach, yet the example given in their Appendix 2 suggests overly personal writing. It is questionable, then, to what extent the conclusions drawn from these studies apply to long and complex academic texts that university students are required to write on their degree programmes. It follows that further research is needed on feedback on academic genres.

Another characteristic of TESOL research on feedback that limits its usefulness to EAP is its **preoccupation with language accuracy**. An extreme form of this preoccupation is the Dynamic Written Corrective Feedback, an approach that involves regular short personal writing tasks and feedback with a strong emphasis on language accuracy and on error detection in particular (e.g. Evans et al. 2010; Kurzer 2018). In a nutshell, the writing process as conceptualized in this approach 'begins with a 10-minute paragraph and ends with an error-free writing sample' (Evans et al. 2010: 454). Overfocusing on accuracy in pedagogy might send EAP students the wrong message that good academic writing equals error-free writing, which is problematic for two reasons. First, expectation of error-free writing is not only unrealistic for many L2 English writers but also unsubstantiated when the purpose of writing is to communicate content rather than to demonstrate language mastery. Second, such an approach disregards other aspects of academic writing, from language complexity to following genre conventions.

The consequence of overfocusing on accuracy in research is that feedback on other areas of relevance to EAP, such as criticality, textual organization and use of sources, has received very little attention. That these areas require more research attention is suggested, for instance, by Green's (2019) case study, in which the student participant showed a good understanding of feedback on language and conventions, some understanding of feedback on structure and use of sources, but only a limited understanding of feedback on content (e.g. equating criticality with criticism). I therefore call on EAP practitioners to conduct more research into these areas of academic writing.

With the above caveats in mind, I will now turn to the findings of TESOL research on feedback. A central concern of TESOL research on feedback has been the question of whether **feedback on grammatical errors** is conducive to reducing these errors in subsequent writing. Truscott (1996, 2007) reviewed a number of relevant studies and concluded that, regardless of type of feedback and students' language proficiency, correction of grammatical errors in feedback on writing is ineffective and even detrimental, because overfocusing on linguistic accuracy might reduce linguistic complexity, and because error correction might be distracting and demotivating for students. Truscott's conclusion, however, is based on several problematic assumptions. One problem is that Truscott seems to take into account findings which are not statistically significant (such as Sheppard 1992, cited in Truscott 2007), and thus to draw conclusions of difference between samples that are most likely due to chance (see Section 1.3). The second problem with Truscott's conclusion is that he dismisses findings of positive effect of error correction due to observed improvement in accuracy being non-linear, i.e. improvement followed by a temporary decline before further improvement (Bitchener, Young & Cameron, cited in Truscott 2007). Such non-linearity, however, is characteristic of language development, as shown by a number of studies in the CDST (e.g. Rosmawati, 2024; see also Chapter 2.4). Similarly, Truscott rejects studies showing a positive effect of feedback on grammar errors on the basis of interpreting improvement in student writing as a result of student motivation or out-of-class exposure rather than as a result of error correction: 'this study indicated that the students were very serious about dealing with the corrections they received (much more so than was found in previous studies) and were quite successful in incorporating them in their subsequent revisions. Thus, these very modest results were obtained under unusually favourable circumstances' (Truscott 2007: 267). Truscott's speculation is a complete dismissal of viewing a learner holistically and of the importance of psychological research for language teaching (e.g.

Williams & Burden 1997). On the contrary, HE research on feedback shows the significance of affective factors for uptake of feedback (see Section 7.2).

Unsurprisingly, Truscott's (1996, 2007) controversial papers sparked a heated debate on the effectiveness of feedback (e.g. Ferris 1999 followed by Truscott 1999; Chandler 2003 followed by Truscott 2004 and Chandler 2004; Bruton 2009a, 2009b followed by Truscott 2010 and Bruton 2010) and stimulated extensive research investigating the effect of grammar correction feedback. Subsequently, a number of studies have proved the effectiveness of correction feedback for improving grammatical accuracy (e.g. Bitchener 2008; Bitchener & Knoch 2010; Chandler 2003; Ellis et al. 2008; Ferris & Roberts 2001; Sheen 2007), contra Truscott (1996, 2007). However, these studies typically focus on a limited number of language structures and a restricted range of their uses: Most studies (Bitchener 2008; Bitchener & Knoch 2010; Ellis et al. 2008; Sheen 2007) investigate the effect of grammar correction feedback on very basic uses of English articles (i.e. *a* for first mention and *the* for subsequent mention). It remains an open question, therefore, to what extent this effect translates into authentic learner writing that contains grammatical errors of various types. In fact, research investigating several different language structures has found that the effect of grammar correction feedback partly depends on the language structure in question: language structures governed by grammatical rules, such as the use of the definite article and past tense, are more easily addressed by feedback than idiosyncratic language structures, such as prepositions and sentence structure (Bitchener, Young & Cameron 2005; Ferris & Roberts 2001).

Error correction studies have also ruled out Truscott's (2007) speculation that an observed improvement in accuracy is due to error avoidance rather than acquisition of language structures (e.g. Ellis et al. 2008) and demonstrated that grammar correction feedback is effective not only for revisions of the same text (e.g. Ferris & Roberts 2001) but also for new texts produced in response to the same task (Bitchener 2008; Bitchener & Knoch 2010; Bitchener, Young & Cameron 2005; Ellis et al. 2008). It remains unknown, however, if the positive effect of feedback is transferred to tasks of different types and new genres. Moreover, improvement in accuracy does not necessarily mean improvement in the overall quality of text, as Chandler (2003: 210) shows: in her words, 'writing quality is slow to show measurable effects'.

TESOL research has also paid considerable attention to the question as to what types of feedback are more effective, especially in terms of direct and indirect feedback and accompanying explanation of grammatical rules. Ferris (2010: 189) defines direct feedback as 'explicit corrections provided by the teacher or another reader' and indirect feedback as 'an error called to the student's attention (whether through more or less explicit means) but left for the student to correct'. The results of available research are inconclusive: some studies suggest that direct and indirect corrective feedback are equally effective (Bitchener & Knoch 2010; Ferris & Roberts 2001), while others suggest that direct correction of errors increases language accuracy more effectively than indirect feedback (Chandler 2003; Shute 2008). Students, while finding direct corrective feedback easier to implement, feel they learn more from indirect feedback that indicates the type of error (Chandler 2003; Ferris & Roberts 2001). This might be because indirect corrective feedback elicits more engagement than direct correction (Storch & Wigglesworth 2010), and engagement in turn increases efficacy of feedback (Wingate 2010). The effectiveness of corrective feedback is further increased by oral feedback given, in addition to written feedback, in individual consultations or as collective class feedback (Bitchener 2008; Bitchener, Young & Cameron 2005).

The effect of additional written metalinguistic explanation of errors accompanying correction is also unclear: Bitchener and Knoch (2010) conclude that metalinguistic explanation does not increase the effectiveness of corrective feedback, contra Sheen (2007). The effect of metalinguistic explanation may depend on students' previous linguistic knowledge: if students lack knowledge of a particular language structure, instruction will be more effective than feedback. Language errors in writing do not necessarily mean a lack of knowledge, however: a study by Ferris and Roberts (2001) suggests that students' linguistic knowledge plays a greater role in the revision stage than in the production stage. This suggests that students should be trained to revise before submission.

To sum up this section, we can see that TESOL research on feedback is characterized by inconsistencies and gaps, which has implications for both teaching practice and research. In particular, more attention needs to be paid to giving feedback on content, structure, use of sources and genre conventions.

7.4 Recommendations

Based on the discussion in the previous sections, this section provides recommendations for practice, both at the level of teacher feedback and at the level of curriculum design. For teacher feedback, I propose the following recommendations:

1. Feedback should be tailored to the respective **institutional context**. What I mean here by institutional context is not only at the level of the HE (or another) institution but also at the level of individual departments, as feedback practices may vary from one department to another, which needs to be taken into account when working with subject lecturers. Considering one's institutional context includes taking into account teachers' time allocation for providing feedback and institutional values regarding academic writing (Goldstein 2004). In other words, teachers need to ask themselves

what is perceived as good academic writing in their given context and comment on various areas accordingly (e.g. how much importance is given to language accuracy or the use of sources), and to take into account how much time they have for giving feedback.

2. Feedback should be related to **assessment criteria and instruction**. Research shows that students find it frustrating when feedback is not explicitly related to assessment criteria (Weaver 2006), but less attention has been paid to the relation of feedback to previous instruction. For instance, a student participant quoted in Price, Handley and Millar's (2011: 891) study found feedback on criticality unhelpful because, while it pointed out a lack of analysis in student writing, it did not explain what analysis is or how to improve analytical skills. I would argue, however, that analytical skills should be defined, exemplified and practised as part of instruction, prior to students' submission of an assignment in which they need to demonstrate these skills.

   Admittedly, this conceptualization of feedback as related to instruction raises questions around feedback on language in EAP: while even advanced L2 English writers might make basic errors in their writing (e.g. subject–verb agreement errors), EAP classes cannot devote much time to instruction on such areas, as other areas need to be prioritized. However, it can be assumed that EAP students will have received instruction on basic grammar previously, as they typically have been learners of English – although not learners of academic English and literacy – for several years. Therefore, if individual students have gaps in their knowledge of basic grammar, they can be given relevant explanation in consultations, referred to further resources and encouraged to focus on the area in their independent learning. Should a particular language area appear to be problematic for the majority of a class, it might be useful to provide collective in-class feedback with further explanation and exemplification (Bitchener 2008).

3. Feedback on writing should be **individualized**. This means considering the ability and affect of individual learners as well as the specifics of a given task – as Shute (2008: 182) puts it, 'there is no "best" type of formative feedback for all learners and learning outcomes'. Individualization of feedback might involve the overall amount and focus of feedback, the ratio of direct and indirect feedback and the ratio of positive and negative feedback. Individualized feedback relates a specific text to assessment criteria, showing how and why the text meets the criteria or not. Individualized feedback can also acknowledge whether a particular problem is persistent for a particular student writer or whether the

student has made progress in this area compared to his/her previous work. Of course, individualized feedback can be further reinforced by collective feedback addressing common problems.

4. Feedback should be **selective**. Ferris (1999) argues that selection and prioritization improve accuracy and efficiency of feedback. Exhaustive feedback can be unnecessarily time consuming for teachers and counterproductively overwhelming for students. Selecting the most important areas for improvement therefore helps teachers to align with the institutional context and to provide more individualized feedback. However, little is said in literature about how to identify areas for prioritization. Assuming that feedback is related to assessment criteria at all times, as discussed above, I suggest the following factors for teachers to consider:

   a. Impact on students' academic **success**. As a consequence, for instance, plagiarism and lack of criticality take precedence over inaccurate language.

   b. **Intelligibility**. Language errors which interfere with intelligibility need to be prioritized. In practice, this might mean not paying attention to errors which do not interfere with intelligibility in feedback on a text that suffers from numerous intelligibility problems.

   c. **Learnability**. Some problems can be addressed rather quickly once brought to students' attention, while others take time for students to overcome. For example, mechanical aspects of writing, such as punctuation and formatting of references, are easier to master than grammatical accuracy. Similarly, some language areas are easier to master than others: for instance, rule-governed errors respond to feedback better than idiosyncratic errors (Bitchener, Young & Cameron 2005). I am not, however, suggesting that feedback should only focus on areas that are easy to rectify. Instead, learnability should be considered by teachers in terms of to what extent a particular area receives attention, especially when giving feedback regularly. For instance, in the case of serious mechanical problems, these can be paid careful attention in initial feedback on student writing and be simply mentioned in subsequent feedback, referring to previous feedback. In contrast, complex grammatical errors will likely require continuous attention in feedback on a number of assignments, and teachers cannot expect immediate improvement.

   d. **Exemplification**. This factor involves considering how many instances of a particular area need to be singled out in feedback. Generally, I suggest feedback should exemplify errors rather than proofread the text, i.e. it should draw the student's attention to several instances rather than to point out every single instance. This, however, will depend on the overall frequency and type of error, as well as the student writer's self-revision ability. Feedback should therefore be tailored to individual student's needs, for example, by providing direct correction of error, or just by identifying the type of error without correction, or by simply asking the student to check for this error in the text, or any combination of these approaches.

Admittedly, these factors can sometimes be in conflict. Typically, areas that are easy to learn will not have a great impact on students' success, and vice versa. It is therefore necessary to find balance to enable students to work on challenging areas of writing as well as to experience success. For instance, although mechanical problems do not have a great impact on students' success or text's intelligibility, early intervention can enable students experience rapid progress and thus be motivating. Therefore, teachers need to consider each student's strengths, needs and confidence individually and prioritize feedback accordingly. Ideally, formative feedback will be given repeatedly over a period of time rather than on a single occasion before summative assessment, and therefore teachers might decide to postpone feedback on certain areas to future assignments.

5. Feedback should be **explicit**. Students might misinterpret indirectly worded feedback (Hyland & Hyland 2001) and find feedback lacking in detail unhelpful (Weaver 2006). An additional way of clarifying feedback is oral dialogue between student and teacher about written feedback, which has been shown to promote improvement in academic writing (Schillings et al. 2023). It has to be borne in mind that it is not only negative feedback and suggestions for improvement that need to be explicit – positive feedback needs to be explicit and specific as well, not only because students find praise worded in formulaic ways insincere (Hyland & Hyland 2001) but also because positive feedback reinforces learning by identifying examples of good writing. This is particularly important in two cases. One is when a student is trying a new strategy or structure in a piece of writing and needs to know whether the attempt was successful or not – in other words, when s/he is testing a hypothesis about language and/or writing. Another case is when a novice writer feels a section of text which is actually well written is not good enough and needs to be re-written, and s/he removes good features of the text in an attempt to revise it. Clearly, in this case the student writer does not have a firmly developed understanding of (a particular area of) good writing. This understanding can be

developed by explicit acknowledgement of what makes his/her text effective.

6. Feedback should **feed forward**. For students to find feedback useful, it needs to evaluate current performance on a task at hand and inform future assignments (Walker 2009; Weaver 2006). Carless et al. (2011: 397) call such 'dialogic processes and activities which can support and inform the student on the current task, whilst also developing the ability to self-regulate performance on future tasks' *sustainable* feedback. In other words, feedback needs to provide suggestions on how to close the gap between the current performance and the target performance (Shute 2008). While it may be argued that feedback comments accompanying summative assessment are redundant, I would argue that even summative assessment should serve a feed-forward function, and thus foster a lifelong learning approach in students.

I now turn to recommendations for curriculum design. Research has shown that the effect of feedback largely depends on student engagement with the feedback (Storch & Wigglesworth 2010; Wingate 2010), yet, as Goldstein (2004: 69) points out, we cannot assume students know how to use feedback effectively. This points to a need to develop students' **feedback literacy**, or 'the ability to read, interpret and use written feedback', as defined by Sutton (2012: 31). Carless and Boud (2018) propose that feedback literacy should be embedded in curriculum and developed systematically. I now propose what areas the development of feedback literacy should address.

1. **Teacher feedback.** Students on each programme should be inducted as to what the purpose of teacher feedback is, how it is given and what students are expected to do with it (Price, Handley & Millar 2011). Induction on feedback can include navigating technology used in feedback practice, guidance on the use of codes used in feedback (if any), discussion of how to interpret indirectly worded feedback and expectations of following up on teacher feedback.

2. **Negotiating expectations.** Induction needs to be coupled with dialogue between the teacher and students, in which students are asked about their expectations of feedback and preferences for particular approaches to feedback (Goldstein 2004), e.g. direct and indirect corrective feedback or balance of positive and negative feedback. It can be expected that some student preferences might run counter to pedagogical principles – such a situation should be used to discuss the rationale for giving feedback in a certain way (e.g. for giving selective rather than exhaustive feedback). In other situations, students should be given a voice and opportunity to negotiate feedback practices.

3. **Handling affect.** As affect has been shown to have impact on the effect of feedback (Hattie & Timperley 2007; Young 2000), feedback literacy development should also include developing strategies for handling negative emotions upon receiving feedback (Carless & Boud 2018; Sutton 2012). This can involve creating a positive learning atmosphere in which students feel free to take risks and reminding students that feedback is a constructive critique of a piece of work rather than a criticism of themselves. Carless and Boud (2018) suggest that teachers should openly discuss with students how they handle negative emotions experienced during peer review process when writing for publication and how they act on feedback. By implication, EAP practitioners should engage in scholarship and subject themselves to peer review in order to develop deep empathy with students and to serve as role models in handling negative affect related to feedback.

4. **Taking action.** Students should be trained to **interpret and implement feedback** (Sutton 2012). This is particularly important for EAP students reading feedback in their L2. Supporting students to understand feedback and to take appropriate action might include induction mentioned above, individual support in consultations, peer discussions of feedback and teacher-supported collaborative re-writing of a text using feedback.

5. **Appropriation and resistance.** Bearing in mind that feedback might result in text appropriation (Tardy 2019; see Section 7.2), the induction and teacher–student dialogue on feedback should also include the questions of appropriation and agency. Students should be given an option to resist feedback, but such resistance should be an informed decision well supported with arguments. For instance, resisting teacher feedback on language accuracy or clarity would be a missed opportunity for improvement. In contrast, students should feel free to make stylistic choices (see Chapter 4.6) and should be recognized as content experts in ESAP. Nevertheless, they should acknowledge unfavourable responses from their reader (as represented by teacher feedback), as a counterargument if applicable, and mitigate these by, for instance, rebutting or providing additional explanation in the text. Assuming agency and implementing or resisting feedback as appropriate is a skill particularly important for academics writing for publication. Developing this skill in student writers might be empowering, and EAP practitioners will be best placed to help students develop this skill if they develop it themselves through writing for publication.

6. **Analytical and evaluative skills.** When students analyse and evaluate texts written by others as well as by themselves, they become less

reliant on teacher feedback and their writing improves. Relevant analytical and evaluative skills can be developed in the following ways:

a. Using **exemplars**. Exemplars, or samples of previous student work matched for the genre that students are expected to produce, illustrate how writing can be made effective in various ways (Carless & Boud 2018). Exemplars do not need to be samples of good writing only; students can be presented with successful and less successful samples of student writing and apply the course's marking criteria to evaluate them and to compare their judgement to teacher's evaluation of the same samples (Kostopoulou 2021).

b. **Peer review.** Peer review develops learner autonomy and empowers students, yet arguably its greatest value rests in the development of evaluative skills that then can be applied to one's own writing (Nicol, Thomson & Breslin 2014). To help students provide quality feedback, training is needed on what makes effective peer feedback and what areas to focus on (for instance, L2 English writers are typically more confident providing reader response than language feedback). To provide a richer feedback-giving and feedback-receiving experience, it might be beneficial for students to provide feedback on the writing of several peers. Peer feedback should be followed by writers deciding what feedback to implement and how, and revising their text accordingly. This can be supported by a teacher in class.

c. **Self-evaluation and self-revision.** While revising and editing play a vital role in the writing process, not all students have yet developed the habit of evaluating and improving their own work before submission: Wingate and Harper (2021) show that less successful writers spend considerably less time on revision than more successful writers. It follows, then, that EAP students should be trained to evaluate their own work against a set of criteria or a checklist and to improve their text accordingly before receiving feedback from peers or a teacher.

It needs to be recognized, however, that as analysing and evaluating are cognitive skills subordinate to creating (Anderson et al. 2001; see Chapter 2.2), analytical and evaluative skills might enable students (and teachers!) to recognize instances of effective and less effective writing but they might not be sufficient for writers to know how to create a better text. For instance, Nygaard (2021) describes how she struggled to write her own dissertation even after years of coaching academic writers. For this reason, analysis and evaluation need to be accompanied with teaching students how to improve texts using feedback, as suggested above.

This section has proposed a number of recommendations for good feedback-giving practice and for developing students' feedback literacy. It has to be recognized, however, that these are 'ideal world' recommendations, and their implementation is likely to be met with some difficulties in certain institutional contexts, as discussed previously. Nevertheless, where circumstances are favourable to good feedback practice, research and scholarship conducted to prove its positive effect on student learning could be used to advocate for a positive change in other contexts.

7.5 Summary

This chapter has discussed extensive existing research on feedback in HE and language learning in order to draw implications for good practice. I have advocated a differentiated approach to feedback, one that recognizes individual students' needs as well as institutional values and constraints, yet one that understands academic writing as more than a mere demonstration of language mastery. I have argued for empowering students by giving them a voice in feedback practices, by developing their feedback literacy and by encouraging students to maintain ownership of their texts. I have called for more EAP-specific research into feedback on texts' content, structure, use of sources and genre conventions. I have suggested that EAP practitioners should themselves engage in writing for publication to gain a deeper understanding of the experience of receiving feedback.

Many areas have not been addressed in this chapter due to its limited scope. These include detailed discussion of peer feedback and self-revision and the use of technology to enhance feedback, such as the use of similarity checkers, audio feedback or corpus concordance lines. The reason for these omissions is that the chapter aims to provide general pedagogical principles for feedback on writing rather than to provide the reader with specific tools for feedback-giving. It is hoped that despite its limitations the chapter has been an inspiration for improving feedback on writing on EAP courses.

NOTES

Chapter 1

1 For this reason, the recency of a corpus was not considered relevant.
2 The examples from the corpora and published writing are presented in their original form without changes to punctuation. Only italics and/or bold have been added to some examples to highlight particular structures. The TECCL (2015) corpus was accessed with AntConc (Anthony 2014), the BAWE (2004–7) corpus with Intellitext, the MICUSP (2009) with MICUSP Simple Beta interface and the BNC (2007) with the BNC-web CQP-interface.

Chapter 3

1 See Bruce (2008a) for an in-depth discussion and application of schema theory.

Chapter 4

1 I would argue that including *side* as a necessary component of argument is reductive, as it fosters dichotomous *for or against* type of argument and excludes more complex arguments.
2 Moore and Morton's (2005) rhetorical functions are comparison, description, explanation, evaluation, prediction, summarization, hortation, instruction and recommendation. Bruce's (2008a) cognitive genres are report, explanation, discussion and recount. Fahnestock and Secor's (1988) stases are facts, definition, cause/effect, value/evaluation and policy/procedure.
3 Short in-text examples (in italics) are constructed. The numbered examples are occasionally constructed (in which case this is indicated) but typically they are taken from an authentic text (indicated with a citation) or from a corpus. The examples from corpora are labelled with an abbreviation of the name of the corpus and text (and possibly sentence) identifier.
4 The use of asterisk indicates ungrammaticality.
5 For this syntactic flexibility of collocations I distinguish between collocations and lexical bundles, contra Hyland (2008) – while the latter collocate, i.e. frequently occur together, they are not treated as collocations here as they are not syntactically flexible.

6 Contra Timmis (2015: 26), I do not distinguish between bundles and chunks by the criterion of semantic completeness or pragmatic function but treat them together instead, for pedagogical reasons.

Chapter 5

1 The paper is, after all, only three pages long.
2 Meade and Ellis (1971: 76) characterize additional comment paragraph literally as 'statements were related to a paragraph's central idea in such a general way that they could not be characterized by any of the other methods'.
3 I am using the FSP framework, which does not assume that *theme*, or given information, has to occupy sentence-initial position, in contrast to the understanding of theme in SFL (see Chapter 2.3). Accordingly, contra Lovejoy and Lance (1991), I do not consider sentence-initial adverbials (e.g. However) and prepositional phrases (e.g. *In this respect*), or anticipatory *it* (*It has been suggested that*) as deviations from the expected known-to-new pattern.

Chapter 6

1 It has to be borne in mind, however, that the choice of formatting will often follow a prescribed stylesheet, and thus it does not necessarily represent the writer's voice.
2 At this point I would like to clarify my own choice of third person singular pronouns for generic reference. As I strongly believe in gender equality, I do not wish to 'silence' gender in my text by using gender-neutral *they* as exemplified in Example (4). Therefore, I opt to use gender-balanced combinations of pronouns, without promoting one gender at the expense of the other (as in Examples 1 and 2), even if my choice is considered stylistically 'cumbersome' (Zapletalová 2009: 180). By using *s/he* (feminine–masculine) alongside *his/her* (masculine–feminine), I attempt to challenge the usual order that puts the masculine pronoun first (as in Example 3) and to further balance gender in my text. My choice of third person singular pronouns for generic reference, as an example of the writer's voice, thus reflects my personal beliefs about gender equality and style and their relative importance in a text to me.
3 Jiang and Hyland (2015) consider only complement noun constructions but I would argue that the evaluative value rests in the semantics of the nouns rather than in the complementation, and I therefore consider them as stance nouns even without complementation.
4 While pedagogical materials typically mention avoiding *personal pronouns* in academic writing, this term is imprecise for two reasons. First, the term *personal pronouns* does not, technically speaking, include possessive pronouns such as *my* and *our*, which might equally be used for self-mention. Second, the term *personal pronouns* includes not only first- and second-person pronouns, whose position in academic text might be contested, but also third person

pronouns, such as *he* and *they*. This might seem like a minor point but in my teaching practice I have been repeatedly asked by students if the rule of avoiding personal pronouns applies to third person pronouns as well. For these reasons, I use the term *self-mention pronouns* rather than *personal pronouns*. This section is only concerned with reader-exclusive pronouns; reader-inclusive pronouns are discussed in Section 6.7.
5 Obviously, the possibility of self-citations is largely limited to previously published authors.
6 I would suggest that Hyland's (1999a) explanation is an oversimplification, since integral citations can foreground or background cited authors depending on whether the citation is used in the main clause or a subordinate clause – compare, for instance, examples (67) and (70). See also Teaching activity 6.13.
7 This section does not discuss paraphrasing/summarizing skills but see Chapter 4.4.

REFERENCES

Abasi, A. R., N. Akbari and B. Graves (2006), 'Discourse Appropriation, Construction of Identities, and the Complex Issue of Plagiarism: ESL Students Writing in Graduate School', *Journal of Second Language Writing*, 15 (2): 102–17.
Abdollahzadeh, E. (2011), 'Poring over the Findings: Interpersonal Authorial Engagement in Applied Linguistics Papers', *Journal of Pragmatics*, 43 (1): 288–97.
Ädel, A. (2023), 'Adopting a "Move" Rather Than a "Marker" Approach to Metadiscourse: A Taxonomy for Spoken Student Presentations', *English for Specific Purposes*, 69 (January): 4–18.
Ädel, A. and G. Garretson (2006), 'Citation Practices across the Disciplines: The Case of Proficient Student Writing', in C. Pérez-Llantada, R. Plo-Alastrué and C. P. Neumann (eds), *Academic and Professional Communication in the 21st Century: Genres, Rhetoric and the Construction of Disciplinary Knowledge. Proceedings of the 5th International AELFE Conference*, 271–80, Zaragoza: University of Zaragoza.
Akbas, E. (2012), 'Exploring Metadiscourse in Master's Dissertation Abstracts: Cultural and Linguistic Variations across Postgraduate Writers', *International Journal of Applied Linguistics & English Literature*, 1 (1): 12–26.
Aktas, R. N. and V. Cortes (2008), 'Shell Nouns as Cohesive Devices in Published and ESL Student Writing', *Journal of English for Academic Purposes*, 7 (1): 3–14.
Allison, D. (1994), 'Comments on Sarah Benesch's 'ESL, Ideology, and the Politics of Pragmatism', A Reader Reacts', *TESOL Quarterly*, 28 (3): 618–23.
Anderson, L. W., D. R. Krathwohl, P. W. Airasian, K. A. Cruikshank, R. E. Mayer, P. R. Pintrich, J. Rathsand and M. C. Wittrock (2001), *A Taxonomy for Learning, Teaching, and Assessing: A Revision of Bloom's Taxonomy of Educational Objectives*, abridged edn, London: Longman.
Andrews, R. (2005), 'Models of Argumentation in Educational Discourse', *Text – Interdisciplinary Journal for the Study of Discourse*, 25 (1): 107–27.
Anthony, L. (1999), 'Writing Research Article Introductions in Software Engineering: How Accurate Is a Standard Model?', *IEEE Transactions on Professional Communication*, 42 (1): 38–46.
Anthony, L. (2014), *AntConc*, Version 3.4.4 [Computer Software], Tokyo: Waseda University. Available online: http://www.laurenceanthony.net/software/antconc/ (accessed 9 February 2020).
APA (American Psychological Association) (2019), *APA Publication Manual*, 7th edn, Washington, DC: American Psychological Association.

Appleby, R. (2009), 'The Spatial Politics of Gender in EAP Classroom Practice', *Journal of English for Academic Purposes*, 8 (2): 100–10.

Ashwell, T. (2000), 'Patterns of Teacher Response to Student Writing in a Multiple-draft Composition Classroom: Is Content Feedback Followed by Form Feedback the Best Method?', *Journal of Second Language Writing*, 9 (3): 227–57.

Atasever Belli, S. (2019), 'Frame Markers in Master Thesis Abstracts Written in English and Turkish', *Çukurova Üniversitesi Eğitim Fakültesi Dergisi*, 48 (2): 994–1011.

Aull, L. (2015), 'Linguistic Attention in Rhetorical Genre Studies and First Year Writing', *Composition Forum*, 31: no pagination.

Aull, L. L., D. Bandarage and M. R. Miller (2017), 'Generality in Student and Expert Epistemic Stance: A Corpus Analysis of First-year, Upper-level, and Published Academic Writing', *Journal of English for Academic Purposes*, 26: 29–41.

Aull, L. L. and Z. Lancaster (2014), 'Linguistic Markers of Stance in Early and Advanced Academic Writing: A Corpus-based Comparison', *Written Communication*, 31 (2): 151–83.

Badger, R. and G. White (2000), 'A Process Genre Approach to Teaching Writing', *ELT Journal*, 54 (2): 153–60.

Bailey, R. and M. Garner (2010), 'Is the Feedback in Higher Education Assessment Worth the Paper It Is Written On? Teachers' Reflections on Their Practices', *Teaching in Higher Education*, 15 (2): 187–98.

Bailey, S. (2011), *Academic Writing: A Handbook for International Students*, 3rd edn, London: Routledge.

Basturkmen, H. and J. Von Randow (2014), 'Guiding the Reader (or Not) to Re-create Coherence: Observations on Postgraduate Student Writing in an Academic Argumentative Writing Task', *Journal of English for Academic Purposes*, 16: 14–22.

Bawarshi, A. S. and M. J. Reiff (2010), *Genre: An Introduction to History, Theory, Research, and Pedagogy*, West Lafayette: Parlor Press.

BAWE [The British Academic Writing English Corpus] (2004–2007), compiled by H. Nesi, S. Gardner, P. Thompson and P. Wickens, *The Universities of Warwick, Reading and Oxford Brookes*. Accessed via *Intellitext*, Version 2.6, University of Leeds. Available online: http://corpus.leeds.ac.uk/itweb (accessed 26 April 2023).

Becher, T. and P. R. Trowler (2001), *Academic Tribes and Territories*, 2nd edn, Buckingham: SRHE and Open University Press.

Belcher, D. (1995), 'Writing Critically across the Curriculum', in D. D. Belcher and G. Braine (eds), *Academic Writing in a Second Language: Essays on Research and Pedagogy*, 135–54, Norwood: Ablex.

Belcher, D. and H. S. Yang (2020), 'Global Perspectives on Linguacultural Variation in Academic Publishing', *Journal of English for Research Publication Purposes*, 1(1): 28–50.

Bell, D. M. (2007), 'Sentence-initial *And* and *But* in Academic Writing', *Pragmatics*, 17 (2): 183–201.

Benesch, S. (1993), 'ESL, Ideology, and the Politics of Pragmatism', *TESOL Quarterly*, 27 (4): 705–17.

Bennett, K. (2009), 'English Academic Style Manuals: A Survey', *Journal of English for Academic Purposes*, 8 (1): 43–54.

Bereiter, C. and M. Scardamalia (1987), *The Psychology of Written Composition*. London: Routledge.

Biber, D., B. Gray and K. Poonpon (2022), 'Should We Use Characteristics of Conversation to Measure Grammatical Complexity in L2 Writing Development?', in D. Biber, B. Gray, S, Staples and J. Egbert (eds), *The Register-Functional Approach to Grammatical Complexity: Theoretical Foundation, Descriptive Research Findings*, Application, 291–312, London: Routledge.

Biber, D., S. Johansson, G. Leech, S. Conrad and E. Finegan (1999), *Longman Grammar of Spoken and Written English*, London: Longman.

Bitchener, J. (2008), 'Evidence in Support of Written Corrective Feedback', *Journal of Second Language Writing*, 17 (2): 102–18.

Bitchener, J. and U. Knoch (2010), 'The Contribution of Written Corrective Feedback to Language Development: A Ten Month Investigation', *Applied Linguistics*, 31 (2): 193–214.

Bitchener, J., S. Young and D. Cameron (2005), 'The Effect of Different Types of Corrective Feedback on ESL Student Writing', *Journal of Second Language Writing*, 14 (3): 191–205.

Blagojević, S. and B. Mišić Ilić (2012), 'Interrogatives in English and Serbian Academic Discourse: A Contrastive Pragmatic Approach', *Brno Studies in English*, 38 (2): 17–35.

Bloor, M. (1998). 'Variations in the Methods Sections of Research Articles across Disciplines: The Case of Fast and Slow Text', *Issues in EAP Writing, Research and Instruction*, 84–106, Reading: CALS.

BNC [The British National Corpus] (2007), Version 3 (BNC XML Edition). Distributed by Bodleian Libraries, University of Oxford, on behalf of the BNC Consortium. URL: http://www.natcorp.ox.ac.uk/ Available as the CQP-edition of BNCweb (2018), Version 4.4. developed by S. Hoffmann and S. Evert. Available online: http://bncweb.lancs.ac.uk/ (accessed 26 April 2023).

Bodin-Galvez, J. and A. Ding (2019), 'Interdisciplinary EAP: Moving Beyond Aporetic English for General Academic Purposes', *The Language Scholar*, 4: 78–88.

Borg, E. (2000), 'Citation Practices in Academic Writing', in P. Thompson (ed.), *Patterns and Perspectives: Insights into EAP Writing Practice*, 26–42, Reading: Centre for Applied Language Studies.

Bowman, M. (2021), 'Good Academic Reflective Writing in Dentistry', in M. Whong and J. Godfrey (eds), *What is Good Academic Writing?: Insights Into Discipline-Specific Student Writing*, 111–33, London: Bloomsbury.

Braddock, R. (1974), 'The Frequency and Placement of Topic Sentences in Expository Prose', *Research in the Teaching of English*, 8 (3): 287–302.

Brett, P. (1994), 'A Genre Analysis of the Results Section of Sociology Articles', *English for Specific Purposes*, 13 (1): 47–59.

British Council (2023), 'What is IELTS?'. Available online: https://takeielts.britishcouncil.org/take-ielts/what-ielts (accessed 14 September 2023).

Brooke, M. (2014), 'Attribution and Authorial (Dis)Endorsement in High- and Low-rated Undergraduate ESL Students' English Academic Persuasive Essays', *English Linguistics Research*, 3 (1): 1–11.

Brown, P. and S. C. Levinson (1987), *Politeness: Some Universals in Language Usage*, Cambridge: Cambridge University Press.

Bruce, I. (2008a), *Academic Writing and Genre: A Systematic Analysis*, London: Bloomsbury.
Bruce, I. (2008b), 'Cognitive Genre Structures in Methods Sections of Research Articles: A Corpus Study', *Journal of English for Academic Purposes*, 7 (1): 38–54.
Bruce, I. (2010), 'Textual and Discoursal Resources Used in the Essay Genre in Sociology and English', *Journal of English for Academic Purposes*, 9 (3): 153–66.
Bruce, I. (2020), *Expressing Critical Thinking through Disciplinary Texts: Insights from Five Genre Studies*, London: Bloomsbury.
Bruce, I. (2021), 'Towards an EAP without Borders: Developing Knowledge, Practitioners, and Communities', *International Journal of English for Academic Purposes: Research and Practice*, Spring: 23–37.
Bruton, A. (2009a), 'Designing Research into the Effects of Grammar Correction in L2 Writing: Not So Straightforward', *Journal of Second Language Writing*, 18 (2), 136–40.
Bruton, A. (2009b), 'Improving Accuracy Is Not the Only Reason for Writing, and Even if It Were . . .', *System*, 37 (4): 600–13.
Bruton, A. (2010), 'Another Reply to Truscott on Error Correction: Improved Situated Designs over Statistics', *System*, 38 (3): 491–8.
Bubaš, G. and A. Čižmešija (2023), 'A Critical Analysis of Students' Cheating in Online Assessment in Higher Education: PostCOVID-19 Issues and Challenges Related to Conversational Artificial Intelligence', in D. Cisic, N. Vrcek, M. Koricic et al. (eds), *Proceedings of 2023 46th ICT and Electronics Convention (MIPRO)*, 22–26 May, Opatija: MIPRO.
Bunton, D. (2002), 'Generic Moves in PhD Thesis Introductions', in J. Flowerdew (ed.), *Academic Discourse*, 57–75, Harlow: Longman.
Bunton, D. (2005), 'The Structure of PhD Conclusion Chapters', *Journal of English for Academic Purposes*, 4 (3): 207–24.
Burbules, N. C. and Berk, R. (1999), 'Critical Thinking and Critical Pedagogy: Relations, Differences, and Limits', in T. S. Popkewitz and L. Fendler (eds), *Critical Theories in Education: Changing Terrains of Knowledge and Politics*, 45–65, London: Routledge.
Burgess, S. and M. Cargill (2013), 'Using Genre Analysis and Corpus Linguistics to Teach Research Article Writing', in V. Matarese (ed.), *Supporting Research Writing: Roles and Challenges in Multilingual Settings*, 55–71, Oxford: Chandos.
Burneikaitė, N. (2009), 'Endophoric Marker in Linguistics Master's Theses in English L1 & L2', *Žmogus ir žodis*, 11 (3): 11–16.
Burrough-Boenisch, J. (2005), 'NS and NNS Scientists' Amendments of Dutch Scientific English and Their Impact on Hedging', *English for Specific Purposes*, 24 (1): 25–39.
Çakır, H. (2016), 'Native and Non-native Writers' Use of Stance Adverbs in English Research Article Abstracts', *Open Journal of Modern Linguistics*, 6 (2): 85–96.
Campion, G. C. (2016), '"The Learning Never Ends': Exploring Teachers' Views on the Transition from General English to EAP', *Journal of English for Academic Purposes*, 23: 59–70.
Canagarajah, A. S. (1993). 'Critical Ethnography of a Sri Lankan Classroom: Ambiguities in Student Opposition to Reproduction Through ESOL', *TESOL Quarterly*, 27 (4): 601–26.

Çandarlı, D., Y. Bayyurt and L. Martı (2015), 'Authorial Presence in L1 and L2 Novice Academic Writing: Cross-linguistic and Cross-cultural Perspectives', *Journal of English for Academic Purposes*, 20: 192–202.

Cao, F. and G. Hu (2014), 'Interactive Metadiscourse in Research Articles: A Comparative Study of Paradigmatic and Disciplinary Influences', *Journal of Pragmatics*, 66: 15–31.

Carless, D. (2006), 'Differing Perceptions in the Feedback Process', *Studies in Higher Education*, 31 (2): 219–33.

Carless, D. and D. Boud (2018), 'The Development of Student Feedback Literacy: Enabling Uptake of Feedback', *Assessment & Evaluation in Higher Education*, 43 (8): 1315–25.

Carless, D., D. Salter, M. Yang and J. Lam (2011), 'Developing Sustainable Feedback Practices', *Studies in Higher Education*, 36 (4): 395–407.

Carrell, P. L. (1982), Cohesion Is Not Coherence, *TESOL Quarterly*, 16 (4): 479–88.

Carrell, P. L. (1987), 'Content and Formal Schemata in ESL Reading', *TESOL Quarterly*, 21 (3): 461–81.

Carter-Thomas, S. and E. Rowley-Jolivet (2008), 'If-conditionals in Medical Discourse: From Theory to Disciplinary Practice', *Journal of English for Academic Purposes*, 7 (3): 191–205.

Chandler, J. (2003), 'The Efficacy of Various Kinds of Error Feedback for Improvement in the Accuracy and Fluency of L2 Student Writing', *Journal of Second Language Writing*, 12 (3): 267–96.

Chandler, J. (2004), 'A Response to Truscott', *Journal of Second Language Writing*, 4 (13): 345–8.

Chandrasoma, R., C. Thompson and A. Pennycook (2004), 'Beyond Plagiarism: Transgressive and Nontransgressive Intertextuality', *Journal of Language, Identity, and Education*, 3 (3): 171–93.

Chang, Y. Y. and J. Swales (1999), 'Informal Elements in English Academic Writing: Threats or Opportunities for Advanced Non-Native Speakers', in C. N. Candlin and K. Hyland (eds), *Writing: Texts, Processes and Practices*, 145–67. London: Routledge.

Chanock, K. (2008), 'When Students Reference Plagiarised Material: What Can We Learn (and What Can We Do) about Their Understanding of Attribution?', *International Journal for Educational Integrity*, 4 (1): 3–16.

Charles, M. (2003), '"This Mystery . . .": A Corpus-based Study of the Use of Nouns to Construct Stance in Theses from Two Contrasting Disciplines', *Journal of English for Academic Purposes*, 2 (4): 313–26.

Charles, M. (2006), 'Phraseological Patterns in Reporting Clauses Used in Citation: A Corpus-based Study of Theses in Two Disciplines', *English for Specific Purposes*, 25 (3): 310–31.

Charles, M. (2007), 'Argument or Evidence? Disciplinary Variation in the Use of the Noun *that* Pattern in Stance Construction', *English for Specific Purposes*, 26 (2): 203–18.

Chen, C. W. Y. (2006), 'The Use of Conjunctive Adverbials in the Academic Papers of Advanced Taiwanese EFL Learners', *International Journal of Corpus Linguistics*, 11 (1): 113–30.

Chen, Q. (2019), 'Theme-rheme Structure in Chinese Doctoral Students' Research Writing: From the First Draft to the Published Paper', *Journal of English for Academic Purposes*, 37: 154–67.

Cheng, A. (2021), 'The Place of Language in the Theoretical Tenets, Textbooks, and Classroom Practices in the ESP Genre-Based Approach to Teaching Writing', *English for Specific Purposes*, 64: 26–36.

Clugston, M. F. (2008), 'An Analysis of Citation Forms in Health Science Journals', *Journal of Academic Language and Learning*, 2 (1): A11–A22.

Čmejrková, S. (1996), 'Academic Writing in Czech and English', in E. Ventola and A. Mauranen (eds), *Academic Writing: Intercultural and Textual Issues*, 137–52, Amsterdam: John Publishing.

Coe, R. M. (2002), 'The New Rhetoric of Genre: Writing Political Briefs', in A. M. Johns (ed.), *Genre in the Classroom: Multiple Perspectives*, 197–207, Mahwah: Erlbaum.

Coffin, C. and A. Hewings (2003), 'Writing for Different Disciplines', in C. Coffin, M. J. Curry, S. Goodman, A. Hewings, T. Lillis and J. Swann (eds), *Teaching Academic Writing: A Toolkit for Higher Education*, 45–72, London: Routledge.

Connor, U. (1996), *Contrastive Rhetoric: Cross-cultural Aspects of Second Language Writing*, Cambridge: Cambridge University Press.

Connor, U. (2011), *Intercultural Rhetoric in the Writing Classroom*, Ann Arbor: University of Michigan Press.

Connor, U., E. Nagelhout and W. V. Rozycki, eds (2008), *Contrastive Rhetoric: Reaching to Intercultural Rhetoric*, Amsterdam: John Benjamins.

Cortes, V. (2013), 'The Purpose of This Study is to: Connecting Lexical Bundles and Moves in Research Article Introductions', *Journal of English for Academic Purposes*, 12 (1): 33–43.

Cotos, E., S. Huffman and S. Link (2017), 'A Move/Step Model for Methods Sections: Demonstrating Rigour and Credibility', *English for Specific Purposes*, 46: 90–106.

Cowley-Haselden, S. and J. Kukuczka (2019), *TiP Welcome email to BALEAP jiscmail list*, 1 August.

Cowley-Haselden, S. and L. Monbec (2019), 'Emancipating Ourselves from Mental Slavery: Affording Knowledge in Our Practice; in M. Gillway (ed.), *Proceedings of the 2017 BALEAP Conference. Addressing the State of the Union: Working Together = Learning Together*, April 2017, Bristol, 39–46, Reading: Garnet.

Crewe, W. J. (1990), 'The Illogic of Logical Connectives', *ELT Journal*, 44: 316–25.

Crismore, A., R. Markkanen and M. S. Steffensen (1993), 'Metadiscourse in Persuasive Writing: A Study of Texts Written by American and Finnish University Students', *Written Communication*, 10 (1): 39–71.

Crompton, P. (1997), 'Hedging in Academic Writing: Some Theoretical Problems', *English for Specific Purposes*, 16 (4): 271–87.

Crossley, S. A. and D. S. McNamara (2009), 'Computational Assessment of Lexical Differences in L1 and L2 Writing', *Journal of Second Language Writing*, 18 (2): 119–35.

Crossley, S. A. and D. S. McNamara (2016), 'Say More and Be More Coherent: How Text Elaboration and Cohesion Can Increase Writing Quality', *Journal of Writing Research*, 7 (3): 351–70.

Cutting, J. (2012), 'Vague Language in Conference Abstracts', *Journal of English for Academic Purposes*, 11 (4): 283–93.

D'Angelo, F. J. (1986), 'The Topic Sentence Revisited', *College Composition and Communication*, 37 (4): 431–41.

Dafouz-Milne, E. (2008), 'The Pragmatic Role of Textual and Interpersonal Metadiscourse Markers in the Construction and Attainment of Persuasion: A Cross-linguistic Study of Newspaper Discourse', *Journal of Pragmatics*, 40 (1): 95–113.
Daneš, F. (1974), 'Functional Sentence Perspective and the Organization of the Text' in F. Daneš (ed.), *Papers on Functional Sentence Perspective*, 106–28, the Hague: Mouton.
Dastjerdi, H. V. and S. H. Samian (2011), 'Quality of Iranian EFL Learners' Argumentative Essays: Cohesive Devices in Focus', *Mediterranean Journal of Social Sciences*, 2 (2): 65–76.
Davies, M. (2015), 'A Model of Critical Thinking in Higher Education', in M. Paulsen (ed), *Higher Education: Handbook of Theory and Research*, 41–92, Cham: Springer.
Davis, M. (2019), 'Publishing Research as an EAP Practitioner: Opportunities and Threats', *Journal of English for Academic Purposes*, 39: 72–86.
Deroey, K. L. (2018), 'The Representativeness of Lecture Listening Coursebooks: Language, Lecture Authenticity, Research-Informedness', *Journal of English for Academic Purposes*, 34: 57–67.
Ding, A. and I. Bruce (2017), *The English for Academic Purposes Practitioner: Operating on the Edge of Academia*, Cham, Switzerland: Palgrave Macmillan.
Dontcheva-Navratilova, O. (2016a), 'Cross-cultural Variation in the Use of Hedges and Boosters in Academic Discourse', *Prague Journal of English Studies*, 5 (1): 163–84.
Dontcheva-Navratilova, O. (2016b), 'Rhetorical Functions of Citations in Linguistics Research Articles: A Contrastive (English-Czech) Study', *Discourse and Interaction*, 9 (2): 51–74.
Dos Santos, M. B. (1996), 'The Textual Organization of Research Paper Abstracts in Applied Linguistics', *Text & Talk*, 16 (4): 481–500.
Dovey, T. (2010), 'Facilitating Writing from Sources: A Focus on Both Process and Product', *Journal of English for Academic Purposes*, 9 (1): 45–60.
Du, Z., F. Jiang and L. Liu (2021), 'Profiling Figure Legends in Scientific Research Articles: A Corpus-Driven Approach', *Journal of English for Academic Purposes*, 54: 101054.
Dubois, B. L. (1988), 'Citation in Biomedical Journal Articles', *English for Specific Purposes*, 7 (3): 181–93.
Duncan, M. (2007), 'Whatever Happened to the Paragraph?', *College English*, 69 (5): 470–95.
Eden, R. and R. Mitchell (1986), 'Paragraphing for the Reader', *College Composition and Communication*, 37 (4): 416–41.
Elahi, M. and M. T. Badeleh (2013), 'A Contrastive Study on Transitional Markers in English Language Teaching Research Articles Written by English and Persian Academic Writers', *Journal of Language Teaching and Research*, 4 (4): 839–44.
Ellis, R., Y. Sheen, M. Murakami and H. Takashima (2008), 'The Effects of Focused and Unfocused Written Corrective Feedback in an English as a Foreign Language Context', *System*, 36 (3): 353–71.
Evans, N. W., K. J. Hartshorn, R. M. McCollum and M. Wolfersberger (2010), 'Contextualizing Corrective Feedback in Second Language Writing Pedagogy', *Language Teaching Research*, 14 (4): 445–63.

Facione, P. A. (1990), *Critical Thinking: A Statement of Expert Consensus for Purposes of Educational Assessment and Instruction. Research Findings and Recommendations*, Newark: American Philosophical Association. Available online: https://files.eric.ed.gov/fulltext/ED315423.pdf (accessed 27 March 2023).

Faghih, E. and S. Rahimpour (2009), 'Contrastive Rhetoric of English and Persian Written Texts: Metadiscourse in Applied Linguistics Research Articles', *Rice Working Papers in Linguistics*, 1: 92–106.

Fahnestock, J. and M. Secor (1988), 'The Stases in Scientific and Literary Argument', *Written Communication*, 5 (4): 427–43.

Farley, A. F. (2018), 'NNES RAs: How ELF RAs Inform Literacy Brokers and English for Research Publication Instructors', *Journal of English for Academic Purposes*, 33: 69–81.

Farrokhi, F. and S. Emami (2008), 'Hedges and Boosters in Academic Writing: Native vs. Non-native Research Articles in Applied Linguistics and Engineering', *Journal of English Language Pedagogy and Practice*, 1 (2): 62–98.

Ferguson, G. (1997), 'Teacher Education and LSP: The Role of Specialized Knowledge', in R. Howard and G. Brown (eds), *Teacher Education for Languages for Specific Purposes*, 80–9, Clevedon: Multilingual Matters.

Ferris, D. (1999), 'The Case for Grammar Correction in L2 Writing Classes: A Response to Truscott (1996)', *Journal of Second Language Writing*, 8 (1): 1–11.

Ferris, D. and B. Roberts (2001), 'Error Feedback in L2 Writing Classes: How Explicit Does It Need to Be?', *Journal of Second Language Writing*, 10 (3): 161–84.

Ferris, D. R. (2010), 'Second Language Writing Research and Written Corrective Feedback in SLA: Intersections and Practical Applications', *Studies in Second Language Acquisition*, 32: 181–201.

Ferris, D. R. and K. Kurzer (2019), 'Does Error Feedback Help L2 Writers? Latest Evidence on the Efficacy of Written Corrective Feedback', in K. Hyland and F. Hyland (eds), *Feedback in Second Language Writing: Contexts and Issues*, 2nd edn, 106–24, Cambridge: Cambridge University Press.

Firbas, J. (1992), *Functional Sentence Perspective in Written and Spoken Communication*, Cambridge: Cambridge University Press.

Florek, C. S. and G. R. Hendges (2023), 'A Multimodal Move Analysis of Graphical Abstracts in Medicine and Chemistry', *ESP Today*, 11 (2): 237–60.

Flower, L. (1979), 'Writer-based Prose: A Cognitive Basis for Problems in Writing', *College English*, 41 (1): 19–37.

Flowerdew, J. and Y. Li (2007), 'Language Re-use among Chinese Apprentice Scientists Writing for Publication', *Applied Linguistics*, 28 (3): 440–65.

Flowerdew, J. and M. Peacock (2001), 'Issues in EAP: A Preliminary Perspective', in J. Flowerdew and M. Peacock (eds), *Research Perspectives on English for Academic Purposes*, 8–24. Cambridge: Cambridge University Press.

Fogal, G. G. and M. H. Verspoor, eds (2020), *Complex Dynamic Systems Theory and L2 Writing Development*, Amsterdam: John Benjamins.

Gao, X. (2016), 'A Cross-disciplinary Corpus-based Study on English and Chinese Native Speakers' Use of Linking Adverbials in Academic Writing', *Journal of English for Academic Purposes*, 24: 14–28.

Gardner, S. (2012), 'Genres and Registers of Student Report Writing: An SFL Perspective on Texts and Practices', *Journal of English for Academic Purposes*, 11 (1): 52–63.

Gardner, S. and C. Han (2018), 'Transitions of Contrast in Chinese and English University Student Writing', *Educational Sciences: Theory and Practice*, 18 (4): 861–82.

Geisler, C., D. S. Kaufer and E. R. Steinberg (1985), 'The Unattended Anaphoric 'this': When Should Writers Use It?', *Written Communication*, 2 (2): 129–55.

Giora, R. (1985), 'A Text-based Analysis of Non-narrative Texts', *Theoretical Linguistics*, 12 (2–3): 115–35.

Giora, R. (1988), 'On the Informativeness Requirement', *Journal of Pragmatics*, 12 (5–6): 547–65.

Goldstein, L. M. (2004), 'Questions and Answers about Teacher Written Commentary and Student Revision: Teachers and Students Working Together', *Journal of Second Language Writing*, 13 (1): 63–80.

Gomez-Laich, M. P., R. T. Miller and S. Pessoa (2019), 'Scaffolding Analytical Argumentative Writing in a Design Class: A Corpus Analysis of Student Writing', *Linguistics and Education*, 51: 20–30.

Goulart, L., D. Biber and R. Reppen (2022). '"In This Essay, I Will . . .": Examining Variation of Communicative Purpose in Student Written Genres', *Journal of English for Academic Purposes*, 59: 101159.

Granger, S. and S. Tyson (1996), 'Connector Usage in the English Essay Writing of Native and Non-native EFL Speakers of English', *World Englishes*, 15 (1): 17–27.

Gray, B. (2010), 'On the Use of Demonstrative Pronouns and Determiners as Cohesive Devices: A Focus on Sentence-initial *This/These* in Academic Prose', *Journal of English for Academic Purposes*, 9 (3): 167–83.

Gray, B. and D. Biber (2012), 'Current Conceptions of Stance', in K. Hyland and C. S. Guinda (eds), *Stance and Voice in Written Academic Genres*, 15–33, London: Palgrave Macmillan.

Green, C. (2012), 'A Computational Investigation of Cohesion and Lexical Network Density in L2 Writing', *English Language Teaching*, 5 (8): 57–69.

Green, C. (2019), 'Enriching the Academic Wordlist and Secondary Vocabulary Lists with Lexicogrammar: Toward a Pattern Grammar of Academic Vocabulary', *System*, 87: 102158.

Green, S. (2019), 'What Students Don't Make of Feedback in Higher Education: An Illustrative Study', *Journal of English for Academic Purposes*, 38: 83–94.

Grice, H. P. (1975), 'Logic and Conversation', in P. Cole and J. L. Morgan (eds), *Syntax and Semantics, Vol. 3: Speech Acts*, 41–58, New York: Academic Press.

Guillen Solano, V. (2016), 'Written Assessment and Feedback Practices in Postgraduate Taught Courses in the UK: Staff and International Students' Perspectives', *Practitioner Research in Higher Education*, 10 (1): 65–80.

Guinda, C. S. and K. Hyland (2012), 'Introduction: A Context-sensitive Approach to Stance and Voice', in K. Hyland and C. S. Guinda (eds), *Stance and Voice In Written Academic Genres*, 1–11, London: Palgrave Macmillan.

Halliday, M. A. K. and R. Hasan (1976), *Cohesion in English*, London: Routledge.

Halliday, M. A. K. and C. M. Matthiessen (2013), *Halliday's Introduction to Functional Grammar*, London: Routledge.

Hamilton, J. (2016), 'Attribution, Referencing and Commencing HE Students as Novice Academic Writers: Giving Them More Time to "Get it"', *Student Success*, 7 (2): 43–9.

Han, Y. and F. Hyland (2019), 'Learner Engagement with Written Feedback: A Sociocognitive Perspective', in K. Hyland and F. Hyland (eds), *Feedback in Second Language Writing: Contexts and Issues*, 2nd edn, 247–64, Cambridge: Cambridge University Press.

Harris, D. P. (1990), 'The Use of 'Organizing Sentences' in the Structure of Paragraphs in Science Textbooks', in U. Connor and A. M. Johns (eds), *Coherence in Writing: Research and Pedagogical Perspectives*, 196–205, Alexandria: Teachers of English to Speakers of Other Languages.

Harrison, M., V. Jakeman and K. Paterson (2016), *Improve Your Grammar: The Essential Guide to Accurate Writing*, 2nd edn, London: Macmillan.

Harwood, N. (2005a), '"We Do Not Seem to Have a Theory . . . The Theory I Present Here Attempts to Fill This Gap': Inclusive and Exclusive Pronouns in Academic Writing', *Applied Linguistics*, 26 (3): 343–75.

Harwood, N. (2005b), 'What Do We Want EAP Teaching Materials for?', *Journal of English for Academic Purposes*, 4(2): 149–61.

Harwood, N. (2006), '(In)Appropriate Personal Pronoun Use in Political Science: A Qualitative Study and a Proposed Heuristic for Future Research', *Written Communication*, 23 (4): 424–50.

Harwood, N. (2009), 'An Interview-based Study of the Functions of Citations in Academic Writing across Two Disciplines', *Journal of Pragmatics*, 41 (3): 497–518.

Harwood, N. and G. Hadley (2004), 'Demystifying Institutional Practices: Critical Pragmatism and the Teaching of Academic Writing', *English for Specific Purposes*, 23 (4): 355–77.

Hashimoto, I. (1987), 'Voice as Juice: Some Reservations about Evangelic Composition', *College Composition and Communication*, 38 (1): 70–80.

Hattie, J. and H. Timperley (2007), 'The Power of Feedback', *Review of Educational Research*, 77 (1): 81–112.

Helms-Park, R. and P. Stapleton (2003), 'Questioning the Importance of Individualized Voice in Undergraduate L2 Argumentative Writing: An Empirical Study with Pedagogical Implications', *Journal of Second Language Writing*, 12 (3): 245–65.

Henry, A. and R. L. Roseberry (1997), 'An Investigation of the Functions, Strategies and Linguistic Features of the Introductions and Conclusions of Essays', *System*, 25 (4): 479–95.

Hewings, M. (2006), 'English Language Standards in Academic Articles: Attitudes of Peer Reviewers', *Revista Canaria de Estudios Ingleses*, 53: 47–62.

Hewings, M. and A. Hewings (2002), '"It Is Interesting to Note That . . .": A Comparative Study of Anticipatory 'It' in Student And Published Writing', *English for Specific Purposes*, 21 (4): 367–83.

Hinds, J. (1987), 'Reader Versus Writer Responsibility: A New Typology', in U. Connor and R. B. Kaplan (eds), *Writing Across Languages: Analysis of L2 Text*, 141–52, Reading, Mass: Addison-Wesley Publishing company.

Hinkel, E. (2002a), *Second Language Writers' Text: Linguistic and Rhetorical Features*, London: Routledge.

Hinkel, E. (2002b), 'Why English Passive is Difficult to Teach (and Learn)', in E. Hinkel and S. Fotos (eds), *New Perspectives on Grammar Teaching in Second Language Classrooms*, 233–59, London: L. Erlbaum Associates.

Hinkel, E. (2005), 'Hedging, Inflating, and Persuading in L2 Academic Writing', *Applied Language Learning*, 15 (1–2): 29–53.

Hinkel, E. (2013), 'Research Findings on Teaching Grammar for Academic Writing', *English Teaching*, 68 (4): 3–21.

Hirvela, A. and D. Belcher (2001), 'Coming Back to Voice: The Multiple Voices and Identities of Mature Multilingual Writers', *Journal of Second Language Writing*, 10 (1–2): 83–106.

Holmes, J. (1982), 'Expressing Doubt and Certainty in English', *RELC Journal*, 13 (2): 9–28.

Hood, S. (2012), 'Voice and Stance as Appraisal: Persuading and Positioning in Research Writing across Intellectual Fields', in K. Hyland and C. S. Guinda (eds), *Stance and Voice in Written Academic Genres*, 51–68, London: Palgrave Macmillan.

Hopkins, A. and T. Dudley-Evans (1988), 'A Genre-Based Investigation of the Discussion Sections in Articles and Dissertations', *English for Specific Purposes*, 7 (2): 113–21.

Hounsell, D. (1997), 'Contrasting Conceptions of Essay-Writing', *The Experience of Learning*, 2 (1): 106–25.

Howard, R. M. (1992), 'A Plagiarism Pentimento', *Journal of Teaching Writing*, 11 (2): 233–45.

Howard, R. M., T. Serviss and T. K. Rodrigue (2010), 'Writing from Sources, Writing from Sentences', *Writing and Pedagogy*, 2 (2): 177–92.

Hu, G. (2018), 'The "Researching EAP Practice" Initiative', *Journal of English for Academic Purposes*, 31: A2.

Hu, G. and F. Cao (2011), 'Hedging and Boosting in Abstracts of Applied Linguistics Articles: A Comparative Study of English- And Chinese-medium Journals', *Journal of Pragmatics*, 43 (11): 2795–809.

Humphrey, S. L. and D. Economou (2015), 'Peeling the Onion: A Textual Model of Critical Analysis', *Journal of English for Academic Purposes*, 17: 37–50.

Hunston, S. and G. Francis (2000), *Pattern Grammar: A Corpus-driven Approach to the Lexical Grammar of English*, Amsterdam: John Benjamins.

Hyland, F. (1998), 'The Impact of Teacher Written Feedback on Individual Writers', *Journal of Second Language Writing*, 7 (3): 255–86.

Hyland, F. and K. Hyland (2001), 'Sugaring the Pill: Praise and Criticism in Written Feedback', *Journal of Second Language Writing*, 10 (3): 185–212.

Hyland, K. (1995), 'The Author in the Text: Hedging Scientific Writing', *Hong Kong Papers in Linguistics and Language Teaching*, 18: 33–42.

Hyland, K. (1996), 'Writing without Conviction? Hedging in Science Research Articles', *Applied Linguistics*, 17(4): 433–54.

Hyland, K. (1998), 'Boosting, Hedging and the Negotiation of Academic Knowledge', *Text*, 18 (3): 349–82.

Hyland, K. (1999a), 'Academic Attribution: Citation and the Construction of Disciplinary Knowledge', *Applied Linguistics*, 20 (3): 341–67.

Hyland, K. (1999b), 'Disciplinary Discourses: Writer Stance in Research Articles', in C. Candlin and K. Hyland (eds), *Writing Texts, Processes and Practices*, 99–121, London: Longman.

Hyland, K. (2001a), 'Bringing in the Reader: Addressee Features in Academic Articles', *Written Communication*, 18 (4): 549–74.

Hyland, K. (2001b), 'Humble Servants of the Discipline? Self-Mention in Research Articles', *English for Specific Purposes*, 20 (3): 207–26.

Hyland, K. (2002a), 'Activity and Evaluation: Reporting Practices in Academic Writing', in J. Flowerdew (ed.), *Academic Discourse*, 115–30, London: Routledge.

Hyland, K. (2002b), 'Authority and Invisibility: Authorial Identity in Academic Writing', *Journal of Pragmatics*, 34(8): 1091–112.

Hyland, K. (2002c), 'Directives: Argument and Engagement in Academic Writing', *Applied Linguistics*, 23 (2): 215–39.

Hyland, K. (2002d), 'What Do They Mean? Questions in Academic Writing', *Text*, 22 (4): 529–58.

Hyland, K. (2003a), 'Genre-based Pedagogies: A Social Response to Process', *Journal of Second Language Writing*, 12 (1): 17–29.

Hyland, K. (2003b), 'Self-citation and Self-reference: Credibility and Promotion in Academic Publication', *Journal of the American Society for Information Science and Technology*, 54 (3): 251–9.

Hyland, K. (2004a), 'Disciplinary Interactions: Metadiscourse in L2 Postgraduate Writing', *Journal of Second Language Writing*, 13 (2): 133–51.

Hyland, K. (2004b), 'Praise and Criticism: Interactions in Book Reviews', in K. Hyland (ed.), *Disciplinary Discourses: Social Interactions in Academic Writing*, 41–62, Ann Arbor: The University of Michigan Press.

Hyland, K. (2005), 'Representing Readers in Writing: Student and Expert Practices', *Linguistics and Education*, 16 (4): 363–77.

Hyland, K. (2006), *English for Academic Purposes: An Advanced Resource Book*, London: Routledge.

Hyland, K. (2007), 'Applying a Gloss: Exemplifying and Reformulating in Academic Discourse', *Applied Linguistics*, 28 (2): 266–85.

Hyland, K. (2008), 'Academic Clusters: Text Patterning in Published and Postgraduate Writing', *International Journal of Applied Linguistics*, 18 (1): 41–62.

Hyland, K. (2009), 'Corpus Informed Discourse Analysis: The Case of Academic Engagement', in M. Charles, S. Hunston and D. Pecorari (eds), *Academic Writing: At the Interface of Corpus and Discourse*, 110–28, London: Continuum.

Hyland, K. (2010a), 'Community and Individuality: Performing Identity in Applied Linguistics', *Written Communication*, 27 (2): 159–88.

Hyland, K. (2010b), 'Metadiscourse: Mapping Interactions in Academic Writing', *Nordic Journal of English Studies*, 9 (2): 125–43.

Hyland, K. (2012), 'Undergraduate Understandings: Stance and Voice in Final Year Reports', in K. Hyland and C. S. Guinda (eds), *Stance and Voice in Written Academic Genres*, 134–50, London: Palgrave Macmillan.

Hyland, K. (2017), 'Metadiscourse: What Is It and Where Is It Going?', *Journal of Pragmatics*, 113: 16–29.

Hyland, K. (2019a), *Metadiscourse: Exploring Interaction in Writing*, 2nd edn, London: Bloomsbury.

Hyland, K. (2019b), 'What Messages Do Students Take from Teacher Feedback?', in K. Hyland and F. Hyland (eds), *Feedback in Second Language Writing: Contexts and Issues*, 2nd edn, 265–84, Cambridge: Cambridge University Press.

Hyland, K. and G. Diani, eds (2009), *Academic Evaluation: Review Genres in University Settings*, London: Palgrave Macmillan.
Hyland, K. and C. S. Guinda, eds (2012), *Stance and Voice in Written Academic Genres*, London: Palgrave Macmillan.
Hyland, K. and F. Hyland (2019), 'Interpersonality and Teacher-written Feedback', in K. Hyland and F. Hyland (eds), *Feedback in Second Language Writing: Contexts and Issues*, 2nd edn, 165–83, Cambridge: Cambridge University Press.
Hyland, K. and F. K. Jiang (2017), 'Is Academic Writing Becoming More Informal?', *English for Specific Purposes*, 45: 40–51.
Hyland, K. and J. Milton (1997), 'Qualification and Certainty in L1 and L2 Students' Writing', *Journal of Second Language Writing*, 6 (2): 183–205.
Hyland, K. and P. Tse (2005a), 'Evaluative That Constructions: Signalling Stance in Research Abstracts', *Functions of Language*, 12 (1): 39–63.
Hyland, K. and P. Tse (2005b), 'Hooking the Reader: A Corpus Study of Evaluative That in Abstracts', *English for Specific Purposes*, 24 (2): 123–39.
Hyland, K. and P. Tse (2007), 'Is there an "Academic Vocabulary"?', *TESOL Quarterly*, 41 (2): 235–53.
Hyland, K. and H. J. Zou (2020), 'In the Frame: Signalling Structure in Academic Articles and Blogs', *Journal of Pragmatics*, 165: 31–44.
Hyon, S. (1996), 'Genre in Three Traditions: Implications for ESL', *TESOL Quarterly*, 30 (4): 693–722.
Intaraprawat, P. and M. S. Steffensen (1995), 'The Use of Metadiscourse in Good and Poor ESL Essays', *Journal of Second Language Writing*, 4: 253–72.
Ivanič, R. (2004), 'Discourses of Writing and Learning to Write', *Language and Education*, 18 (3): 220–45.
Ivanič, R. and D. Camps (2001), 'I am How I Sound: Voice as Self-representation in L2 Writing', *Journal of Second Language Writing*, 10 (1–2): 3–33.
Jabulani, S. (2014), 'An Analysis of the Language of Attribution in University Students' Academic Essays', *South African Journal of Education*, 34 (3): 1–10.
Jamieson, S. (2013), 'Reading and Engaging Sources: What Students' Use of Sources Reveals About Advanced Reading Skills', *Across the Disciplines*, 10 (4): n.p.
Jiang, F. and K. Hyland (2015), '"The Fact That": Stance Nouns in Disciplinary Writing', *Discourse Studies*, 17 (5): 529–50.
Jomaa, N. J. and S. J. Bidin (2017), 'Perspectives of EFL Doctoral Students on Challenges of Citations in Academic Writing', *Malaysian Journal of Learning and Instruction*, 14(2): 177–209.
Kaplan, R. B. (1966), 'Cultural Thought Patterns in Inter-cultural Education', *Language Learning*, 16 (1–2): 1–20.
Khoutyz, I. (2013), 'Engagement Features in Russian and English: A Cross-cultural Analysis of Academic Written Discourse', *Working Papers in TESOL & Applied Linguistics*, 13 (1): 1–20.
Kirk, S. E. (2018), *Enacting the Curriculum in English for Academic Purposes: A Legitimation Code Theory Analysis*, PhD diss., Durham University, Durham.
Kitagawa, C. and A. Lehrer (1990), 'Impersonal Uses of Personal Pronouns', *Journal of Pragmatics*, 14 (5): 739–59.
Knoch, U. (2007), '"Little Coherence, Considerable Strain for Reader": A Comparison between Two Rating Scales for the Assessment of Coherence', *Assessing Writing*, 12 (2): 108–28.

Kostopoulou, S. (2021), 'Sustainable Feedback and Assessment for Autonomous Learning within and beyond the EAP Writing Classroom', paper presented at the 2021 Baleap Conference: Exploring Pedagogical Approaches in EAP Teaching, 6–10 April, University of Glasgow.

Koutsantoni, D. (2004), 'Attitude, Certainty and Allusions to Common Knowledge in Scientific Research Articles', *Journal of English for Academic Purposes*, 3 (2): 163–82.

Koyalan, A. and S. Mumford (2011), 'Changes to English as an Additional Language Writers' Research Articles: From Spoken to Written Register', *English for Specific Purposes*, 30 (2): 113–23.

Kuo, C. H. (1995), 'Cohesion and Coherence in Academic Writing: From Lexical Choice to Organization', *RELC Journal*, 26 (1): 47–62.

Kurzer, K. (2018), 'Dynamic Written Corrective Feedback in Developmental Multilingual Writing Classes', *TESOL Quarterly*, 52 (1): 5–33.

Kwan, B. S. (2006), 'The Schematic Structure of Literature Reviews in Doctoral Theses of Applied Linguistics', *English for Specific Purposes*, 25 (1): 30–55.

Kwon, M. H., S. Staples and R. S. Partridge (2018), 'Source Work in the First-year L2 Writing Classroom: Undergraduate L2 Writers' Use of Reporting Verbs', *Journal of English for Academic Purposes*, 34: 86–96.

Lafuente-Millán, E. (2014), 'Reader Engagement across Cultures, Languages and Contexts of Publication in Business Research Articles', *International Journal of Applied Linguistics*, 24 (2): 201–23.

Lafuente Millán, E. L. (2010), '"Extending This Claim, We Propose . . ." The Writer's Presence in Research Articles from Different Disciplines', *Ibérica*, 20: 35–56.

Lai, E. R. (2011), 'Critical Thinking: A Literature Review', *Pearson's Research Reports*, 6: 40–1. Available online: https://citeseerx.ist.psu.edu/document?repid=rep1&type=pdf&doi=b42cffa5a2ad63a31fcf99869e7cb8ef72b44374 (accessed 27 March 2023).

Larsen-Freeman, D. (1997), 'Chaos/Complexity Science and Second Language Acquisition', *Applied Linguistics*, 18 (2): 141–65.

Larsen-Freeman, D. (2001), 'Teaching Grammar', in M. Celce-Murcia (ed.), *Teaching English as a Second or Foreign Language*, 3rd edn, 25–66, London: Heinle & Heinle.

Larsen-Freeman, D. (2003), *Teaching Language: From Grammar to Grammaring*, Boston: Thomson Heinle.

Larsen-Freeman, D. (2012), 'Complex, Dynamic Systems: A New Transdisciplinary Theme for Applied Linguistics?', *Language Teaching*, 45 (2): 202–14.

Larsen-Freeman, D. (2015), 'Research into Practice: Grammar Learning and Teaching', *Language Teaching*, 48 (2): 263–80.

Le, T. N. P. and M. Harrington (2015), 'Phraseology Used to Comment on Results in the Discussion Section of Applied Linguistics Quantitative Research Articles', *English for Specific Purposes*, 39: 45–61.

Lea, M. R. and B. V. Street (1998), 'Student Writing in Higher Education: An Academic Literacies Approach', *Studies in Higher Education*, 23 (2): 157–72.

Lea, M. R. and B. V. Street (2006), 'The "Academic Literacies" Model: Theory and Applications', *Theory into Practice*, 45 (4): 368–77.

Leader, J. W. (2019), 'SCOPE for Criticality in HE: The Critical Thinker as Curator'. Paper presented at *Questioning Criticality: What is Criticality in Higher Education?* Symposium held at the University of Leeds, 19 December.

Lee, I. (2002), 'Teaching Coherence to ESL Students: A Classroom Inquiry', *Journal of Second Language Writing*, 11 (2): 135–59.

Lee, J. J. and L. Deakin (2016), 'Interactions in L1 and L2 Undergraduate Student Writing: Interactional Metadiscourse in Successful and Less-successful Argumentative Essays', *Journal of Second Language Writing*, 33: 21–34.

Lee, J. J., C. Hitchcock and J. E. Casal (2018), 'Citation Practices of L2 University Students in First-year Writing: Form, Function, and Stance', *Journal of English for Academic Purposes*, 33: 1–11.

Lei, L. (2012). 'Linking Adverbials in Academic Writing on Applied Linguistics by Chinese Doctoral Students', *Journal of English for Academic Purposes*, 11: 267–75.

Leńko-Szymańska, A. (2004), 'Demonstratives as Anaphora Markers in Advanced Learners' English', in G. Aston, S. Bernardini and D. Stewart (eds), *Corpora and Language Learners*, 89–107. Amsterdam: John Benjamins.

Liardét, C. L. and S. Black (2019), '"So and So" Says, States and Argues: A Corpus-assisted Engagement Analysis of Reporting Verbs', *Journal of Second Language Writing*, 44: 37–50.

Lillis, T. (2003), 'Student Writing as 'Academic Literacies': Drawing on Bakhtin to Move from Critique to Design', *Language And Education*, 17 (3): 192–207.

Lillis, T. and J. Tuck (2016), 'Academic Literacies: A Critical Lens on Writing and Reading in the Academy', in K. Hyland and P. Shaw (eds), *The Routledge Handbook of English for Academic Purposes*, 30–43, London: Routledge.

Lim, J. M. H. (2006), 'Method Sections of Management Research Articles: A Pedagogically Motivated Qualitative Study', *English for Specific Purposes*, 25 (3): 282–309.

Liu, C. and M. Y. Tseng (2021), 'Paradigmatic Variation in Hedging and Boosting: A Comparative Study of Discussions in Narrative Inquiry and Grounded Theory Research', *English for Specific Purposes*, 61: 1–16.

Liu, D. (2008), 'Linking Adverbials: An Across-register Corpus Study and its Implications', *International Journal of Corpus Linguistics*, 13 (4): 491–518.

Liu, J. (2020), 'Research Video Abstracts in the Making: A Revised Move Analysis', *Journal of Technical Writing and Communication*, 50 (4): 423–46.

Liu, M. and G. Braine (2005), 'Cohesive Features in Argumentative Writing Produced by Chinese Undergraduates', *System*, 33 (4): 623–36.

Liu, M. and G. Wang (2011), 'Paragraph-level Errors in Chinese Undergraduate EFL Learners' Compositions: A Cohort Study', *Theory and Practice in Language Studies*, 1 (6): 584–93.

Liu, Y. and L. Buckingham (2018), 'The Schematic Structure of Discussion Sections in Applied Linguistics and the Distribution of Metadiscourse Markers', *Journal of English for Academic Purposes*, 34: 97–109.

Loan, N. T. T. and I. Pramoolsook (2015), 'Reporting Verbs in Literature Review Chapters of TESOL Master's Theses Written by Vietnamese Postgraduates', *ESP Today*, 3 (2): 196–215.

Logan, J. K. and M. J. Kieffer (2018), 'Academic Vocabulary Instruction: Building Knowledge about the World and How Words Work', in D. Lapp and D. Fisher (eds), *Handbook of Research on Teaching the English Language Arts*, 4th edn, 162–82, London: Routledge.

Lorés, R. (2004), 'On RA Abstracts: From Rhetorical Structure to Thematic Organisation', *English for Specific Purposes*, 23 (3): 280–302.
Lovejoy, K. B. (1991), 'Cohesion and Information Strategies in Academic Writing: Analysis of Passages in Three Disciplines', *Linguistics and Education*, 3 (4): 315–43.
Lovejoy, K. B. and D. M. Lance (1991), 'Information Management and Cohesion in the Study of Written Discourse', *Linguistics and Education*, 3 (3): 251–73.
Lu, X., J. Yoon and O. Kisselev (2021), 'Matching Phrase-Frames to Rhetorical Moves in Social Science Research Article Introductions', *English for Specific Purposes*, 61: 63–83.
MacDiarmid, C. and J. J. MacDonald, eds (2021), *Pedagogies in English for Academic Purposes: Teaching and Learning in International Contexts*, London: Bloomsbury.
Macqueen, S. S. and U. Knoch (2020), 'Adaptive Imitation: Formulaicity and the Words of Others in L2 English Academic Writing', in G. G. Fogal and M. H. Verspoor (eds), *Complex Dynamic Systems Theory and L2 Writing Development*, 81–108, Amsterdam: John Benjamins.
Magyar, A. E. (2012), 'Plagiarism and Attribution: An Academic Literacies Approach', *Journal of Learning Development in Higher Education*, 4: n.p.
Maher, P. and S. Milligan (2019), 'Teaching Master Thesis Writing to Engineers: Insights from Corpus and Genre Analysis of Introductions', *English for Specific Purposes*, 55: 40–55.
Mansourizadeh, K. and U. K Ahmad (2011), 'Citation Practices among Non-native Expert and Novice Scientific Writers', *Journal of English for Academic Purposes*, 10 (3): 152–61.
Maschler, Y. and D. Schiffrin (2015), 'Discourse Markers: Language, Meaning, and Context', in D. Tannen, H. E. Hamilton and D. Schiffrin (eds), *The Handbook of Discourse Analysis*, 2nd edn, 189–221, Malden: Wiley Blackwell.
Master, P. (1991), 'Active Verbs with Inanimate Subjects in Scientific Prose', *English for Specific Purposes*, 10 (1): 15–33.
Matsuda, P. K. (2001), 'Voice in Japanese Written Discourse: Implications for Second Language Writing', *Journal of Second Language Writing*, 10 (1–2): 35–53.
Matsuda, P. K. and C. M. Tardy (2007), 'Voice in Academic Writing: The Rhetorical Construction of Author Identity in Blind Manuscript Review', *English for Specific Purposes*, 26 (2): 235–49.
Mauranen, A. (1996), 'Discourse Competence: Evidence from Thematic Development in Native and Non-native Texts', in E. Ventola and A. Mauranen (eds), *Academic Writing: Intercultural and Textual Issues*, 195–230, Amsterdam: John Benjamins.
Mauranen, A. (1997), 'Hedging in Language Revisers' Hands', in R. Markkanen and H. Schröder (eds), *Hedging and Discourse: Approaches to the Analysis of a Pragmatic Phenomenon*, 115–33, Berlin: de Gruyter.
Maxwell, C. (2020), 'Exploring Clarity in the Discipline of Design', in M. Whong and J. Godfrey (eds), *What is Good Academic Writing?: Insights into Discipline-Specific Student Writing*, 57–82, London: Bloomsbury.
McCulloch, S. (2012), 'Citations in Search of a Purpose: Source Use and Authorial Voice in L2 Student Writing', *International Journal for Educational Integrity*, 8 (1): 55–69.

McEnery, T. and N. A. Kifle (2002), 'Epistemic Modality in Argumentative Essays of Second-language Writers', in J. Flowerdew (ed.), *Academic Discourse*, 182–95, London: Routledge.

McGrath, L. (2016), 'Self-mentions in Anthropology and History Research Articles: Variation Between and within Disciplines', *Journal of English for Academic Purposes*, 21: 86–98.

McGrath, L. and M. Kuteeva (2012), 'Stance and Engagement in Pure Mathematics Research Articles: Linking Discourse Features to Disciplinary Practices', *English for Specific Purposes*, 31 (3): 161–73.

McKinley, J. and H. Rose (2018), 'Conceptualizations of Language Errors, Standards, Norms and Nativeness in English for Research Publication Purposes: An Analysis of Journal Submission Guidelines', *Journal of Second Language Writing*, 42: 1–11.

Meade, R. A. and W. G. Ellis (1971), 'The Use in Writing of Textbook Methods of Paragraph Development', *The Journal of Educational Research*, 65 (2): 74–6.

Meisuo, Z. (2000), 'Cohesive Features in the Expository Writing of Undergraduates in Two Chinese Universities', *RELC Journal*, 31 (1): 61–95.

Metsä-Ketelä, M. (2012), 'Frequencies of Vague Expressions in English as an Academic Lingua Franca', *Journal of English as a Lingua Franca*, 1 (2): 263–85.

Meurer, J. L. (2003), 'Relationships between Cohesion and Coherence in Essays and Narratives', *Fragmentos: Revista de Língua e Literatura Estrangeiras*, 25: 147–54.

MICUSP [Michigan Corpus of Upper-level Student Papers] (2009), Ann Arbor: The Regents of the University of Michigan. Available online: https://micusp.elicorpora.info/ (accessed 26 April 2023).

Miller, R. T. and S. Pessoa (2016), 'Where's Your Thesis Statement and What Happened to Your Topic Sentences? Identifying Organizational Challenges in Undergraduate Student Argumentative Writing', *TESOL Journal*, 7 (4): 847–73.

Mitrasca, M. (2009). 'The Split Infinitive in Electronic Corpora: Should There Be a Rule?', *Concordia Working Papers in Applied Linguistics*, 2: 99–131.

Molinari, J. (2022), *What Makes Writing Academic: Rethinking Theory for Practice*, London: Bloomsbury.

Molino, A. (2010), 'Personal and Impersonal Authorial References: A Contrastive Study of English and Italian Linguistics Research Articles', *Journal of English for Academic Purposes*, 9 (2): 86–101.

Moore, T. and J. Morton (2005), 'Dimensions of Difference: A Comparison of University Writing and IELTS Writing', *Journal of English for Academic Purposes*, 4(1): 43–66.

Moreno, A. I. and L. Suárez (2008), 'A Study of Critical Attitude across English and Spanish Academic Book Reviews', *Journal of English for Academic Purposes*, 7 (1): 15–26.

Motta-Roth, D. (1995), *Rhetorical Features and Disciplinary Cultures: A Genre-Based Study of Academic Book Reviews in Linguistics, Chemistry, and Economics*, PhD thesis, Universidade Federal de Santa Catarina, Florianópolis.

Mur Dueñas, P. (2007), '"I/We Focus on . . .": A Cross-cultural Analysis of Self-mentions in Business Management Research Articles', *Journal of English for Academic Purposes*, 6 (2): 143–62.

Mur Dueñas, P. (2009), 'Designing EAP Materials Based on Intercultural Corpus Analyses: The Case of Logical Markers in Research Articles', *Revista de Lingüística y Lenguas Aplicadas*, 4: 125–35.
Mur Dueñas, P. (2010), 'Attitude Markers in Business Management Research Articles: A Cross-cultural Corpus-driven Approach', *International Journal of Applied Linguistics*, 20 (1): 50–72.
Mur-Dueñas, P. and J. Šinkūnienė (2016), 'Self-reference in Research Articles across Europe and Asia: A Review of Studies', *Brno Studies in English*, 42 (1): 71–92.
Myers, G. (1989), 'The Pragmatics of Politeness in Scientific Articles', *Applied Linguistics*, 10 (1): 1–35.
Narita, M., C. Sato and M. Sugiura (2004), 'Connector Usage in the English Essay Writing of Japanese EFL Learners', Paper presented at the Fourth International Conference on Language Resources and Evaluation, Lisbon, 26–28 May. Available online: http://www.lrec-conf.org/proceedings/lrec2004/pdf/48.pdf (accessed 26 April 2023).
Nesi, H. and E. Moreton (2012), 'EFL/ESL Writers and the Use of Shell Nouns', in R. Tang (ed.), *Academic Writing in a Second or Foreign Language: Issues and Challenges Facing ESL/EFL Academic Writers in Higher Education Contexts*, 126–45, London: Continuum.
Nesi, H. and S. Gardner (2012), *Genres across the Disciplines: Student Writing in Higher Education*, Cambridge: Cambridge University Press.
Nicol, D. (2010), 'From Monologue to Dialogue: Improving Written Feedback Processes in Mass Higher Education', *Assessment & Evaluation in Higher Education*, 35 (5): 501–17.
Nicol, D., A. Thomson and C. Breslin (2014), 'Rethinking Feedback Practices in Higher Education: A Peer Review Perspective', *Assessment & Evaluation in Higher Education*, 39 (1): 102–22.
Noble, W. (2010), 'Understanding Metadiscoursal Use: Lessons from a "Local" Corpus of Learner Academic Writing', *Nordic Journal of English Studies*, 9 (2): 145–69.
Nygaard, L. P. (2021), 'Into the Fray: Becoming an Academic in My Own Right', in M. Savva and L. P. Nygaard (eds), *Becoming a Scholar: Cross-cultural Reflections on Identity and Agency in an Education Doctorate*, 121–35, London: UCL Press.
Obeng, B., A. A. Wornyo and C. Hammond (2023), 'Variations in Rhetorical Moves and Metadiscourse Elements in Conference Abstracts: A Genre Analysis', *European Journal of Applied Linguistics Studies*, 6 (1): 126–48.
OPAL (n.d.), *Oxford Phrasal Academic Lexicon*, Oxford: Oxford University Press. Available online: https://www.oxfordlearnersdictionaries.com/wordlists/opal (accessed 5 January 2023).
Oxford Collocations Dictionary for Students of English (2002), Oxford: Oxford University Press.
Paltridge, B. (1997), *Genre, Frames and Writing in Research Settings*, Amsterdam: John Benjamins.
Paquot, M., H. Hasselgård and S. O. Ebeling (2013), 'Writer/reader Visibility in Learner Writing across Genres: A Comparison of the French and Norwegian Components of the ICLE and VESPA Learner Corpora', in S. Granger, G. Gilquin and F. Meunier (eds), *Twenty Years of Learner Corpus Research:*

Looking Back, Moving Ahead. Proceedings of the First Learner Corpus Research Conference, 377–87, Louvain: Presses Universitaires de Louvain.

Parkinson, J. (2017), 'The Student Laboratory Report Genre: A Genre Analysis', *English for Specific Purposes*, 45: 1–13.

Parkinson, J. and J. Musgrave (2014), 'Development of Noun Phrase Complexity in the Writing of English for Academic Purposes Students', *Journal of English for Academic Purposes*, 14: 48–59.

Pavičić Takač, V. and T. Vakanjac Ivezić (2019), 'Frame Markers and Coherence in L2 Argumentative Essays', *Discourse and Interaction*, 12 (2): 46–71.

Peacock, M. (2002), 'Communicative Moves in the Discussion Section of Research Articles', *System*, 30 (4): 479–97.

Peacock, M. (2010), 'Linking Adverbials in Research Articles across Eight Disciplines', *Ibérica*, 20: 9–33.

Peacock, M. (2011), 'The Structure of the Methods Section in Research Articles across Eight Disciplines', *The Asian ESP Journal*, 7 (2): 99–124.

Pecorari, D. (2003), 'Good and Original: Plagiarism and Patchwriting in Academic Second-Language Writing', *Journal of Second Language Writing*, 12 (4): 317–45.

Pecorari, D. (2006), 'Visible and Occluded Citation Features in Postgraduate Second-Language Writing', *English for Specific Purposes*, 25 (1): 4–29.

Pecorari, D. (2008), *Academic Writing and Plagiarism: A Linguistic Analysis*, London: Bloomsbury.

Pennycook, A. (1997), 'Vulgar Pragmatism, Critical Pragmatism, and EAP', *English for Specific Purposes*, 16 (4): 253–69.

Perales-Escudero, M. D. (2011), 'To Split or To Not Split: The Split Infinitive Past and Present', *Journal of English Linguistics*, 39 (4): 313–34.

Petrić, B. (2007), 'Rhetorical Functions of Citations in High- and Low-rated Master's Theses', *Journal of English for Academic Purposes*, 6 (3): 238–53.

Petrić, B. (2012), 'Legitimate Textual Borrowing: Direct Quotation in L2 Student Writing', *Journal of Second Language Writing*, 21 (2): 102–17.

Pho, P. D. (2008), 'Research Article Abstracts in Applied Linguistics and Educational Technology: A Study of Linguistic Realizations of Rhetorical Structure and Authorial Stance', *Discourse Studies*, 10 (2): 231–50.

Popken, R. L. (1987), 'A Study of Topic Sentence Use in Academic Writing', *Written Communication*, 4 (2): 209–28.

Price, M., K. Handley and J. Millar (2011), 'Feedback: Focusing Attention on Engagement', *Studies in Higher Education*, 36 (8): 879–96.

Price, M., K. Handley, J. Millar, and B. O'Donovan (2010), 'Feedback: All That Effort, but What Is the Effect?', *Assessment & Evaluation in Higher Education*, 35 (3): 277–89.

Prior, P. (2001), 'Voices in Text, Mind, and Society: Sociohistoric Accounts of Discourse Acquisition and Use', *Journal of Second Language Writing*, 10 (1–2): 55–81.

Quirk, R., S. Greenbaum, G. Leech and J. Svartvik (1985), *A Comprehensive Grammar of the English Language*, London: Longman.

Ramanathan, V. and D. Atkinson (1999), 'Individualism, Academic Writing, and ESL Writers', *Journal of Second Language Writing*, 8 (1): 45–75.

Ravelli, L. J. (2004), 'Signalling the Organization of Written Texts: Hyper-Themes in Management and History Essays', in L. Ravelli and R. A. Ellis (eds),

Analysing Academic Writing: Contextualized Frameworks, 104–25, London: Continuum.

Reid, J. (1994), 'Responding to ESL Students' Texts: The Myths of Appropriation', *TESOL Quarterly*, 28 (2): 273–92.

Riazi, A. M., H. Ghanbar and I. Fazel (2020), 'The Contexts, Theoretical and Methodological Orientation of EAP Research: Evidence from Empirical Articles Published in the Journal of English for Academic Purposes', *Journal of English for Academic Purposes*, 48: 100925.

Richards, J. C. and R. Schmidt (2010), *Longman Dictionary of Language Teaching and Applied Linguistics*, 4th edn, London: Routledge.

Roig, M. (2001), 'Plagiarism and Paraphrasing Criteria of College and University Professors', *Ethics & Behavior*, 11 (3): 307–23.

Rosmawati (2024), 'Applying Complex Dynamic Systems Theory in EAP Curriculum Design and Teaching Practice: Challenges and Possibilities', in M. Walková (ed.), *Linguistic Approaches in English for Academic Purposes: Expanding the Discourse*, 117–141, London: Bloomsbury.

Ryan, M. (2011), 'Improving Reflective Writing in Higher Education: A Social Semiotic Perspective', *Teaching in Higher Education*, 16 (1): 99–111.

Ryan, M. and M. Ryan (2013), 'Theorising a Model for Teaching and Assessing Reflective Learning in Higher Education', *Higher Education Research & Development*, 32 (2): 244–57.

Samraj, B. (2002), 'Introductions in Research Articles: Variations across Disciplines', *English for Specific Purposes*, 21 (1): 1–17.

Samraj, B. (2005), 'An Exploration of a Genre Set: Research Article Abstracts and Introductions in Two Disciplines', *English for Specific Purposes*, 24 (2): 141–56.

Samraj, B. (2008), 'A Discourse Analysis of Master's Theses across Disciplines with a Focus on Introductions', *Journal of English for Academic Purposes*, 7 (1): 55–67.

Sawaki, T. (2024), 'Conceptual Metaphors as a Resource to Build a Coherent Text: A Socio-Cognitive Approach to EAP', in M. Walková (ed.), *Linguistic Approaches in English for Academic Purposes: Expanding the Discourse*, 193–218, London: Bloomsbury.

Schillings, M., H. Roebertsen, H. Savelberg and D. Dolmans (2023), 'A Review of Educational Dialogue Strategies to Improve Academic Writing Skills', *Active Learning in Higher Education*, 24 (2): 95–108.

Schmid, H. J. (2018), 'Shell Nouns in English: A Personal Roundup', *Caplletra: Revista Internacional de Filologia*, 64: 109–28.

Schneider, M. and U. Connor (1990), 'Analyzing Topical Structure in ESL Essays: Not All Topics Are Equal', *Studies in Second Language Acquisition*, 12 (4): 411–27.

Shaw, P. (1992), 'Reasons for the Correlation of Voice, Tense, and Sentence Function in Reporting Verbs', *Applied Linguistics*, 13 (3): 302–19.

Shaw, P. (2009), 'Linking Adverbials in Student and Professional Writing in Literary Studies: What Makes Writing Mature', in M. Charles, S. Hunston and D. Pecorari (eds), *Academic Writing: At the Interface of Corpus and Discourse*, 215–35, London: Continuum.

Sheen, Y. (2007), 'The Effect of Focused Written Corrective Feedback and Language Aptitude on ESL Learners' Acquisition of Articles', *TESOL Quarterly*, 41 (2): 255–83.

Sheldon, E. (2009), 'From One I to Another: Discursive Construction of Self-representation in English and Castilian Spanish Research Articles', *English for Specific Purposes*, 28 (4): 251–65.

Shin, Y. K., V. Cortes and I. W. Yoo (2018), 'Using Lexical Bundles as a Tool to Analyze Definite Article Use in L2 Academic Writing: An Exploratory Study', *Journal of Second Language Writing*, 39: 29–41.

Shute, V. J. (2008), 'Focus on Formative Feedback', *Review of Educational Research*, 78 (1): 153–89.

Sinclair, J. (1991), *Corpus, Concordance, Collocation*, Oxford: Oxford University Press.

Sloane, B. S. (2003), 'Say It Straight: Teaching Conciseness', *Teaching English in the Two Year College*, 30 (4): 429–33.

Small, F. and K. Attree (2016), 'Undergraduate Student Responses to Feedback: Expectations and Experiences', *Studies in Higher Education*, 41 (11): 2078–94.

Soler-Monreal, C. (2016), 'A Move-Step Analysis of the Concluding Chapters in Computer Science PhD Theses', *Ibérica: Revista de La Asociación Europea de Lenguas Para Fines Específicos*, 32: 105–32.

Staples, S., J. Egbert, D. Biber, and B. Gray (2022), 'Academic Writing Development at the University Level: Phrasal and Clausal Complexity across Level of Study, Discipline, and Genre', in D. Biber, B. Gray, S. Staples and J. Egbert (eds), *The Register-Functional Approach to Grammatical Complexity: Theoretical Foundation, Descriptive Research Findings, Application*, 333–59, London: Routledge.

Stapleton, P. (2002), 'Critiquing Voice as a Viable Pedagogical Tool in L2 Writing: Returning the Spotlight to Ideas', *Journal of Second Language Writing*, 11 (3): 177–90.

Stapleton, P. and Y. A. Wu (2015), 'Assessing the Quality of Arguments in Students' Persuasive Writing: A Case Study Analyzing the Relationship Between Surface Structure and Substance', *Journal of English for Academic Purposes*, 17: 12–23.

Stock, I. and N. L. Eik-Nes (2016), 'Voice Features in Academic Texts: A Review of Empirical Studies', *Journal of English for Academic Purposes*, 24: 89–99.

Storch, N. and G. Wigglesworth (2010), 'Learners' Processing, Uptake, and Retention of Corrective Feedback on Writing: Case Studies', *Studies in Second Language Acquisition*, 32: 303–34.

Sullivan, P., Y. Zhang and F. Zheng (2012), 'College Writing in China and America: A Modest and Humble Conversation, with Writing Samples', *College Composition and Communication*, 306–31.

Sultan, A. H. (2011), 'A Contrastive Study of Metadiscourse in English and Arabic Linguistics Research Articles', *Acta Linguistica*, 5: 28–41.

Sutton, P. (2012), 'Conceptualizing Feedback Literacy: Knowing, Being, and Acting', *Innovations in Education and Teaching International*, 49 (1): 31–40.

Swales, J. (1990), *Genre Analysis: English in Academic and Research Settings*, Cambridge: Cambridge University Press.

Swales, J. M. (2004), *Research Genres: Explorations and Applications*, Cambridge: Cambridge University Press.

Swales, J. M. (2005), 'Attended and Unattended 'this' in Academic Writing: A Long and Unfinished Story', *ESP Malaysia*, 11 (1): 1–15.

Swales, J. M. (2014), 'Variation in Citational Practice in a Corpus of Student Biology Papers: From Parenthetical Plonking to Intertextual Storytelling', *Written Communication*, 31 (1): 118–41.

Swales, J. M. (2019), 'The Futures of EAP Genre Studies: A Personal Viewpoint', *Journal of English for Academic Purposes*, 38: 75–82.

Swales, J. M., U. K. Ahmad, Y. Y. Chang, D. Chavez, D. F. Dressen and R. Seymour (1998), 'Consider This: The Role of Imperatives in Scholarly Writing', *Applied Linguistics*, 19 (1): 97–121.

Swales, J. M. and C. B. Feak (2000), *English in Today's Research World: A Writing Guide*, Ann Arbor: University of Michigan Press.

Swales, J. M. and C. B. Feak (2004), *Academic Writing for Graduate Students: Essential Tasks and Skills*, Ann Arbor: University of Michigan Press.

Tadros, A. (1993), 'The Pragmatics of Text Averral and Attribution in Academic Texts', in M. Hoey (ed.), *Data, Description, Discourse: Papers on the English Language in Honour of John McH Sinclair on His Sixtieth Birthday*, 98–114, London: Harper Collins.

Tang, R. and S. John (1999), 'The "I" in Identity: Exploring Writer Identity in Student Academic Writing through the First Person Pronoun', *English for Specific Purposes*, 18: S23–S39.

Tangkiengsirisin, S. (2010), 'Promoting Cohesion in EFL Expository Writing: A Study of Graduate Students in Thailand', *International Journal of Arts and Sciences*, 3 (16): 1–34.

Tapper, M. (2005), 'Connectives in Advanced Swedish EFL Learners' Written English: Preliminary Results', in F. Heinat and E. Klingvall (eds), *The Department of English in Lund: Working Papers in Linguistics*, Vol. 5, 115–44, Lund: Lund University.

Tarasova, E. and N. Baliaeva (2024), 'The Role of Morphological Knowledge in EAP Writing: Evidence-based Study', in M. Walková (ed.), *Linguistic Approaches in English for Academic Purposes: Expanding the Discourse*, 63–88, London: Bloomsbury.

Tardy, C. (2019), 'Appropriation, Ownership, and Agency: Negotiating Teacher Feedback in Academic Settings', in K. Hyland and F. Hyland (eds), *Feedback in Second Language Writing: Contexts and Issues*, 2nd edn, 64–82, Cambridge: Cambridge University Press.

Tardy, C. M. and P. K. Matsuda (2009), 'The Construction of Author Voice by Editorial Board Members', *Written Communication*, 26 (1): 32–52.

TECCL [Ten-thousand English Compositions of Chinese Learners Corpus] (2015), Version 1.1, compiled by X. Xue. Beijing: Beijing Foreign Studies University. Available online: corpus.bfsu.edu.cn/content/teccl-corpus (accessed 22 October 2020).

Therova, D. (2020), 'Review of Academic Word Lists', *TESL-EJ*, 24 (1). Available online: http://tesl-ej.org/wordpress/issues/volume24/ej93/ej93a5/ (accessed 5 January 2023).

Thomas, S. and T. P. Hawes (1994), 'Reporting Verbs in Medical Journal Articles', *English for Specific Purposes*, 13 (2): 129–48.

Thompson, G. and Y. Ye (1991), 'Evaluation in the Reporting Verbs Used in Academic Papers', *Applied Linguistics*, 12 (4): 365–82.

Thompson, P. (2005), 'Points of Focus and Position: Intertextual Reference in PhD Theses', *Journal of English for Academic Purposes*, 4 (4): 307–23.

Thompson, P. and C. Tribble (2001), 'Looking at Citations: Using Corpora in English for Academic Purposes', *Language Learning & Technology*, 5 (3): 91–105.

Thompson, S. A. (1985), 'Grammar and Written Discourse: Initial vs. Final Purpose Clauses in English', *Text – Interdisciplinary Journal for the Study of Discourse*, 5 (1–2): 55–84.

Thornbury, S. (2006), *An A–Z of ELT: A Dictionary of Terms and Concepts*, London: Macmillan.

Timmis, I. (2015), *Corpus Linguistics for ELT: Research and Practice*, London: Routledge.

Timmis, I. (2018), 'A Text-based Approach to Grammar Practice', in C. Jones (ed.), *Practice in Second Language Learning*, 79–108, Cambridge: Cambridge University Press.

Todd, R. W., S. Khongput and P. Darasawang (2007), 'Coherence, Cohesion and Comments on Students' Academic Essays', *Assessing Writing*, 12 (1): 10–25.

Toulmin, S. E. ([1958] 2003), *The Uses of Argument*, updated edn, Cambridge: Cambridge University Press.

Tribble, C. (2009), 'Writing Academic English: A Survey Review of Current Published Resources', *ELT Journal*, 63(4): 400–17.

Truscott, J. (1996), 'The Case Against Grammar Correction in L2 Writing Classes', *Language Learning*, 46 (2): 327–69.

Truscott, J. (1999), 'The Case for 'The Case Against Grammar Correction in L2 Writing Classes': A Response to Ferris', *Journal of Second Language Writing*, 8 (2): 111–22.

Truscott, J. (2004), 'Evidence and Conjecture on the Effects of Correction: A Response to Chandler', *Journal of Second Language Writing*, 13 (4): 337–43.

Truscott, J. (2007), 'The Effect of Error Correction on Learners' Ability to Write Accurately', *Journal of Second Language Writing*, 16 (4): 255–72.

Truscott, J. (2010), 'Some Thoughts on Anthony Bruton's Critique of the Correction Debate', *System*, 38 (2): 329–35.

Tseng, M. Y. (2018), 'Creating a Theoretical Framework: On the Move Structure of Theoretical Framework Sections in Research Articles Related to Language and Linguistics', *Journal of English for Academic Purposes*, 33: 82–99.

Tuck, J. (2012), 'Feedback-giving as Social Practice: Teachers' Perspectives on Feedback as Institutional Requirement, Work and Dialogue', *Teaching in Higher Education*, 17 (2): 209–21.

University of Technology Surrey (n.d.), *Reporting Verbs and Your "Writer's" Voice*, Surrey: University of Technology Surrey, Available online: https://www.uts.edu.au/sites/default/files/article/downloads/reporting-verbs-2.pdf (accessed 19 November 2020).

Vande Kopple, W. J. (1985), 'Some Exploratory Discourse on Metadiscourse', *College Composition and Communication*, 36 (1): 82–93.

Vassileva, I. (1998), 'Who Am I/Who Are We in Academic Writing? A Contrastive Analysis of Authorial Presence in English, German, French, Russian and Bulgarian', *International Journal of Applied Linguistics*, 8 (2): 163–85.

Vassileva, I. (2001), 'Commitment and Detachment in English and Bulgarian Academic Writing', *English for Specific Purposes*, 20 (1): 83–102.

Vázquez Orta, I. V. (2010), 'A Contrastive Analysis of the Use of Modal Verbs in the Expression of Epistemic Stance in Business Management Research Articles in English and Spanish', *Ibérica*, 19: 77–95.

Vladimirou, D. (2007), '"I Suggest That We Need More Research": Personal Reference in Linguistics Journal Articles', in C. Gabrielatos, R. Slessor and J. W. Unger (eds), *Papers from the Lancaster University Postgraduate Conference in Linguistics and Language Teaching, Vol. 1: Papers from LAEL PG 2006*, 139–57, Lancaster: Lancaster University.

Vold, E. T. (2006), 'Epistemic Modality Markers in Research Articles: A Cross-linguistic and Cross-disciplinary Study', *International Journal of Applied Linguistics*, 16 (1): 61–87.

Walker, M. (2009), 'An Investigation into Written Comments on Assignments: Do Students Find Them Usable?', *Assessment & Evaluation in Higher Education*, 34 (1): 67–78.

Walková, M. (2014), 'Students' Academic Writing Skills in English: Where Do They Err?', in I. Lacko and L. Otrísalová (eds), *Slovak Studies in English IV: Cross-Cultural Challenges in British and American Studies*, 277–87, Bratislava: Stimul.

Walková, M. (2017), 'Citačné zvyklosti v slovenských a anglických jazykovedných štúdiách [Citation Practices in Slovak and English Linguistic Research Papers]', *Jazykovedný časopis*, 68 (3): 435–57.

Walková, M. (2018), 'Author's Self-representation in Research Articles by Anglophone and Slovak Linguists', *Discourse and Interaction*, 11 (1): 86–105.

Walková, M. (2019), 'A Three-dimensional Model of Personal Self-mention in Research Papers', *English for Specific Purposes*, 53: 60–73.

Walková, M. (2020), 'Transition Markers in EAP Textbooks', *Journal of English for Academic Purposes*, 46: 100874.

Walková, M. and J. Bradford (2022), Constructing an Argument in Academic Writing across Disciplines, *ESP Today*, 10 (1): 22–42.

Walsh Marr, J. (2019), 'Making the Mechanics of Paraphrasing More Explicit through Grammatical Metaphor', *Journal of English for Academic Purposes*, 42: 100783.

Warchał, K. (2010), 'Moulding Interpersonal Relations through Conditional Clauses: Consensus-Building Strategies in Written Academic Discourse', *Journal of English for Academic Purposes*, 9 (2): 140–50.

Weaver, M. R. (2006), 'Do Students Value Feedback? Student Perceptions of Tutors' Written Responses', *Assessment & Evaluation in Higher Education*, 31 (3): 379–94.

Weissberg, R. C. (1984). 'Given and New: Paragraph Development Models from Scientific English', *TESOL Quarterly*, 18 (3): 485–500.

Wikborg, E. (1985), 'Unspecified Topic in University Student Essays', *Text: Interdisciplinary Journal for the Study of Discourse*, 5 (4): 359–70.

Williams, M. and R. L. Burden (1997), *Psychology for Language Teachers: A Social Constructivist Approach*, Cambridge: Cambridge University Press.

Wingate, U. (2006), 'Doing Away with "Study Skills"', *Teaching in Higher Education*, 11 (4): 457–69.

Wingate, U. (2010), 'The Impact of Formative Feedback on the Development of Academic Writing', *Assessment & Evaluation in Higher Education*, 35 (5): 519–33.

Wingate, U. (2012a), '"Argument!" Helping Students Understand What Essay Writing is About', *Journal of English for Academic Purposes*, 11 (2): 145–54.

Wingate, U. (2012b), 'Using Academic Literacies and Genre-based Models for Academic Writing Instruction: A "Literacy" Journey', *Journal of English for Academic Purposes*, 11 (1): 26–37.

Wingate, U. and R. Harper (2021), 'Completing the First Assignment: A Case Study of the Writing Processes of a Successful and an Unsuccessful Student', *Journal of English for Academic Purposes*, 49: 100948.

Wingate, U. and C. Tribble (2012), 'The Best of Both Worlds? Towards an English for Academic Purposes/Academic Literacies Writing Pedagogy', *Studies in Higher Education*, 37 (4): 481–95.

Wolfe, C. R. (2011), 'Argumentation across the Curriculum', *Written Communication*, 28 (2): 193–219.

Wolfe, C. R., M. A. Britt and J. A. Butler (2009), 'Argumentation Schema and the Myside Bias in Written Argumentation', *Written Communication*, 26 (2): 183–209.

Wong, A. T. (2005), 'Writers' Mental Representations of the Intended Audience and of the Rhetorical Purpose for Writing and the Strategies That They Employed When They Composed', *System*, 33 (1): 29–47.

Wulff, S., U. Römer and J. Swales (2012), 'Attended/unattended *this* in Academic Student Writing: Quantitative and Qualitative Perspectives', *Corpus Linguistics and Linguistic Theory*, 8 (1): 129–57.

Wyatt, M. (2024), 'How Does Academic Writing Produced for the Abstracts of Articles in More and Less Prestigious Journals Reflect Grice's Maxims?', in M. Walková (ed.), *Linguistic Approaches in English for Academic Purposes: Expanding the Discourse*, 145–167, London: Bloomsbury.

Yakhontova, T. (2002), '"Selling" or "Telling"? The Issue of Cultural Variation in Research Genres', in J. Flowerdew (ed.), *Academic Discourse*, 216–32. Harlow: Longman.

Yang, R. and D. Allison (2003), 'Research Articles in Applied Linguistics: Moving from Results to Conclusions', *English for Specific Purposes*, 22 (4): 365–85.

Yang, Y. (2013), 'Exploring Linguistic and Cultural Variations in the Use of Hedges in English and Chinese Scientific Discourse', *Journal of Pragmatics*, 50 (1): 23–36.

Young, P. (2000), '"I Might as Well Give Up": Self-esteem and Mature Students' Feelings About Feedback on Assignments', *Journal of Further and Higher Education*, 24 (3): 409–18.

Zapletalová, G. (2009), *Academic Discourse and the Genre of Research Article*, Banská Bystrica: Univerzita Mateja Bela v Banskej Bystrici.

Zhang, Z. V. and K. Hyland (2022), 'Fostering Student Engagement with Feedback: An Integrated Approach', *Assessing Writing*, 51: 100586.

Zhao, C. G. and L. Llosa (2008), 'Voice in High-stakes L1 Academic Writing Assessment: Implications for L2 Writing Instruction', *Assessing Writing*, 13 (3): 153–70.

Sources of numbered examples and texts used in teaching activities

Amez, S. and S. Baert (2020), 'Smartphone Use and Academic Performance: A Literature Review', *International Journal of Educational Research*, 103: 101618.

Anthony, L. (2014), *AntConc*, Version 3.4.4 [Computer Software], Tokyo: Waseda University. Available online: http://www.laurenceanthony.net/software/antconc/ (accessed 9 February 2020).

Aull, L. L., D. Bandarage and M. R. Miller (2017), 'Generality in Student and Expert Epistemic Stance: A Corpus Analysis of First-year, Upper-level, and Published Academic Writing', *Journal of English for Academic Purposes*, 26: 29–41.

BAWE [The British Academic Writing English Corpus] (2004–2007), compiled by H. Nesi, S. Gardner, P. Thompson and P. Wickens, The Universities of Warwick, Reading and Oxford Brookes. Accessed via Intellitext, Version 2.6, University of Leeds. Available online: http://corpus.leeds.ac.uk/itweb (accessed 26 April 2023).

BNC [The British National Corpus] (2007), Version 3 (BNC XML Edition). Distributed by Bodleian Libraries, University of Oxford, on behalf of the BNC Consortium. URL: http://www.natcorp.ox.ac.uk/ Available as the CQP-edition of BNCweb (2018), Version 4.4. developed by S. Hoffmann and S. Evert. Available online: http://bncweb.lancs.ac.uk/ (accessed 26 April 2023).

Brown, A. L., A. J. Bakke and H. Hopfer (2020), 'Understanding American Premium Chocolate Consumer Perception of Craft Chocolate and Desirable Product Attributes Using Focus Groups and Projective Mapping', *PLOS One*, 15 (11): e0240177.

Bryan, J. and P. Moriano (2023), 'Graph-based Machine Learning Improves Just-in-time Defect Prediction', *PLOS One*, 18 (4): e0284077.

Cox, E. G., W. Dieperink, R. Wiersema, F. Doesburg, I. C. van der Meulen and W. Paans (2020), 'Temporal Artery Temperature Measurements Versus Bladder Temperature in Critically Ill Patients: A Prospective Observational Study', *PLOS One*, 15 (11): e0241846.

Fisher, M., V. Nyabaro, R. Mendum and M. Osiru (2020), 'Making it to the PhD: Gender and Student Performance in Sub-Saharan Africa', *PLOS One*, 15 (12): e0241915

Gillett, A., A. Hammond and M. Martala (2009), *Successful Academic Writing*, Harlow: Pearson.

Grigoriev, I. and A. Sokolova (2019), 'Corpus Based Analysis of First-person Pronouns in Research Proposals Written by Russian Students', *Journal of Teaching English for Specific and Academic Purposes*, 7 (4): 423–30.

Guinda, C. S. (2012), 'Proximal Positioning in Students' Graph Commentaries', in K. Hyland and C. S. Guinda (eds), *Stance and Voice in Written Academic Genres*, 166–83, London: Palgrave Macmillan.

Howard, R. M., T. Serviss and T. K. Rodrigue (2010), 'Writing from Sources, Writing from Sentences', *Writing and Pedagogy*, 2 (2): 177–92.

Hulme, A. (2021), 'Uncovering the Principles Behind EAP Programme Design: Do we Do What we Say we're Going to Do?', *ESP Today*, 9 (2): 206–28.

Hyland, K. (2001), 'Humble Servants of the Discipline? Self-Mention in Research Articles', *English for Specific Purposes*, 20 (3): 207–26.

Janigová, S. (2016), 'Non-agent Cognitive Alignment Frames in Selected European Languages', *SKASE Journal of Theoretical Linguistics*, 13 (3): 70–103.

Jordan, T. R., H. A. K. Yekani and M. Sheen (2020), 'Further Investigation of the Effects of Wearing the Hijab: Perception of Female Facial Attractiveness by Emirati Muslim Men Living in Their Native Muslim Country', *PLOS One*, 15 (10): e0239419.

Kaplan, R. B. (2002), 'Foreword', in E. Hinkel, *Second Language Writers' Text: Linguistic and Rhetorical Features*, ix–xvi, London: Routledge.

Krayushkin, M. M., M. A. Kalik and V. A. Migulin (2009), 'McMurry Reaction in the Synthesis of Photochromic Dihetarylethenes', *Russian Chemical Reviews*, 78 (4): 329–36.

Lee, H. R., K. A. Kim, B. Y. Kim, Y. J. Park, Y. B. Lee and K. S. Cheon (2022), 'The Complete Chloroplast Genome Sequences of Eight Orostachys Species: Comparative Analysis and Assessment of Phylogenetic Relationships', *PLOS One*, 17 (11): e0277486.

Lee, K. and L. Ranta (2014), 'Facebook: Facilitating Social Access and Language Acquisition for International Students?', *TESL Canada Journal*, 31 (2): 22–50.

Li, H., Q. Wu, B. Xing, W. Wang (2023), 'Exploration of the Intelligent-auxiliary Design of Architectural Space Using Artificial Intelligence Model', *PLOS One*, 18 (3): e0282158.

Mazepus, H., M. Osmudsen, M. Bang-Petersen, D. Toshkov and A. Dimitrova (2023), 'Information Battleground: Conflict Perceptions Motivate the Belief in and Sharing of Misinformation about the Adversary', *PLOS One*, 18 (3): e0282308.

MICUSP [Michigan Corpus of Upper-level Student Papers] (2009), Ann Arbor: The Regents of the University of Michigan. Available online: https://micusp.elicorpora.info/ (accessed 26 April 2023).

Mulvey, K. L., L. McGuire, A. J. Hoffman, E. Goff, A. Rutland, M. Winterbottom, F. Balkwill, M. J. Irvin, G. E. Fields, K. Burns and M. Drews (2020), 'Interest and Learning in Informal Science Learning Sites: Differences in Experiences with Different Types of Educators', *PLOS One*, 15 (7): e0236279.

Ruffman, T., R. Then, C. Cheng and K. Imuta (2019), 'Lifespan Differences in Emotional Contagion while Watching Emotion-Eliciting Videos', *PLOS One*, 14 (1): e0209253.

TECCL [Ten-thousand English Compositions of Chinese Learners Corpus] (2015), Version 1.1, compiled by X. Xue. Beijing: Beijing Foreign Studies University. Available online: corpus.bfsu.edu.cn/content/teccl-corpus (accessed 22 October 2020). Accessed with Anthony (2014).

Tripto, N. I., M. Kabir, M. S. Bayzid and A. Rahman (2020), 'Evaluation of Classification and Forecasting Methods on Time Series Gene Expression Data', *PLOS One*, 15 (11): e0241686.

Troost, A. A., M. van Ham and D. J. Manley (2023), 'Neighbourhood Effects on Educational Attainment: What Matters More: Exposure to Poverty or Exposure to Affluence?', *PLOS One*, 18 (3): e0281928.

Vousden, N., K. Bunch, M. Knight and UKOSS Influenza Co-Investigators Group (2021), 'Incidence, Risk Factors and Impact of Seasonal Influenza in Pregnancy: A National Cohort Study', *PLOS One*, 16 (1): e0244986.

Walková, M. (2019), 'A Three-dimensional Model of Personal Self-mention in Research Papers', *English for Specific Purposes*, 53: 60–73.

Weber, D., R. K. McGrail, A. E. Carlisle, J. D. Harwood, R. L. McCulley (2023), 'Climate Change Alters Slug Abundance but Not Herbivory in a Temperate Grassland', *PLOS One*, 18 (3): e0283128.

Williams, J. and F. Condon (2016), 'Translingualism in Composition Studies and Second Language Writing: An Uneasy Alliance', *TESL Canada Journal*, 33 (2): 1–18.

Xu G., X. Xin, C. Zheng (2013), 'GPS2 Is Required for the Association of NS5A with VAP-A and Hepatitis C Virus Replication', *PLOS One* 8 (11): e78195.

Yang, H., Z. Han, Y. Cao, D. Fan, H. Li, H. Mo, Y. Feng, L. Liu, Z. Wang, Y. Yue and S. Cui (2012), 'A Companion Cell–dominant and Developmentally Regulated H3K4 Demethylase Controls Flowering Time in Arabidopsis via the Repression of FLC Expression', *PLOS Genetics*, 8 (4): e1002664.

INDEX

abstract 5, 25–6, 34–5, 38, 57
academic integrity 57
Academic Literacies 21–2, 109
academic socialization 21–2, 26, 28, 53, 110
academic vocabulary lists 19
access to theory, first/second/third hand 2–3
accurate/cy 63, 65–6, 73, 87, 97, 103, 155, 165–70, 173
active voice, *see* voice
Ädel, A. 16, 116, 149–50
adjectives 17, 36, 69–73, 77–8, 122, 139, *see also* adjectives; stance
describing emotions 47
temporal 39
adverbial 47, 67, 78, 90
adverbs 17, 47, 67, 77, 93, 96, 98–9, 121, *see also* adverbs; stance
frequency 8
temporal 39
affect 52, 111, 114, 116, 161–2, 169, 173
appraisal 111, 116
appropriateness 8, 16, 63, 80, 118, 155, 159
argument/ation 3, 5, 26, 51–6, 66, 76, 84, 96, 108, 110–11, 129, 131, 137, 143–4, 149, 151, 173
article 15, 69, 74, 94, 133, 167
assessment criteria 89, 169–70
attitude markers 17, 36, 38–9, 44–5, 47, 54, 114–20
attribution 114–16, 142–4, 152–3
audience 5, 31–2, 34–6, 89–90, 103, 111, 114–15
expectations 4, 13
international 8, 109

authentic/ity 6, 31–5, 43, 48, 59, 79–87, 97, 105, 142, 165, 167
averral 142–3, 152

Bailey, S. 128, 151
Biber, D. 31, 63, 66, 69, 71, 73, 111, 114, 116, 120
Bitchener, J. 164–70
Bloom's revised taxonomy 12, 56
book review 25, 31, 34–6, 43, 53
booster/ing 17, 38, 44–5, 114–16, 120–6, 141
Bruce, I. 1–3, 26–8, 42–3, 45–6, 53–5, 96, 177

citations
integral 58, 62, 116, 146–9, 155–7
non integral 58, 62, 146–9, 155–6
clarity 23, 77, 102, 105, 111, 173
clause
finite 44, 66, 68, 70, 91
main 15, 66, 154, 157, 179
non-finite 29, 36, 39, 42, 66, 68–70
participle 29, 42, 66–8
subordinate 66, 153–4, 157, 179
to–infinitive 36, 39, 42, 67, 73, 114
code glosses 17, 44, 95, 99, 102
cognitive genres 26, 55
coherence 16, 64, 65, 88–93, 97, 103, 147
cohesive/on 71, 87, 89–90, 92–4, 97, 101–3, 118, 149
collocation 19, 62, 73, 80, 93, 120
comparison 44, 47, 56–7, 82, 84, 93–4, 96, 98
Complex Dynamic Systems Theory (CDST) 11, 20, 166

complexity 5, 12, 34, 60, 63, 68, 72, 76, 82, 103, 137, 166
conciseness 81, 90, 102–4
conclusion section 25, 34, 41, 43, 45, 57, 63, 122, 140
conditionals 36, 46–7, 66
context
   institutional 164, 168, 170
   linguistic 28, 71, 73, 129
   social 18, 26, 28, 48, 109
contractions 74, 79
conventions 4, 8, 23, 27, 32, 41, 63, 74, 79–80, 110, 127, 166
counterargument 55, 173
Critical EAP 22, 52
Critical Pragmatic EAP 22, 27, 32–3, 48, 163
critical/ity 5, 23, 33, 35, 51–8, 60, 77, 96–7, 99, 110–12, 125, 128, 143–4, 158–9, 166, 169–70
   Onion model 53, 56–7

definite article, *see* article
determiner 69, 70, 73, 77, 94, 118
Ding, A. 1–3, 53
direct quotations 146, 150
disciplinary differences 14, 21, 41, 116, 129, 131
discussion section 25–6, 34, 37, 41, 43–4, 57, 122

endophoric markers 17, 36–9, 44–5, 95, 99–102
engagement markers 17, 36, 114–15, 137, 139–41
English for General Academic Purposes (EGAP) 21, 53, 140
English for Specific Academic Purposes (ESAP) 2, 53, 140, 163, 173
epistemology/ical 12, 14, 55, 59, 123
essay 3–5, 7, 8, 21, 25, 31–4, 43, 45–6, 48, 54, 56, 89, 91, 131
evaluation 36, 52–4, 56–7, 111, 113, 116–17, 121, 142–4, 174–5
evidence 3–5, 44–6, 48, 52, 54–7, 74, 78, 125–6, 128
evidentials 17, 38–9, 44, 46, 81, 95, 114–15, 142, 155

exclamation 74
explanation 26, 33, 52, 55–7, 77, 131

face-threatening act 18, 74, 121, 139, 158
feedback 20, 30, 32, 105, 109, 145, 161–75
   appropriation 163, 173
   corrective 167–8, 172
   peer feedback 32, 164, 174–5
   literacy 164, 172–3, 175
   student expectations 162, 164
Ferris, D. 162, 165, 167–8, 170
formal/ity 5, 60, 74–6, 79–80, 109, 141–2, 155, *see also* informal/ity
frame markers 17, 37, 42, 44–6, 95, 99–100, 102
Functional Sentence Perspective (FSP) 15–16, 78, 90

Gardner, S. 22, 31–4, 43, 46–8, 96–7
genre 3–4, 15, 25–35, 37–43, 53–8, 63, 85, 110, 130–1, 144–5, 163, 165–8, 174–5
   analysis 27–8, 33, 49
   EAP genre paradox 27, 31–3, 48, 58, 87, 128
   genre approach to writing 18
   process genre approach to writing 19, 27, 48
   theories/approaches 25–8, 48
grammar 19–21, 62, 79, 166–7, 169, *see also* lexicogrammar
   correction 167
   grammaring 20, 163
Gray, B. 69, 77, 111, 114, 116, 120

Halliday, M. A. K. 11, 15, 93, 102
hard disciplines/sciences 14, 33–4, 41, 75, 83, 96, 100–2, 116, 123, 129, 139–41, 149–51, 157, 158
Harwood, N. 1, 11, 14, 18, 22, 31–2, 127, 129, 132, 137–8, 143
hedge/ing 5, 8, 12, 14, 17–18, 36, 38, 44–7, 54, 75, 94, 114–16, 120–7, 141, 163
Hewings, M. 48, 63, 117–19
Hinkel, E. 4, 8, 63, 75, 123–4, 128

Hyland, K. 1, 8, 11, 14, 17–19, 31, 35, 37, 74–6, 81, 95–6, 99–102, 107, 109, 111, 114–17, 119–24, 127–30, 133, 137–42, 149–50, 152, 157–9, 162–4, 171, 177

idiom principle 19
imperative 14, 89, 139, 141
impersonal/ity 108, 123, 127–9, 133–4, 136, 138–40
implications 45–6, 56–7
inanimate subject 46, 121, 133–4, 136, 137
indefinite article, see article
informal/ity 74–6, 78–9, 97, 109, 129, 138, 140, see also formal/ity
information structure 15–16, 89–93, 149
interactional metadiscourse, see metadiscourse
interactive metadiscourse, see metadiscourse
intercultural rhetoric 22–3, 96
International English Language Testing System (IELTS) 4–5, 165
intertextuality 5, 48
introduction section 34–5, 37, 39–41, 45, 57

journal article 8, 31–3, 35, 37, 55, 83, 123, 144–5

knowledge
  EAP knowledge base 2, 6, 11, 14, 23
  shared 41, 58, 90, 104, 121, 123, 137, 141
  subject 47, 52–3, 87, 125, 144
  knowledge–telling 4, 7, 13, 40, 45, 143, 150, 151
  knowledge–transformation 4, 13, 40, 45, 143, 150, 151

L2 English writers 8, 96, 104, 110, 123, 133, 138, 143, 150, 164, 166, 169, 174
lab report 5, 34, 41

Lea, M. R. 11, 21, 58
lexical bundles 19, 44, 58–9, 73, 80
lexico–grammar/tical 15, 19, 27, 51, 62, 63, 71, 74, 80–1, 121
lexis 9, 19, 51, 62, 74–5
literature review 4–5, 34–5, 38, 40–1, 45, 53, 57

meaning making 21–2
metadiscourse
  fuzzy concept 17
  interactional 17–18, 107, 116, 159
  interactive 17–18, 81, 95, 99, 103, 107, 137
methods section 28–30, 41–3, 57, 140
modal verbs, see verbs
modifier 17, 69–70, 154
move structure 28–30, 35–48

Nesi, H. 31–4, 43, 46–8, 71
nominalization 54, 60, 62, 71–2, 85, 108
nouns 69, 72, 77–8, 93, 99, 114, 118–20, 148
  head noun 64, 69
  shell noun 71
noun phrase 15, 42, 65–7, 69–70, 77–8, 84, 93, 99, 153–4

open choice principle 19

paragraph 58, 81–90, 101, 106, 140, 151
paraphrase/ing 12, 34, 57–62, 146–7, 150–2
passive voice, see voice
peer feedback, see feedback
personal essay/writing 3–4, 7, 165
plagiarism 32, 57–8, 60, 143, 151, 170
politeness theory 18, 121
power 8–9, 21–2, 25, 31–2, 48, 52, 138, 144, 161–3
Pragmatic EAP 22
Prague School of Linguistics 15
prediction 46, 56–7, 63

preposition stranding   75
prepositional phrases   70, 75, 90, 93, 96, 119, 153–4
process approach to writing   18, 40, 48
process genre approach to writing, *see* genre
product approach to writing   18
pronoun
   first person plural   127, 137–8
   first person singular   110, 127, 132
   possessive   93, 127
   second person   137–8, 141
   self-mention   127–32, 152
   third person   13, 108, 128, 132–3
proposition   13, 45–6, 54–7, 66, 83–4, 87, 89, 102, 111, 120
purpose   3, 5, 8–9, 25–8, 31–43, 54, 60, 62, 67, 71, 73–4, 76, 83, 89, 103, 130–1, 150–2

question   29, 38–9, 42, 45–6, 56, 77, 79, 82, 97, 137, 140–1, 163

reader-based prose   12–13
reader references   36, 137–9, 141
reader-responsible rhetorical cultures   23
reflective writing   5, 25, 32, 47–8
register   15, 32, 73, 79, 111, 124
reporting verb   17, 20, 111, 115–16, 142, 146–9, 153–9
research report   4, 28, 34–5, 37–9, 41–5, 54, 57, 131
results and discussion section   25–6, 41, 43–4, 57, 122
rheme, *see* theme and rheme
rhetorical functions   4, 55, 79, 84, 128–32, 143

Second Language Acquisition (SLA)   7, 165
self-mention   17, 36, 38–9, 42, 46–7, 114–16, 127–32, 134, 136, 142, 152, *see also* pronoun
sentence fragment   13, 75, 100, 102, 141

sentence initial position   76–7, 97, 178
shared knowledge, *see* knowledge
soft disciples/sciences   14, 41, 74, 83, 96, 100–2, 116, 123, 129, 140–1, 149, 151, 158
split infinitive   77–8
stance   17, 35, 40, 52, 67, 71, 77, 81, 111–21, 127, 128, 137, 142, 158–9
   adjective   77, 113–14, 117–20
   adverb   113–14, 117–18
   attitudinal   114–17, 120
   epistemic   114–16, 120–1, 123–4
   noun   77, 113–14, 118–19
   verb   113–15, 119, 133, 158
statistics/al   7, 38, 42, 44, 123
Street, B. V.   11, 21, 58
student genres   7, 25, 31–3, 41, 43, 48, 58, 131
study skills   12, 21, 109
subject knowledge, *see* knowledge
subject–verb agreement   65, 154, 157, 169
summary   34–5, 40, 60, 151, *see also* paraphrase/ing
Swales, J.   1–2, 14, 26–8, 35, 37, 39, 41, 74, 76–8, 127, 148–9, 153–4, 158
synthesis/ing   4, 35, 40, 60, 152
Systemic Functional Linguistics (SFL)   6, 15–17, 19–20, 26, 28, 84, 90, 111, 163

Teaching English to Speakers of Other Languages (TESOL)   7, 164–8
tense
   future simple   37, 44, 46–7, 63, 64
   past simple   20, 38, 42, 44–7, 63, 64, 147, 159
   present perfect   38–9, 45, 63, 64, 158
   present simple   20, 36, 38–9, 44, 46, 63–5, 133, 147, 158, 159
theme and rheme   15–16, 90
topic sentence   4, 31, 82–9
transferrable skill   21, 29, 53, 109
transition markers   5, 17, 44, 46, 76, 85, 86, 95–100, 104, 108
   addition   96, 98–100

comparison and contrast 37, 39, 47, 54, 96, 99
consequence/cause and effect 42, 47, 54, 96, 98
Truscott, J. 166–7

unattended *this/these* 77, 118
use of sources 4, 53, 57–60, 144, 151, 166, 168–9, 175

vague language 5, 75
verbs, *see also* reporting verbs
   lexical 17, 114
   modal 17, 36–7, 47, 66, 114, 122, 124–5

vocabulary, *see* academic vocabulary lists; lexis
voice, *see also* writer's voice
   active 29, 36, 63–6, 93, 108, 147, 153–4, 156
   passive 16, 29, 36, 38–9, 42, 44, 64–6, 70, 75, 92, 93, 108, 119, 121, 133–4, 136–7, 147, 153–4

word families 19, 73, 93–4
wordy/iness 103–4
writer-based prose 12–13
writer-responsible rhetorical cultures 23
writer's voice 59, 107–9, 116, 159
writing for publication 9, 173, 175